Vocabulary and Writing in a
First and Second Language

Vocabulary and Writing in a First and Second Language
Processes and Development

Dorte Albrechtsen
University of Copenhagen

Kirsten Haastrup
Copenhagen Business School

and

Birgit Henriksen
University of Copenhagen

Foreword
Alister Cumming

ISBN 978-1-349-52007-7   ISBN 978-0-230-59340-4 (eBook)
DOI 10.1007/978-0-230-59340-4

© Dorte Albrechtsen, Kirsten Haastrup and Birgit Henriksen 2008
Foreword © Alister Cumming 2008

Softcover reprint of the hardcover 1st edition 2008

All rights reserved. No reproduction, copy or transmission of this
publication may be made without written permission.

No paragraph of this publication may be reproduced, copied or transmitted
save with written permission or in accordance with the provisions of the
Copyright, Designs and Patents Act 1988, or under the terms of any licence
permitting limited copying issued by the Copyright Licensing Agency, 90
Tottenham Court Road, London W1T 4LP.

Any person who does any unauthorised act in relation to this publication
may be liable to criminal prosecution and civil claims for damages.

The authors have asserted their rights to be identified as
the authors of this work in accordance with the Copyright,
Designs and Patents Act 1988.

First published in 2008 by
PALGRAVE MACMILLAN
Houndmills, Basingstoke, Hampshire RG21 6XS and
175 Fifth Avenue, New York, N.Y. 10010
Companies and representatives throughout the world.

PALGRAVE MACMILLAN is the global academic imprint of the Palgrave
Macmillan division of St. Martin's Press, LLC and of Palgrave Macmillan Ltd.
Macmillan® is a registered trademark in the United States, United Kingdom
and other countries. Palgrave is a registered trademark in the European
Union and other countries.

ISBN 978–1–4039–3966–1 hardback

This book is printed on paper suitable for recycling and made from fully
managed and sustained forest sources. Logging, pulping and manufacturing
processes are expected to conform to the environmental regulations of
the country of origin.

A catalogue record for this book is available from the British Library.

Library of Congress Cataloging-in-Publication Data

Albrechtsen, Dorte.
    Vocabulary and writing in a first and second language : processes
  and development / Dorte Albrechtsen, Kirsten Haastrup, and Birgit
  Henriksen ; foreword, Alister Cumming.
        p. cm.
    Includes index.
    ISBN 978–1–4039–3966–1 (alk. paper)

    1. English language – Study and teaching – Danish speakers. 2. Danish
  language – Study and teaching. 3. Second language acquisition.
    I. Haastrup, Kirsten. II. Henriksen, Birgit. III. Title.
PE1129.S2A346 2007
428.2'43981071—dc22   2007025505

10 9 8 7 6 5 4 3 2 1
17 16 15 14 13 12 11 10 09 08

Transferred to Digital Printing in 2009

Contents

List of Tables	viii
List of Figures	x
Acknowledgements	xi
Foreword by Alister Cumming	xiii

1	**Introduction**	**1**
	1.1 What is this book about?	1
	1.2 The linguistic situation and educational setting in Denmark	3
	1.3 Focus of the study	5
	1.4 Informants	6
	1.5 Introspective methods	9
	1.6 Tasks	10
	1.7 The data collection procedure	11
	1.8 Theoretical framework and key constructs	13
	1.9 Research questions	18
	1.10 How this book is organized	18
2	**Declarative Lexical Knowledge**	**22**
	Birgit Henriksen	
	2.1 Zooming in on learners' lexical competence	22
	2.2 Lexical competence – with a focus on network knowledge	26
	2.3 Different ways of investigating lexical network knowledge	32
	2.4 Investigating the learners' network knowledge	39
	2.5 Looking at the informants' vocabulary size	57
	2.6 Correlations between the lexical measures	61
	2.7 Concluding remarks	62

v

vi *Contents*

3 **Lexical Inferencing Procedures in Two Languages**   **67**
Kirsten Haastrup
  3.1   Situating the study within the field of
        lexical inferencing research   68
  3.2   The lexical inferencing study   72
  3.3   Results   91
  3.4   Discussion   97
  3.5   Perspectives on research design and teaching   108

4 **Writing in Two Languages**   **112**
Dorte Albrechtsen
  4.1   Previous research   114
  4.2   Theoretical background   117
  4.3   The study   120
  4.4   A qualitative analysis of the verbalizations
        of three informants   143
  4.5   Discussion and implications   153

5 **Lexical Knowledge, Lexical Inferencing
and Writing**   **160**
  5.1   Bringing the three studies together   161
  5.2   Correlations across the studies   163
  5.3   Learner profiles   172
  5.4   Summary and discussion of main findings   190

6 **Implications for Research and Instruction**   **195**
  6.1   Research implications   195
  6.2   Perspectives on instruction   198

Appendices   **203**
  A.1   Statistics   203
  A.1.1   Description of the statistical procedures   203
  A.1.2   Statistical details for Chapter 4   203
  A.2   Description of response types in the
        word association data   206
  A.3   Lexical inferencing   207
  A.3.1   Think-aloud instructions   207
  A.3.2   The L2 lexical inferencing task   208
  A.3.3   Description of the interscorer procedure
        for lexical inferencing   209

Contents   vii

A.4	Writing	210
A.4.1	Writing prompts	210
A.4.2	Transcription conventions for verbal protocols in the writing study	211
A.4.3	Interscorer reliability for the analysis of the verbal protocols and for the assessment of the essays	211

References   213

Index   222

List of Tables

1.1	Characteristics of the three informant groups	7
1.2	Order of presentation of the various tasks	12
2.1	Examples of informants' word association responses	23
2.2	Response types identified in word association research	33
2.3	Stimulus words included in the word association task	41
2.4	WCT scores	44
2.5	Scores awarded to different response types	50
2.6	Overall word association score	51
2.7	Differences in response types in L1 and L2	52
2.8	L2 and L1 vocabulary size scores	59
2.9	Informants' acquisition level on the vocabulary size test	60
2.10	Correlations between the lexical measures in L2 and L1	62
3.1	Illustration of the matching of topics in three texts	73
3.2	Levels of lexical inferencing success	90
3.3	Advanced processing across languages and educational levels	93
3.4	Adaptability across languages and educational levels	94
3.5	Inferencing success across languages and educational levels	95
3.6	Distribution of processing in relation to sections on the continuum	104
4.1	Attention to aspects of writing in L1 and L2	129
4.2	Problem solving in L1 and L2	130
4.3	Essay assessment results for L1 and L2 for each grade level	131
4.4	Attention to aspects of writing: means and standard deviations for the *Danish* data	132
4.5	Problem solving: means and standard deviations for the *Danish* data	133
4.6	Attention to aspects of writing: means and standard deviations for the *English* data	134
4.7	Problem solving: means and standard deviations for the *English* data	136
4.8	Assessment ratings: means and standard deviations for the *Danish* data and the *English* data	137
4.9	Spearman correlations for process versus product	138

List of Tables ix

4.10	Spearman correlations for the selected variables	139
4.11	Results for three informants	144
5.1	Correlations between lexical inferencing and network knowledge for Grade 7	167
5.2	Correlations between vocabulary size and inferencing measures	168
5.3	L2 reading, lexical inferencing and lexical knowledge	170
5.4	Combinations of the four process results	175
5.5	Combinations of the four vocabulary results	176
5.6	Combinations of the four product results	177
5.7	Informants with results within the same sections for all L1 and L2 measures	177
5.8	Lexical results for the three Grade 10 informants	179
A.3.1	Interscorer reliability	210

List of Figures

2.1	Links between and within the three levels of lexical representation	29
2.2	The word associates format	36
2.3	Example of a task sheet from Grade 7	40
2.4	The word connection task	42
2.5	Response types identified in the word association data	48
3.1	A hierarchy of cue levels	80
3.2	The processing continuum with eight main types	81

Acknowledgements

This book is dedicated to the late Claus Færch, mentor and friend. His seminal research has made a lasting contribution to the field of foreign language acquisition both in Denmark and abroad, and his visionary idea of involving young language students actively in the research process has been an inspiration in setting up the research project on which this book is based. Building on the legacy of Claus Færch, we have carried out the research project as teamwork. From the start of the project and throughout the process, the three of us have worked together on every aspect of the study.

The research project was made possible through a generous three-year grant (2001–2004), and the authors gratefully acknowledge this financial support from the Danish National Research Council for the Humanities.

Our thanks are due to a number of colleagues from abroad. We are highly indebted to Alister Cumming and Razika Sanaoui for their generous advice concerning the planning of the project and for discussing our work with us at various stages of the project. Our thanks also go to a number of colleagues who have acted as consultants, providing us with ideas, insights and valuable advice: Jan Hulstijn and his colleagues from the Nelson project, Håkan Ringbom, John Read, David Singleton, Jerry Andriessen and the late Pierre Coirier. We wish to thank Norbert Schmitt for his invaluable help with the validation of a Danish vocabulary test. For expert assistance with statistics, we are especially grateful to Ming-Wei Ernest Lee. Finally, Graham Caie kindly helped us collect native speaker norming data. Naturally, any errors or shortcomings remain entirely our responsibility.

From the Danish research environment, we would like to give special thanks to Frans Gregersen whose support encouraged us to start on this project and to Inger Mees, friend and colleague, who helped us in many ways, drawing on her experience with international publication. For help on statistical analyses, we are indebted to Yakov Safir and Henning Ørum. Moreover, we would like to thank Jan Meiding for advice on Danish reading tests as well as Elisabeth Arnbak and Carsten Elbro for permission to use their Danish reading test.

Informants are at the core of an empirical study. Without their co-operation and enthusiasm, the project would not have been possible. Our thanks go to all participating students, as well as to the many teachers

xii *Acknowledgements*

at schools and colleges who assisted us. Numerous graduate students from the University of Copenhagen acted as research assistants, and they worked diligently and conscientiously during the many hours of data collection, transcription and coding. We wish to express our sincere gratitude to Sanne Larsen, who functioned as our project secretary with competence and great dedication. We benefited not only from her talent for organization, but also from her insightful ideas and comments on our research.

The project was carried out as a collaboration between two institutions: the University of Copenhagen and the Copenhagen Business School. There has been considerable support from the former English departments at both institutions. This support enabled us to set up a project environment that functioned well, and we appreciate the funding for the final proofreading, which has been carried out so expertly by Jimmi Østergaard Nielsen. We also wish to thank our colleague, Solveig von Bressendorf for the copying of data. We are grateful to the President of the Copenhagen Business School, Finn Junge-Jensen, whose generous contribution made it possible to arrange two research seminars. This funding also enabled us to recruit assistants for some of the data analysis.

Last but not least, we wish to thank our publisher, Palgrave Macmillan, and Jill Lake, who encouraged us to write this book and supported us during the long writing process.

A large-scale empirical project is extremely time-consuming, and there has been very little time for family and friends. We are therefore very grateful for all the caring support from our families, not least from Yakov and Per, and for the few, but nourishing, breaks arranged by our friends.

Foreword

Alister Cumming

In his widely-cited theory of multiple intelligences, Howard Gardner (1983) proclaimed 'linguistic intelligence' to be the 'pre-eminent instance of human intelligence' (p. 79), exemplified in the exceptional sensitivity to words that poets display in their writing:

> In the poet, then, one sees at work with special clarity the core operations of language. A sensitivity to the meaning of words, whereby an individual appreciates the subtle shades of difference between spilling ink 'intentionally,' 'deliberately,' or 'on purpose.' A sensitivity to the order among words – the capacity to follow rules of grammar, and, on carefully selected occasions, to violate them. At a somewhat more sensory level – a sensitivity to the sounds, rhythms, inflections, and meters of words – that ability which can make even poetry in a foreign tongue beautiful to hear. And a sensitivity to the different functions of language – its potential to excite, convince, stimulate, convey information, or simply to please.
>
> (Gardner, 1983, p. 77)

Dorte Albrechtsen, Kirsten Haastrup, and Birgit Henriksen certainly did not conceive the research presented in this book as an investigation of Gardner's, or any other theory of, intelligence – nor of poetry for that matter. But they have probed systematically into the complex qualities of vocabulary knowledge, reasoning about words, writing, and first and second language development in ways that little previous research has attempted. Their findings illuminate much about young people's acquisition of languages and literacy, akin to Gardner's fascination with words, reasoning, and writing, but revealing far more about these capacities than Gardner ventured to describe.

Three characteristics of this research project are especially notable: its elegant, collaborative research design; the complementary perspectives on multiple aspects of the development of language and literacy during adolescence; and findings that are useful for educational policies and practices. In prefacing this book, I will comment briefly on characteristics then pose some general questions that the book raised for me.

xiii

Research design and multiple facets of language and literacy

Albrechtsen, Haastrup, and Henriksen present the results of a multi-year project that described and assessed Danish students' acquisition – in both Danish and English, as well as cross-sectionally at grades 7, 10, and 13 – of vocabulary knowledge, skills for inferring the meaning of unfamiliar words while reading, and abilities to compose short argumentative texts. These three areas of inquiry build upon the established expertise of the three researchers, as well as their mutual concerns for first and second language learning: Henriksen on vocabulary acquisition and networks; Haastrup on inferencing processes while reading; and Albrechtsen on composing and text discourse. Each area is conceptualized in respect of relevant theories and informed by numerous prior studies. The three areas are distinct but interrelated. Collectively, they constitute well-defined dimensions of language and literacy development rather than any comprehensive or explanatory theory.

The research was designed with precision, purpose, and symmetry. This is the result of careful teamwork, considerable planning, prior experience with these topics, advance piloting of instruments and procedures, and long-term funding for the research. (The close friendship among Dorte, Kirsten, and Birgit no doubt also aided and propelled this process.) Parallel tasks were implemented across languages, at each of three age levels, and in respect of declarative (knowing that) as well as procedural (knowing how) dimensions of each of the three abilities. This multi-method design permitted numerous analyses, both within each aspect of inquiry as well as across them for the same student populations. Key distinctions were examined through relevant statistical techniques. Detailed qualities of students' performance are described through profiles of typical learners with contrasting abilities. Amid an abundance of data, the researchers rightly exercised caution in selecting and interpreting results, and in judging the significance of their implications.

The research demonstrates the multi-faceted nature of language and literacy development. Not all of the analyses turned out neatly, but an impressive number of them did. Particularly notable are developmental trends by age and years of education as well as the extension of abilities to the second language that appeared initially at earlier ages in the first language. As the authors observe, their study is one of several large-scale inquiries into multiple aspects of language and literacy recently undertaken in Europe, such as the NELSON project in Amsterdam

Foreword xv

(Gelderen et al., 2004). This pursuit follows the spirit of Dorte's, Kirsten's, and Birgit's former mentor, Claus Færch, to whom the book is respectfully dedicated.

Educational relevance

All this offers much of value for education. First, the research focuses on the crucial years of adolescence. Educators around the world have recently bemoaned how little empirical inquiry has addressed this age group, compared with the ample research on literacy among children in elementary schools or adults at work or in universities (e.g., August and Shanahan, 2006; Partnership for Reading, 2004). Albrechtsen, Haastrup, and Henriksen provide detailed benchmark data on the writing, reading, and vocabulary knowledge in first and second languages among students between ages 13 and 20 in the Copenhagen area. Intriguingly, the data show distinct achievements, consistently for most measures and in both languages, between grades 7 and 10. In contrast, limited progress appeared between grade 10 and the start of university. A challenge for educational policy is to determine whether there is a lag that might be addressed in learning and instruction during the latter years of secondary schooling. But as the authors rightly observe, there are two related challenges for future research to determine: might great spurts of language and literacy development just naturally occur in the early years of adolescence and secondary schooling, then level out in the years leading into university studies? Alternatively, might the trends observed be an artifact of the research tasks, which necessarily had to span a wide range of abilities and age groups (and so may have discriminated more among the younger than the older learners)?

The important point is that this project did identify and verify distinct indicators of language and literacy development. I will let the authors themselves tell you what these are. But suffice it to say that the book provides ample, substantiated information to guide curricula, pedagogical materials, and teaching practices on strategies worth promoting among students to develop their vocabulary, to refine their abilities to infer the meanings of new words from context, and to direct their thinking strategically while composing. Furthermore, the research shows that development in the second language tends to follow and mirror development in comparable areas in the first language. So approaches to instruction appropriate for first-language development in these domains are probably also appropriate for second-language teaching. For foreign language education, a further implication is to promote the development xvi *Foreword*

of language and literacy abilities in the first language then to facilitate their transfer later to second languages. Further evidence of the educational worth of this project is evident in the numerous graduate students who assisted in collecting and analyzing data, learning themselves in the process to conduct empirical research on language and literacy learning.

Some questions

Reading the completed manuscript gave me great personal pleasure, having conferred with Dorte, Kirsten, and Birgit over several years while they planned, analyzed, and interpreted their research. I am delighted, as they must also be, to know that they accomplished the ambitious, landmark project that they set out to conduct. Reflecting on the results of this research raised some questions for me that other readers too may wish to ponder as they read this book, mull over its many, intriguing findings, and consider how they might act on them.

First, should we conceive of language and literate abilities, not as monolithic capacities – in the ways that educational curricula tend to define them, for example, as language arts, reading, writing, or language learning – but rather as the acquisition of particular, interdependent sub-systems of performance? The bulk of evidence in the present research suggests this. Students progressively acquire, over their years of secondary education, relatively discrete vocabulary knowledge, inferencing skills, and composing abilities. These in turn build on each other and on additional knowledge and skills they accumulate. A componential view of literacy makes sense of the many complex, integrated abilities that have to be acquired for reading (Koda, 2007) and writing (Mellow and Cumming, 1994; Sasaki, 2004) in first and second languages, as well as individual differences that appear among students in respect to specific abilities. Moreover, a construction–integration model of text comprehension (e.g., Kintsch, 1998) coupled with emergentist views of learning (e.g., Ellis and Larsen-Freeman, 2006) may be the only way to reconcile satisfactorily the innumerable items and qualities involved in vocabulary development with the development of heuristic strategies to infer word meanings and write compositions effectively.

Second, are these abilities relatively encapsulated within specific task domains? Are, for example, the reasoning skills required to make inferences about unfamiliar words restricted to the domain of reading comprehension, rather than extending to other domains such as searching heuristically for precise phrases while composing a text? The distinctiveness between these two types of reasoning (for reading and

Foreword xvii

for writing) seems to be a conclusion from the present research, particularly evident in the lack of correlations in performance across tasks domains. At the same time, there is evidence in the present research that certain abilities do extend over time and across periods of development in, for instance, the gradual appearance of abilities in the second language that have previously been established in the first language. Likewise, there appear to be facilitating effects of expanding vocabulary knowledge on inferencing skills and writing abilities. What might restrict or facilitate these extensions, I wonder?

Third, will studies such as the present one lead to substantial recommendations for teaching language and literacy that are developmentally appropriate to students' ages, years of education, and language proficiency? This Piagetian notion has long been articulated for intellectual abilities and narrative interests in schools (e.g., Case, 1985; Egan, 1990). However, language and literacy development varies on so many dimensions, particularly in multilingual contexts, that it has defied such generalizations for education except in close scrutiny to local contexts (Hornberger, 2003). The patterns of development that emerge from the present study seem legitimately able to pinpoint, for example, at what grade levels and in which languages, Danish students could profit from instruction about specific aspects of inferencing, composing, or word-learning. These are implications worth investigating in instructional studies and in other contexts of education and learning.

Ontario Institute for Studies in Education,
University of Toronto
March 21, 2007

1
Introduction

1.1 What is this book about?

Had we but world enough and time ... we would want to trace foreign language learners' development with respect to all aspects of their communicative competence in the target language and in their first language. And we would like to do so year by year from their very first steps in the acquisition process until they are able to attend conferences and business meetings in the foreign language. But, alas, we have neither the time nor the finances for all this. However, the authors of this book have been fortunate enough to obtain funding[1] for a relatively large research project, which has enabled us to describe three groups of language learners on a number of language traits in both their L1 and their L2, and we are eager to share our results with the reader. We imagine our readers to be teachers, graduate students, postgraduate students and researchers who, as we do, wonder what goes on in the minds of language learners.

Not being able to cover all aspects of communicative competence, this book focuses on lexical competence and writing skills in L1 and L2. It is based on an empirical study of young Danes who are learning English as a foreign language, and we have adopted a comprehensive view by studying the same learner with respect to a number of skills and several learners at different stages of development.

The aims of the study are threefold: first, to investigate the relationship between a number of different skills for the same individual, second, to study the degree of mastery of these skills in the L1 and L2 for the same individual and, third, to investigate these issues for different learner groups from three educational levels.

We believe that these aims reveal the unique features of the project. With respect to the first aim, we study a number of skills for the same

2 Vocabulary and Writing in L1 and L2

individual. It is often deplored that only a few studies include more than one of the skills that together constitute competence in a foreign language. A typical research project focuses, for instance, either on writing skills or vocabulary knowledge. Over the last decades, research has become increasingly specialized, with the study of vocabulary acquisition and writing serving as clear examples of research areas arranging their own conferences and having their own international journals. Such specialization has advantages – or may even be necessary – but it certainly also has shortcomings; for instance, as pointed out by Haastrup and Henriksen (2001) in relation to vocabulary research. We believe that studies that allow for an investigation of the relationship between a set of skills are essential for achieving a better understanding of language acquisition (cf., for instance, the Trinity College Project (Singleton, 1999) and the Dutch Nelson project (Gelderen et al., 2004)). This is why the present project deals with three areas, not as isolated fields of research but as complementary research areas. In the study reported in this book, we have tried to bridge the gap between highly specialized areas by studying the relationship between various skills in a within-subjects design.

In relation to the second aim of our project, we find it optimal to adopt a comprehensive perspective, in this case by studying the same aspects of communicative competence in both the L1 and the L2 for the same individuals. In our view, such a within-subjects approach is ideal from a research standpoint as well as from a teaching perspective. In relation to the latter, the cross-linguistic issue is essential, considering the many contexts in which the first and foreign languages are acquired concurrently within a school setting. With the third aim of our study, we leave the within-subjects design in order to compare how learners at different grade levels manage with regard to the skills forming the focus of our study. The cross-sectional design enables us to describe how learners in comprehensive schools and in sixth-form colleges and students at university level operate on identical tasks in the foreign and the first language.

Viewed from the perspective of educational policy, curriculum planning and syllabus design for language teaching, our research addresses important questions such as: What is common in L1 and L2 and what is different? What are the similarities and differences between learners at different grade levels? At which level do significant developmental changes set in? In other words, we believe that the field of language teaching needs research of the kind reported in this book. With the large body of learner data that we collected and analyzed, we hope that insights from our study will inform language teachers about what to expect concerning learner competence and development at different educational levels.

1.2 The linguistic situation and educational setting in Denmark

Before presenting an overview of the project forming the basis of this book, we need to define the context in which it is set. Denmark is a small country of five million people. Although a number of immigrants have come to the country during the past 20 years, Danish is the mother tongue of the great majority of the population and is the primary language of instruction. Throughout history, foreign languages have played an important role for a small country such as ours, which is dependent on trade with its neighbouring countries. The situation for English in Denmark can adequately be compared to that of other small European countries such as Norway, Sweden, Finland and Holland, where the first language is understood by few people beyond the national borders. Consequently, proficiency in a foreign language is essential.

Since the middle of the twentieth century, English has become the dominant foreign language both inside and outside the educational sphere, enjoying very high status. Most Danes are, therefore, highly motivated to learn the language and parents keenly ensure that their children receive proper instruction. Most Danish families frequently spend their holidays abroad, and, at an early age, children therefore experience a need to be able to communicate in English, often in communicative situations with people who use English as a lingua franca. The exposure to American and British English in the media is overwhelming and, as in most other western countries, people are bombarded with media products in English, teenagers being an especially targeted group. Moreover, TV programmes and films are subtitled rather than dubbed, and it is, therefore, no exaggeration to say that Danish teenagers experience a high degree of exposure to English, particularly spoken English, through television and films.

The informants of our study are Danish teenagers and young adults who are currently receiving formal language instruction at different educational levels. We therefore need to look into formal language education in Denmark, especially English as a school subject. Due to the influence of the Danish linguist Otto Jespersen, we have a long tradition of emphasizing the spoken language in the teaching of English. As early

4 *Vocabulary and Writing in L1 and L2*

as 1886, he was one of the founders of a Scandinavian association seeking reform in the teaching of languages, recommending the use of a natural or direct method, and his keen interest in the practical aspects of language tuition resulted in the publication of a series of school books. English enjoys the status of being the first foreign language in Denmark and, until recently, has been taught from grades 4 to 9 as a compulsory subject, placing it among the most important subjects in compulsory education.[2] One of our informant groups is drawn from comprehensive schools (Grade 7). In these schools, the aims specified for the subject, English, give clear priority to English language proficiency, including the development of all four skills, but with writing skills given the least attention. The official guidelines and aims reflect a communicative approach to teaching.

A second informant group comes from sixth-form colleges (here referred to as Grade 10).[3] At this level, the syllabus objectives for English emphasize literacy skills. In relation to reading at this level, more attention is paid to text analysis, literary appreciation and cultural knowledge about English speaking countries. Finally, writing plays a major role, which is reflected in teaching as well as in testing.

Whereas we can offer the reader a broad characterization of the objectives of the teaching of English in the Danish educational system, it is not possible to give an account of a typical English lesson in our schools at any of the levels described. Unlike many other countries, our national syllabi are best characterized as very broad frameworks with learning objectives that are formulated in general rather than specific terms and with a number of guidelines for teaching. Teachers enjoy a high degree of freedom with respect to teaching approaches, including the choice of teaching materials.

Our third informant group includes university level students of English (here referred to as Grade 13) who are in the first year of their studies. Studying English at university level in Denmark is, of course, different from studying English in the USA and in Great Britain. Our university curricula reflect the fact that the students are non-native speakers of English and, therefore, there is much emphasis on linguistics, including instruction in grammar and phonetics with a contrastive focus, and university students receive instruction aimed at improving their written and spoken proficiency in the foreign language.

All in all, this leads us to the following conclusion concerning the Danish context and the expected influence on our informants' English language proficiency: all Danes, especially young people, receive con-siderable English input in their everyday lives, and the English language enjoys high status in Danish society at large, including its position as the first foreign language taught in schools. Young people's motivation for learning English is high, and the fact that the typological relationship between Danish and English is close, in that they are both Germanic languages, makes the acquisition of English in Denmark a less daunting task compared with most other countries.

1.3 Focus of the study

As noted above, we wished to study several traits of individual learners' language competence, and these traits were to be studied in both the learners' L1 (Danish) and L2 (English). Moreover, an important aim was to describe the interplay between different areas of the individual students' competence and the interplay between their abilities in the first and the foreign languages.

Of the many skills that are important for learners' communicative competence in a first as well as in a foreign language, we focus on lexical competence and writing skills. The last two decades have seen a growing acknowledgement of the crucial role played by the lexical component of learners' communicative competence, reflected in the range of research publications within this area. There is an increasing awareness that not only the size but also the structural qualities of the lexicon are important features in vocabulary acquisition (cf. Meara, 1996; Henriksen, 1999; Read, 2004). In light of this fact, we decided that our study should include two aspects of declarative lexical knowledge, focusing on the size and organization of the learners' lexicon. Our study offers an in-depth analysis of the organizational aspect, exploring the learners' network knowledge in L1 and L2. Moreover, we focus on the procedural aspect of lexical competence by including a comprehensive study of the learners' lexical inferencing processes; that is, the procedures used when learners attempt to work out the meaning of unfamiliar words in a text.

Along with reading skills, writing competence constitutes the core of literacy training. Writing is normally the last of the four skills acquired and is viewed by learners and teachers as the most difficult area of language use. In teaching, as well as in testing, much attention is given to the actual product of informants' writing efforts, for obvious reasons. In this research study, however, we wanted to go deeper and have therefore explored the processes involved in essay writing, the aim being to learn more about the similarities and differences between processes in L1 and L2 writing.

6 Vocabulary and Writing in L1 and L2

In deciding which skills to include in the project, we considered the comprehension–production dimension. Along with the productive literacy skill of writing, we wanted to include a receptive literacy skill and chose to study lexical inferencing processes in L1 and L2. This is a prototypical learning-task, in that it is generally assumed that learners pick up many words incidentally while reading. It is our contention that the lexical inferencing study can be characterized as being placed at the intersection between a comprehension study (reading) and a vocabulary study (word comprehension and word acquisition).

In sum, the investigations of the three main areas mentioned above allow us to deal with the learners' declarative knowledge, in the form of lexical knowledge, and with their procedural knowledge, as studied in their writing processes and lexical inferencing procedures. Thus, the project reported in this book is a psycholinguistic study. We have no means of knowing how our informants have acquired their knowledge and skills, so readers looking for direct links to educational practice will have to stretch their imagination. Studies of classroom interaction have provided crucial insight into many aspects of second language learning. However, the outstanding feature of our study is that several skills are studied across the two languages in the same individuals, and that we are able to focus on learners' individual processes – a hidden feature in studies of classroom interaction. The study thus gives teachers insights into the competence and skills of learners across different levels in the educational system.

1.4 Informants

Let us start with a brief characterization of our foreign language learners. By definition, the adult learners of a foreign language have a number of skills in place compared with children acquiring their first language. Their conceptual framework is highly developed: they have knowledge of the world, of language and of discourse, and they have acquired first language literacy skills. However, the foreign language learners in this study (see Table 1.1) are not all adults; they are all young people ranging from teenagers to people in their early twenties, differing in age, maturity and educational experience with English. Therefore, with respect to conceptual and first language literacy development, our informants are also at various stages of learning.

The Grade 7[4] informants are young learners from comprehensive schools who have had three years of instruction in English, and they are still very much in the process of acquiring L1 literacy skills, developing

Introduction 7

Table 1.1 Characteristics of the three informant groups

Level	Educational group	Age	Years of English	Proficiency in English
Grade 7	Comprehensive school Not streamed	13–14	3	Beginners
Grade 10	Sixth-form college students Streamed	16–17	6	Intermediate
Grade 13	University undergraduates Students of English Streamed	Early 20s	9	Advanced

their conceptual framework and consolidating their L1 vocabulary knowledge.

The Grade 10 informants are in their first year at sixth-form college and have received instruction in English as a foreign language for about six years. They are likely to represent an intermediate stage of learning in the process of refining their literacy skills and their conceptual knowledge to prepare them for university entrance. Regarding Grade 10, we had to consider whether we wanted to choose our group from vocationally oriented or more academically oriented schools. Selecting the latter, we undertook a further screening procedure, in that we chose our informants from the group of students who had opted for arts subjects with a focus on language studies rather than students who had selected science subjects.

The university group comprises undergraduates who have just started studying English at a university or at a business school. They are in their early twenties and they have received formal instruction in English for at least nine years. The university students who have English as their primary subject are at a stage at which they experience their initial exposure to the discourse demands of academia proper.

In addition to the grouping according to grade level, we introduced a sub-division of the informants at each grade level, establishing high ability and low ability groups. In order to meet our objective of gaining insight into the processes used by our learner groups, we found it essential to employ introspective methods. However, since the analysis of verbal protocols is known to be extremely time-consuming, a consequence of this choice was that we had to give up the idea of working with very large informant populations. We settled for a moderate selection of

8 *Vocabulary and Writing in L1 and L2*

30 informants from each educational level. Still, our goal was – even with such a limited group size – to make sure that the informants would come from the extreme ends of the student population at a particular educational level. Thus, we had to identify the students who belonged to the high and low ability groups within each educational level. The procedure that is normally followed when dividing informants according to ability is to use intelligence tests; however, as such tests are not available in the Danish educational setting, we decided to use reading tests in L1[5] (Danish) instead. This means that the high and low groups represent good L1 readers and poor L1 readers, respectively. Although this procedure is not ideal, grouping the students according to their L1 reading abilities tallies with our focus on literacy skills.

Our informants were selected from whole classes and from a number of different schools: nine Danish comprehensive schools for the Grade 7 informants, eleven Danish sixth-form colleges for the Grade 10 informants. The first-year university students of English were recruited from a university and a business school. Due to the moderate size of the data we were able to include in our study, we decided to exclude all students for whom Danish was their second language, to avoid introducing an additional research variable.

As mentioned above, the informants were selected based on their L1 reading skills, but we also took into consideration their ability to verbalize their thinking. The latter was essential, since the majority of our data comprises verbal protocols. The actual selection of the informants was therefore carried out in two stages. First, the L1 reading tests were administered to whole classes at the 20 different comprehensive schools and sixth-form colleges by their class teachers, who had been instructed in the administration of the tests at meetings with the researchers. Based on the results of the L1 reading test, we selected an equal number of potential informants; that is, a number of learners with low reading scores and a number with high reading scores. In the second stage, a team of student-assistants visited the 20 schools in order to test how willingly the selected informants verbalized their thinking. This was carried out by administering three small tasks, which they were to solve while verbalizing their thoughts simultaneously. A similar selection and screening procedure was used for the university informants.

Inspired by Ericsson and Simon (1993), the students had to: (1) close their eyes and say how many windows they had at home; (2) multiply two numbers without the use of pen and paper (for instance, $28 \times 32 = ?$); and (3) create as many words as possible from a string of letters without the use of pen and paper. Audio recordings were made of these tasks and the recordings formed the basis of the final selection of the informants, eliminating learners who were not inclined to verbalize. In addition, performing these tasks served as a training exercise in verbalization for our informants.

Out of the many students who were screened for L1 reading skills and verbalization ability, 140 informants[6] took part in the actual data collection, and 90 of these informants were selected as our core informants, yielding 30 informants at each grade level for analysis.

1.5 Introspective methods

As the majority of our data comprises verbal protocols, some attention will be paid to introspective methods in this general introduction. Extensive use of introspective methods is made in the form of concurrent think aloud and retrospection. The main advantage of these methods is that they give access to the informants' processing, which is not reflected in the final product and therefore cannot be inferred from the analysis of the product only.

In the three studies, we used think aloud and retrospection in slightly different ways and combinations. An illustrative example is given here, using the lexical inferencing study as a case in point. The reader should envisage informants who are confronted with a written text that includes a number of words that are unknown to them, their task being to offer suggestions for the meanings of these words. We first applied concurrent think aloud in order to uncover which knowledge sources the informants activated in their attempts to arrive at a proposed meaning for a particular word. However, since think aloud is known to have certain shortcomings – such as incomplete reporting and protocols that are difficult to interpret – the think-aloud session was immediately followed by a retrospection session, in which informants were asked to report on what had helped them arrive at their proposed meaning for a word. In the analysis phase, the researchers adopted a combined method; the retrospection data were regarded as a supplement to the think-aloud data. As expected, the addition of the retrospection session greatly improved the validity of the protocol analysis. The use of introspective methods in the studies will be accounted for in Chapters 2 to 4.

With regard to validity, we are fully aware that introspective methods have advantages and disadvantages (cf. Ericsson and Simon, 1993; Smagorinsky, 1994). Rather than entering into this important and ongoing discussion, we shall point out what our main assumptions are. First, think aloud gives access to the conscious processes only (see Section

10 *Vocabulary and Writing in L1 and L2*

1.8.2), and what informants report is what they pay attention to. Second, although we assume that there is a close connection between verbalizations and mental processes, we cannot claim that we obtain access to these. When researchers analyze verbal protocols, they are only able to observe what the learners pay attention to and, based on this, they attempt to reconstruct the learners' mental processes. In other words, the use of verbal protocols allows us to get as close as is presently possible to what goes on in our informants' minds while they are solving the many tasks.

1.6 Tasks

The tasks tapping into our learners' procedural knowledge (writing and lexical inferencing) can be characterized as literacy-related school tasks. They are tasks that are more or less familiar in educational settings, but are not so-called real world tasks. As noted above, the task that was chosen to tap into the domain of writing was essay writing, which is a regular and traditional task of the kind we believe is used in schools worldwide. In connection with the analysis of the learners' writing skills, we are able to present an in-depth study of the kinds of processes involved in essay writing, relating the process analysis to the products resulting from the learners' efforts.

In the second type of task, the learners are required to guess the meaning of unfamiliar words in a written text. The task is intended to throw light not only on the procedures that learners engage in to guess at the meaning of a word, but also on the results of their efforts; that is, whether their proposed meanings are correct. Since the lexical inferencing task is embedded in a reading task, the literacy aspect – so important for school learning – is highlighted. The task can be characterized as embracing both text and word comprehension and represents the very first phase of vocabulary acquisition.

As noted earlier, lexical competence was chosen as one of the focus areas for this project. The study of the learners' declarative lexical knowledge includes three different types of task, measuring both the size of the learners' vocabulary and their network knowledge; that is, the structural properties of their lexicon. The vocabulary tasks focus on individual lexical items, which are presented in isolation; that is, without any sentence or text support. While the vocabulary size test is a prototypical school task, the two other tasks are less well-known test instruments in school settings. In one of the network tasks, the learners are asked to supply word associations to a given stimulus word and, in the other task they must select the words they consider most closely related to a number of target words. These elicitation tasks are included in the task battery to enable us to probe into other aspects of the learners' vocabulary knowledge than those usually measured in the better-known tests of vocabulary size.

An important feature of our study is that informants are required to complete all the tasks in both L1 and L2. Thus, parallel versions of all tasks were developed in L1 and L2, allowing us to investigate similarities and differences in the way our informants fare on the different tasks in their first language, Danish, as compared with their first foreign language, English. In addition, to enable a comparison of our informants at the three grade levels, all informants were given identical tasks. This posed a challenge with respect to the development of the tasks. We had to ensure that the tasks could be managed by the Grade 7 students but still would be sufficiently taxing for the university students.

As described above, L1 reading tests were used in the selection of the informants, but L2 readings tests were also included in the task battery proper. Due to the difference in proficiency levels between the three groups of learners, it was, however, deemed necessary to use two different L2 reading tests, one for the Grade 7 informants and one for the two other educational levels.

Let us finally emphasize that while the aim of our study is ambitious, in that we wish to throw light on how learners process and produce language, we are well aware that the tasks are all quite constrained, when viewed in relation to tasks in the real world. We must thus restrict our research ambitions by saying that what we are able to do is to describe carefully the kinds of processes we have investigated and describe the kind of knowledge we have tapped into. We believe that, taken together, the task types included in our study enable us to describe important aspects of our learners' declarative and procedural knowledge.

1.7 The data collection procedure

The data were collected in an experimental setting at the University of Copenhagen, in the period from September to the end of November of 2002. We decided to use language laboratories for two main reasons. First, most of our data required informants to verbalize their thoughts while solving the various tasks, and we required audio recordings this process. Second, the laboratory seating helped us minimize the interaction between the researcher/research assistant and the informant (see, for instance, Smagorinsky, 1994).

12 *Vocabulary and Writing in L1 and L2*

In all, 140 informants participated in the data collection. They were paid by the hour for the time spent at the university, including breaks between the tasks. They were organized in nine groups, each group coming to the university on four separate occasions for four to five hours each time. Their assignments of 15 hours and 30 minutes of time-on-task were completed within a two-week period. Table 1.2 shows the order of presentation of the tasks administered on two consecutive weeks and on two consecutive days each week.

The many tasks that each informant had to complete were given in a particular order. The most important aspect of this ordering procedure was the sequencing of the parallel tasks in L1 and L2. For instance, since each informant was to write an essay in English and another in Danish, we ensured that half of the informant group wrote their Danish essays first and the other half their English essays. The rationale behind this procedure is that experience from writing the first essay may influence the second essay. For all task types, such counterbalancing procedures were taken into account.

On the first day of the data collection, all informants received a general instruction in concurrent think aloud. This took the form of a video presentation showing extracts from a student's thinking aloud while writing an essay in English and an essay in Danish. In addition to this general session, informants received comprehensive task-specific instructions in what to do with respect to the elicitation tasks that included think aloud and retrospection.

Table 1.2 Order of presentation of the various tasks

Week 1: day 1	Week 1: day 2	Week 2: day 1	Week 2: day 2
Demonstration of concurrent verbalization			
Essay writing	Lexical inferencing	Essay writing	Lexical inferencing
Word association[7]	*A writing task	Word association	*A writing task
Danish vocabulary test	Word connection	English vocabulary test	Word connection
		English reading test	*Questionnaire-bio data

Note: * Not reported on in this book

Introduction 13

1.8 Theoretical framework and key constructs

Below, we shall briefly draw attention to the most important theoretical assumptions underlying our study. First, we shall define the way in which we use the terms *declarative* and *procedural* knowledge. Second, we will outline and discuss the distinction between *conscious* and *automatic processes* in writing and lexical inferencing, detailing the type of procedural knowledge addressed in this study.

1.8.1 Declarative and procedural knowledge in reception and production

The present study focuses on the declarative and procedural knowledge of our informants but, since these terms are used differently in the literature, we feel a need to clarify how we understand and use the two terms.

Based on the distinctions proposed by many researchers (for instance, Færch and Kasper, 1983; Wolff, 1994), we view declarative knowledge ('knowing that') as encompassing a wide range of different aspects of factual knowledge: knowledge of the world, knowledge of paralinguistic and extra-linguistic means of communication, linguistic knowledge, pragmatic and discourse knowledge, and socio-cultural knowledge. With respect to aspects of declarative knowledge, we are primarily concerned with describing and measuring our informants' vocabulary knowledge, on the assumption that the size and the organization of language learners' declarative lexical knowledge play an important role for all the four language skills. For instance, when learners encounter an unknown word in a text, their ability to activate relevant lexical cues in the surrounding text and in the unknown word is highly dependent on their degree of declarative lexical knowledge. Moreover, when writing in L2, learners will be spending considerable time finding the appropriate lexical items to express their intended meaning, drawing heavily on their declarative lexical knowledge during the ongoing search procedures.

Procedural knowledge ('knowing how') includes language learners' knowledge of a number of different procedural aspects: reception and production procedures, conversational procedures and communication strategies, and learning procedures. In short, procedural knowledge can be described as the various processes involved in comprehending, producing and learning language. In our study, we deal more narrowly with reception procedures in the form of lexical inferencing processes and with production procedures in the form of writing processes.

14   *Vocabulary and Writing in L1 and L2*

Declarative and procedural knowledge is in focus to varying degrees in the three areas investigated. Thus, the lexical knowledge study exclusively taps into declarative knowledge, whereas the writing study primarily measures procedural knowledge. The lexical inferencing study addresses both declarative and procedural knowledge and the interaction between the two types of knowledge.

As pointed out by Wolff (1994), declarative and procedural knowledge can take the form of both implicit and explicit knowledge. In this connection, it is important to point out that the concept of *proceduralization of knowledge* is used widely in the research literature in a different sense to the understanding of procedural knowledge described in the preceding paragraphs. Procedural or automatic ability to draw on knowledge in communication may, dependent on the learning view adopted by the individual researcher, be seen as the product of either extended practice (and thus automatization of explicit knowledge) or be described as the product of implicit learning procedures. When we use the term *procedural knowledge* here, it is in the sense proposed by Færch and Kasper (1983) and Wolff (1994). The term covers reception and production procedures, and this type of knowledge can be either implicit or explicit.

Since our study addresses the question of the degree to which our informants are able to apply the procedural knowledge they demonstrate in L1 to L2 lexical inferencing and writing, a discussion of learners' procedural knowledge in the native language is highly relevant in our context. In Wolff (1994), it is assumed that procedural knowledge is primarily language neutral and therefore a strong potential candidate for positive transfer. In the L1, procedural knowledge is most often stored as implicit knowledge; that is, native speakers have little conscious awareness of the procedural knowledge they utilize in comprehension and production. Deficiencies in declarative knowledge in the foreign language often prevent learners from transferring their procedural potentials to demanding L2 communicative situations. Moreover, being accustomed to teaching, which focuses on the development of explicit declarative knowledge, many L2 learners do not experience purposeful language use and therefore feel no need to use or develop their procedural knowledge in L2. In short, most learners have no explicit awareness of their procedural knowledge, and they are not likely to draw on their implicit procedural knowledge in L2 situations in which they lack declarative knowledge. They do not see and understand the parallel between L1 and L2 processing, and consequently do not exploit their processing potential in new L2 language contexts. As will be discussed later in connection with the lexical inferencing and the writing study, this may have serious implications for learners' processes in reception and production in L2.

1.8.2 Automatic and conscious processing in reading and writing

Having clarified how we understand the concepts of declarative and procedural knowledge, we now turn to a more detailed specification of the construct of procedural knowledge in the context of the present study. As already stated, processing is directly studied in this project in two areas; that is, in the contexts of writing and lexical inferencing. Although reading processes, as such, are not included in our study, reading theory is relevant to us, in that lexical inferencing forms a subprocess of reading, and the processes pertinent to lexical inferencing can be seen as more local manifestations of the kind of interactive processes that apply to reading in general.

Our investigations focus on conscious processes. However, recent theories of reading and writing have been developed with a much greater emphasis on automatic processing than has previously been the case. We therefore feel a need to position our work in relation to these theories.

Automatic processing

The two models dealt with below both invoke connectionist principles and describe processes as operating within a semantic network. This network responds to new input as a function of the nature of connections between the items of the network. The activation of the network caused by new input goes through a number of circles of activation until the network finds a stable configuration that will tally with the new input.

In reaction to the dominant role played by schema theory in models of reading comprehension, Walter Kintsch (1998) has proposed a theory that places more emphasis on automatic, bottom-level processes. According to Kintsch, comprehension proceeds as a constraint-satisfaction process, as described in his construction–integration model. In this conception of comprehension, the construction of the text base – that is, the reader's mental representation of the text – is seen as essential for the activation of the situation model – that is, the reader's background knowledge. In the construction process, which relates to the text base, it is assumed that, on reading a sentence, all the senses of a given word and associations based on the context in which the word appears will be

16 *Vocabulary and Writing in L1 and L2*

activated. The final selection of the relevant sense for the sentence in question will happen quickly via suppression of the senses and associations that are irrelevant in the context. The model is based on research that measures the time it takes for an informant to arrive at the relevant sense of a word. For instance, for the sentence: 'The townspeople were amazed to find that all the buildings had collapsed except the **mint**.' (Kintsch, 1998: 131), research has shown that all of the following associations are initially activated: 'money', 'candy', 'earthquake' and 'breath'. However, after 350 mss, the relevant sense 'money' remains the only active association. The integration process accounts for how the information from the text base is integrated into the larger discourse context whereby a situation model is created, forming a coherent mental representation of the text. Only if these automatic processes fail will the reader resort to conscious processing.

In a similar vein, David Galbraith (1999) argues for a theory of writing that focuses on automatic text production rather than conscious problem solving. As with Kintsch, his aim is to emphasize the importance of automatic, lower level processes at the expense of the higher level processes associated with problem solving. Where Kintsch's model is a reaction against schema theory, Galbraith's model is a reaction against the problem-solving metaphor that has dominated models of the writing process (for instance, Flower and Hayes, 1984; Bereiter and Scardamalia, 1987). The generally recognized assumption, that composing helps writers understand relationships and ideas that would be lost to them without the use of pen and paper, is attributed to the problem-solving nature of the writing process. The model by Bereiter and Scardamalia specifies the type of problem solving that triggers the acquisition of new knowledge, referred to as *knowledge transforming*. Galbraith does not dispute that writing often leads to discovering new ideas, but he has a quarrel with which mechanism leads to discovery while writing. His claim is that the knowledge-transforming processes described by Bereiter and Scardamalia (1987) do not lead to new insight on the part of the writer, simply because knowledge transforming represents problem solving related to known entities that are typically applied in planning and in textual revision. Instead, he maintains that knowledge is constituted during actual text production, and hence the model is referred to as the knowledge-constituting model. In the knowledge-constituting process, a semantic network is activated that consists of units that are not equivalent to separate ideas, but comprises sub-conceptual units. This network represents the writer's disposition. Information from the writing prompt or the topic feeds into this network and upsets the initial stability of the network. Through repeated activation of the network, and also as a result of input from the actual formulation process, the network eventually settles into a new stable condition. This mechanism is seen to account for how new ideas are created in the process of writing. In other words, it is the non-problem-solving part of the writing process that leads to new knowledge. This spontaneous text production, involving implicit, automatic processes is, however, not likely to lead to a well-organized text. At this point, the explicit processes of problem solving are applied to the already generated text in order to achieve a well-organized and coherent text. Thus, problem solving still has an important role to play in writing, but the implicit processes are responsible for the creation of new knowledge. The model is presented as being in line with the instructional method of multiple drafting. The knowledge-constituting model for writing has not yet been empirically supported to the same degree as Kintsch's comprehension model for reading.

Conscious problem solving

Let us now specify how our study relates to the two models presented above. The lexical inferencing task used in this study has been devised to include words that are unknown to the informants. According to Kintsch's model, multiple senses of a word are activated automatically when reading a text, but are then suppressed quickly by the sense that fits the context. Words that are unknown to the informant are therefore unlikely to activate multiple senses of the type described above, although thematic inferences based on the context are likely to be activated in the process of reading the text. In other words, the lexical inferencing task has been set up to ensure that automatic processes will fail, and hence the task invites conscious problem solving. Obviously, the kind of automatic processing described in Kintsch's model helps us account for poor and good readers, in that their processing of the entire text clearly has implications for their ability to utilize contextual cues to the meanings of the words that are unknown to them. However, automatic processing is not the focus of the present study.

In the writing study, the informants are given the rather taxing task of writing an argumentative essay while thinking aloud. Since writing processes in this project are studied through the use of verbal protocols, the basis for our analyses of the informants' writing processes is constituted by what they attend to during the writing process, and hence we are studying explicit processing in the form of conscious problem solving. The implicit processing, described in Galbraith's knowledge-constituting

18 *Vocabulary and Writing in L1 and L2*

model, will naturally affect the quality of our informants' writing processes, but these automatic processes are not the focus of the present study.

1.9 Research questions

The project is an exploratory study, which is evident from the way in which our research questions are phrased. Although there is much previous research to learn from when it comes to insight into aspects of either L1 or L2 competence, research that cuts across the L1–L2 dimension is not equally well represented with regard to the three main areas investigated here. Thus, there is not a strong research basis for formulating hypotheses concerning the interplay between skills in L1 and L2. Neither do we have access to research on which to form hypotheses as to the interplay of the three studies. Therefore, our main research questions are phrased in rather general terms:

1 For the within-subjects data, are there significant differences between the results for performance on tasks in L1 and L2?
2 For the cross-sectional data, are there significant differences in task performance across grade levels?
3 For the interplay between the three studies, can significant correlations be established between the results of the studies of lexical knowledge, lexical inferencing and writing?
4 Is it possible to set up profiles of the informants as a function of the level of development of their knowledge and skills within the areas studied?

1.10 How this book is organized

Since this book covers a number of areas that might not be of equal interest to all readers, some might prefer to focus on a single study. A chapter is devoted to each of the three studies, and we have made an effort to ensure that readers will benefit from reading any of Chapters 2, 3 and 4 in isolation from the other chapters, the exception being the present chapter, which gives details on our study not included elsewhere.

Chapter 2 details the lexical knowledge study, with an emphasis on the investigation of our learners' network knowledge. This aspect of declarative lexical knowledge has been less widely explored than, for example, language learners' vocabulary size. The chapter therefore opens with a somewhat extensive discussion of the construct of network

Introduction 19

knowledge, and gives a review of different research approaches to studying structural aspects of lexical competence. The second half of the chapter presents the empirical study, which includes investigation of the learners' network knowledge and their vocabulary size.

In Chapter 3, we begin by situating the study of lexical inferencing within the broad field of research that explores the different aspects of guessing the meaning of a word. Whereas few studies include an investigation of the procedural aspects of lexical inferencing, this is a feature that is highlighted in the present study. The main focus of Chapter 3 is thus a presentation of a coding framework for processing types illustrated by extracts from learners' verbal protocols. However, the chapter also includes an investigation of the product dimension of lexical inferencing; that is, the quality of the informants' guesses at the meaning of a word. In our discussion of results in the last part of the chapter, much space is given to qualitative analyses, which support the interpretation of some of our major findings.

Chapter 4 is devoted to an investigation of the writing processes of our informants. Initially, we briefly review previous research pertinent to appreciating our research design and the results of our investigation, followed by a description of the writing models that have informed our study. Then we outline the design of the study, emphasizing the categories applied in the analyses of the verbal protocols, and detailing the quantitative analysis of the data and the interpretation of the findings. Since some of our findings were unexpected, we introduce a qualitative analysis of three selected verbal protocols, allowing the voices of our informants to be heard. In doing so, we find that the learners tell us more than was captured by the quantitative analysis. Thus, they help us arrive at more informed tentative suggestions for future research.

In Chapter 5, we bring together the results of the project and look at possible correlations between different key measures from the three studies outlined in the previous chapters. We also present 'learner profiles' of the informants as a function of how well developed their knowledge and skills are within the areas studied. Finally, we focus more specifically on learners from the intermediate educational level (Grade 10), presenting characteristic features of the language produced by this group of informants at a point that we believe is a transition point in their interlanguage development. A more detailed analysis is given of three learners in order to illustrate how well developed their knowledge and skills are with regard to declarative and procedural lexical knowledge.

As pointed out above, the project is exploratory. We describe a range of knowledge and skills components of learners from three educational

20 Vocabulary and Writing in L1 and L2

levels, operating in both their L1 and their L2. The task of developing comparable research tools in L1 and L2 suitable for informants at very different ages and educational levels has been a challenge. Chapter 6 therefore focuses on the insights gained in relation to the various research instruments used and on possible implications for future research. Our project is psycholinguistic in nature, but we feel that both the quantitative results and the in-depth insights into our learners' processing behaviour, obtained through the hours of verbal protocols analyzed, have pointed to some central issues pertaining to language instruction. The last chapter will therefore include some suggestions for instruction, which may be of interest to language teachers.

Notes

1 We were very fortunate to receive a generous three-year research grant from the Danish Research Council for the Humanities.

2 In 2002, English was introduced into the curriculum for grade 3 learners. However, the informants of the present study started their instruction in English in grade 4.

3 Comprehensive schools include grades 1 to 9. Danish children start school relatively late at seven years of age, and compulsory schooling is not streamed. We use the term sixth-form college to refer to schools for students in grades 10 to 12. For this three-year period, students choose between vocational training colleges and the more academically oriented colleges. The latter qualify students for university entrance. Our informants are drawn from the language line of the academically oriented stream.

4 In this book, we shall refer to the three groups as Grades 7, 10 and 13, although they come from different institutional settings. Regarding their general English proficiency, we use the terms *beginners*, *intermediate* and *advanced* learners as relative terms, basically reflecting the number of years of English instruction. We shall furthermore refer to *mature* and *immature* learners as terms pointing to language proficiency as well as general cognitive development.

5 For the informants from Grade 10 and Grade 13, Professor Carsten Elbro from the Department of Nordic Studies and Linguistics at the University of Copenhagen kindly gave us permission to use a Danish reading test developed by himself and Elisabeth Arnbak. For the Grade 7 informants, a reading test developed for Danish schools by Nielsen and Møller (1998) was used. Significant statistical differences were found between the high and the low achievement groups on the L1 reading test for all three educational levels (T-tests: G.7: t $(29) = -16.927$, $p < .001$; G.10: t $(29) = -14.259$, $p < .001$; G.13: t $(29) = -7.972$, $p < .001$).

6 The reason for the initial collection of data from 140 students was to ensure that we could afford to lose some students for our longitudinal study of the Grade 7 and Grade 10 students. Data analysis for the longitudinal part of our study is still pending. The high number of informants also allowed us to

Introduction 21

exclude cases with missing data. In the final selection procedure, informants with the highest and lowest L1 reading results for each level were, if possible, included as core informants.
7 The productive word association task in one language was always given before the receptive word connection task in the same language.

2
Declarative Lexical Knowledge

Birgit Henriksen

2.1 Zooming in on the learners' lexical competence

The basic building blocks for language use and development are words and lexical phrases. Operating in our native language, we draw on an immense store of lexical items and have in-depth knowledge of the meaning and usage restrictions of many words and lexical expressions. The many lexical entries in our L1 mental lexicon are not stored randomly, but are structured in a well-organized web with connections or pathways between the words; a structural system that enables us to retrieve words rapidly and with ease, because the access routes in the lexical store are varied and well-established. Can the same be said about foreign language learners' mental lexicon at different stages of their interlanguage development? By nature, the L2 learner has had less exposure to the target language; so, one would naturally expect the L2 lexicon to differ from the L1 lexicon – not only in relation to size, but also in relation to the structural properties of the word store. But how different is the L2 lexicon? And can differences be traced across learner groups who differ with respect to age, maturity and educational experience? These are some of the research questions we address in this chapter, where we describe our learners' lexical competence, both in terms of size and the organizational properties of their mental lexicon.

A well-known research technique for probing into the mental lexicon is the word association task. In this task, native speakers and language learners are presented with a stimulus word and are asked to say or write down the first word that comes to mind when hearing or reading that stimulus word. Analyzing the response patterns given in a word association task opens a window into the lexical store and is seen as a way of

Declarative Lexical Knowledge 23

describing different levels of lexical competence, especially in relation to the structural qualities of the learner lexicon. As an illustrative example, let us look at the responses given by the informants from our three learner groups (see Table 2.1) to the stimulus words 'moon' and 'hungry' in a word association task, which was included in the project design. The original spelling has been preserved.

The learners from the three educational levels give a number of identical responses, but interesting differences can also be detected. The more advanced students supply a greater variety of lexical items, and respond with more abstract and superordinate words than the Grade 7 learners. The responses given by the younger informants are more restricted in the semantic fields represented (for instance, four colour terms are given as responses to 'moon') and contain more high-frequent lexical items than the responses from Grade 13 learners. Moreover, some responses are given in L1 by the Grade 7 and Grade 10 informants.

Table 2.1 Examples of informants' word association responses

MOON

Grade 7	sun, stars, night, round, yellow, blue, universe, man, wolf, white, black, shadow, space, light, milkwey, rocket, 3D, cheese, circle, lys (= light), mørk (= dark)
Grade 10	sun, stars, night, round, yellow, blue, universe, man, dark, darkness, honey, shiny, big, pale, howling, sky, heaven, gravity, distance, werewolf, mystery, orange, Tycho Brahe, Gagarin, lys (= light)
Grade 13	sun, stars, night, round, yellow, blue, universe, darkness, sky, heaven, space, helicopter, cake, light, movie, bright, cheese, planet, sixties, full, happy, myth, shadow, mooning, shine, Titan, Pjerrot

HUNGRY

Grade 7	food, eat, thirsty, starving, dinner, burger, honey, drinks, restaurant, dog, family, stomach, person, meat, water, thin, bread, fat, mouth, apple, Pizzahut, Maggie
Grade 10	food, eat, thirsty, starving, dinner, lion, full, need, comfort, candy, child, me, always, cake, stomach, delicious, discomfort, waiting, pain, poor, lunch, Africa, Hungary, fattig (= poor)
Grade 13	food, eat, thirsty, starving, dinner, people, water, paper, bad, always, normal, burger, pasta, eatable, nutrition, lean, starved, negative, feeling, belly, wolf, famine, empty, full, child, country, Africa

24 *Vocabulary and Writing in L1 and L2*

Sometimes the younger learners are not even able to supply a response to the stimulus words.

These differences reflect some quantitative and qualitative characteristics of the lexical competence of the three learners from the three informant groups. A learner's ability to give a response under time constraint, to use a variety of different lexical items and to supply more low frequent and abstract words to a given stimulus word may be an indication of a larger, more advanced and differently structured lexicon, compared with the vocabulary of the learner who seems to be operating within a much smaller frequency range or who even fails to come up with a reply in the foreign language. Descriptions of the mental lexicon elicited by means of word association tasks complement measures of vocabulary size, enabling researchers to obtain a fuller picture of the quality of language learners' lexical knowledge.

2.1.1 The relationship between lexical competence and language skills

The answers to the research questions mentioned above are interesting in themselves but including an investigation of our informants' lexical competence in the project design has also enabled us to supplement the learner data dealt with in the lexical inferencing and the writing studies described in Chapters 3 and 4. When language learners read or listen, they often encounter unknown words in the input. In addition to drawing on their general knowledge of the world, they must rely on lexical cues in the surrounding co-text and in the unknown words themselves in order to come up with a qualified guess concerning the meaning of unfamiliar lexical items. When writing or speaking, learners often experience an inability to find the appropriate words to express the intended meaning immediately and must rely on using either an imprecise word or lexical search procedures – for example, searching their lexical memory or consulting a dictionary.

Undoubtedly, declarative lexical knowledge, both in the form of a large vocabulary store and in terms of a well-organized lexical network, plays a crucial role in coping with real communication situations. Many studies have shown that vocabulary size correlates with language learners' reading abilities (Laufer, 1992; Horst et al., 1998; Henriksen et al., 2004). It has been documented that learners below a certain threshold of L2 vocabulary knowledge are unable to transfer the higher order skills they may have developed in their L1 to L2 tasks (for

Declarative Lexical Knowledge 25

instance, Bossers, 1991; Schoonen et al., 2003). As argued by Laufer (1997a), learners probably need a threshold vocabulary of about 5000 words to be able to read effortlessly in L2 and to achieve adequate text comprehension.

Not only do language learners need a vocabulary of a certain size, but also the organization of their lexicon must be of a certain quality to ensure efficient language use. Lexical items are not stored randomly in the mental lexicon, but are linked together in a network structure that provides access to the lexical items in the process of language use. Correlational evidence from studies of reading and listening that have included measuring of network knowledge – namely, knowledge of synonymy and collocations – has shown that a strong relationship exists between quality of network knowledge and language use (Quian, 1999, 2002; Mecartty, 2000; Stæhr Jensen, 2005). Nassaji (2004) also found a strong relationship between ESL learners' depth of vocabulary knowledge, measured by means of a word associates format (see Section 2.3.2), and the types of strategies they employed when guessing unknown words in a text. It was documented that the informants' degree of network knowledge influenced their ability to achieve inferencing success; that is, to arrive at an understanding of a word's meaning. Depth of vocabulary knowledge was found to be a much stronger predictor of inferencing success than the types of guessing strategies used. This issue will be pursued in Chapter 5, where we investigate possible relationships between our learners' declarative lexical knowledge and their lexical inferencing skills.

2.1.2   The structure of the chapter

Many researchers have focused on the development and use of different tests of vocabulary size (Read, 2000), and a range of valid and well-established test formats already exists for measuring the number of words in a learner's L1 or L2 vocabulary. In contrast, no agreement exists on the exact nature of the types of links found in the mental lexicon and on how to describe the structural properties of the lexicon; that is, the network knowledge of language learners. Productive and receptive word association task formats have been used extensively to investigate the links found in the word net and to describe network knowledge in terms of shifting patterns of organizational structure both in L1 and L2. However, there is no general agreement on the definition of network knowledge, and few valid methods for quantifying qualitative differences have been developed that could be used to compare our informants' L2 and L1 network knowledge. Due to these central research issues

26 *Vocabulary and Writing in L1 and L2*

concerning the construct of network knowledge, we feel a need to outline in some detail the central underlying assumptions, which have informed the study (Section 2.2). Second, an extensive review of research studies that have investigated L2 learners' network knowledge, with an emphasis on specific research approaches that have informed our own study, will be given (Section 2.3). The final, core sections of this chapter (2.4 to 2.7) deal with the empirical study itself, describing the research methods employed and presenting the findings regarding the lexical knowledge of our informants. Readers who are primarily interested in the research study can therefore go directly to the second half of the chapter.

2.2 Lexical competence – with a focus on network knowledge

A central question in lexical research naturally concerns the exact definition of the construct of lexical competence. The dimensions of breadth (vocabulary size) and depth (quality of lexical knowledge) have been described as central properties of the mental lexicon both in the L1 and the L2 (for an overview, see Henriksen, 1999; Read, 2004). A large vocabulary with knowledge of lexical items across a range of frequency bands has been seen as a hallmark of good lexical knowledge; that is, lexical competence has primarily been defined as the number of words in the lexicon.

As pointed out by Henriksen (1999) lexical competence could, however, be envisaged as a complex construct comprising knowledge across three dimensions: *partial to precise knowledge of word meaning, depth of knowledge* and *receptive to productive use ability*. It is hypothesized that a close relationship exists between the three dimensions and that development in one dimension is related to and affects development in the other dimensions. In other words, increase in network knowledge of a specific lexical item is likely to affect the learner's precision of word meaning. Increase in precision of word meaning and network knowledge is, in turn, likely to affect receptive or productive control of the lexical item.

Different approaches to defining the second dimension, the construct of depth or quality of lexical knowledge, have been proposed. Henriksen (1999) primarily defines depth as *network knowledge*, relating this to the acquisitional process of network building. In a recent article, Read (2004) outlines three distinct constructs: *precision of meaning, comprehensive word knowledge* and *network knowledge*. *Precision of meaning* is defined as the elaborated understanding of the semantic content of lexical items that characterizes the lexical entries of the native speaker or the more advanced language learner. The term *comprehensive word knowledge* refers to aspects of word knowledge that go beyond the mere propositional content alluded to in the first construct, echoing the comprehensive lists of both receptive and productive word knowledge components previously outlined in the research literature (Richards, 1976; Nation, 1990, 2001). The third understanding of the construct of depth refers to *network knowledge*, the main research interest in the present lexical study. Meara (1996) argues that vocabulary size is crucial for language beginners but, as the vocabulary grows in terms of size, learners' network knowledge becomes increasingly more important in ensuring effective access to the expanding mental store of lexical items.

2.2.1 The construct of network building

As pointed out by numerous researchers, developing lexical competence does not only involve the process of adding new words to our lexical store and expanding the knowledge we have of these items (item learning). It also includes the important process of developing our network knowledge through the process of creating links between the lexical items found in the mental lexicon (system learning; see Ringbom, 1983). Aitchison (1987) mentions two central processes in L1 lexical acquisition: *mapping* and *network building*. Mapping is the cognitive process of creating links between our conceptual knowledge (the semantic base) and the lexical form of the lexical entry. This process of mapping meaning onto form may be seen as a cumulative development from partial to precise knowledge (Haastrup and Henriksen, 1998; Henriksen, 1999). The lexical inferencing procedures employed by our informants in their attempt to comprehend unknown words in a number of texts reflect the very first crucial steps of the mapping process. Each encounter with the lexical item in new contexts potentially adds more and more precision of meaning and develops comprehensive word knowledge. Simultaneously with the creation of links between the word form and its meaning in the mapping process, it is assumed that a process of network building takes place. Via experience, repeated language exposure and the raising of meta-semantic awareness, the language learner constantly establishes internal links between the lexical items in the mental lexicon.

The network metaphor

The notion of the organization of the mental lexicon as a network is prevalent in both L1 and L2 lexical research (Aitchison, 1987;

28 *Vocabulary and Writing in L1 and L2*

Singleton, 1999; Wilks and Meara, 2002). The network is envisaged as an intricate, multi-layered structure or word web with numerous levels of interconnections between lexical items. Even if the network metaphor has gained almost universal acceptance, we still do not know enough about the structure, hierarchy and complexity (in terms of number and types) of the linkage between the elements in the mental lexicon. This matter will be discussed in 2.2.2 in connection with an outline of different levels of lexical representation.

The conception of a lexical network with numerous relations between words is naturally associated with connectionist accounts of knowledge representation, processing and acquisition. According to this view, both the representation and the acquisition of knowledge are envisaged as the establishment, storage and continuous strengthening and restructuring of neural links in our memory system (Hulstijn, 2002). Singleton (1999) and Hulstijn (2002) have discussed the feasibility of reconciling a connectionist perspective with a more traditional symbolist view of language, suggesting the possibility of adopting a hybrid model of cognitive representation and processing which operates with both lower-order elements of a more connectionist kind as well as higher-order elements in the form of symbols. Lexical items could therefore be stored both in the form of lower-order, sub-lexical connections and as more higher-order elements in the form of symbols. This unified, hybrid understanding is adopted in the present study.

In connectionist terms, the mapping and network building process can be viewed as the strengthening of associations between network nodes. The activation of an item in our memory strengthens and reorganizes the links between the nodes activated. The creation of links between the various lexical items is a continuous process of expansion and restructuring as words occur in different contexts and new items are added to the lexical store. Some associative links gain a canonical status (Murphy, 2003), whereas others may be weakened by lack of activation. This point is developed by Wilks and Meara (2002) who hypothesize that we are not dealing with a constant build-up of links. Some associations may weaken or become dormant as others are formed or strengthened, so what we most probably will be seeing is a constant shift in the relative relationship and activation level of link types; that is, both an addition to and a reorganization of the internal structure of the network. This is why we see a shifting pattern in response behaviour in word association studies (see 2.3.1) both over time and across learner groups.

2.2.2 Different types of lexical links in the lexical network

Before we present the empirical study, we will give an outline of the underlying assumptions concerning lexical representation adopted in the present study. This section will focus on the types of links established both between and within the levels of representation outlined.

Links between and within three levels of lexical representation

A hierarchical conception of mental representation, inspired by theoretical proposals put forward by Kroll and de Groot (1997), Murphy (2003) and Kroll and Tokowicz (2005) is adopted in the present study. According to the view adopted here, three types of lexical knowledge are found in our semantic memory: conceptual knowledge, intra-lexical knowledge in the form of lexical entries, and meta-semantic knowledge (Figure 2.1). It is assumed that links are established between the knowledge elements included within each of the three different layers of representational knowledge, as well as between knowledge elements across the three levels of representation. At least three types of links are envisaged:

Level I contains our conceptual or encyclopaedic knowledge; that is, our background knowledge, derived from experience. Conceptual links are established between the conceptual knowledge elements that organize our background knowledge into schema knowledge. The links are created through co-occurrence or contiguity of objects and actions in

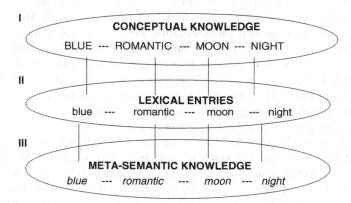

Figure 2.1 Links between and within the three levels of lexical representation

the world as well as through shared or private experiences of events (for instance, the fact that the moon comes out at night and that moonlight creates a romantic atmosphere). We know from our experience of the world that the concept MOON is linked to the concept NIGHT and that there are links to other encyclopaedic knowledge elements specifying what we know about the moon. Conceptual knowledge may comprise both the denotative and connotative experiential links established in our semantic memory.

Level II describes the lexical items; that is, our mental inventory of words or lexical entries. Based on the theories developed by Levelt (1989) and Jiang (2000, 2002, 2004), one could argue that the intra-lexical knowledge base of the lexical entries in Level II contains information about the word's phonemic and graphic form, word class and morphology, syntactical and pragmatic restrictions, and semantic specifications. We are agnostic about the type of semantic information and the level of specification in the lexical entries. Associative memory links between the lexical entries evolve naturally out of language use, and are created and reinforced by repeated exposure to the co-occurrence of these lexical items in natural language. For instance, the lexical item 'moon' has associative links to other lexical entries in our semantic memory; for example, to the words 'star', 'night', 'blue' and 'romantic'.

Level III comprises our meta-knowledge of the semantic relations between lexical items in the language. This comprises knowledge related to specific lexical entries (for example, the knowledge that the lexical items 'moon' and 'sun' and 'planet' are paradigmatically related, that 'moon' is syntagmatically related to 'shine' and 'full', and that 'moon' is analytically[1] related to the lexical items 'yellow' and 'round'). Moreover, it contains more general meta-semantic knowledge (for instance, the knowledge that possible paradigmatic, syntagmatic and analytic relations exist between lexical items; knowledge that words are organized in semantic fields; and knowledge that stylistic and pragmatic conditions restrict word use). This type of knowledge may be taught explicitly or is derived implicitly through a process of analysis and categorization.

Our semantic memory comprises both stronger and weaker connections. Some of the associative links are canonical – that is, prototypical and stable – and are the types of responses that are given by many informants in free word association tasks (see Section 2.3). Others may be less common and more context-dependent. As will be discussed later, it is assumed that different test formats and the time restrictions induced by the elicitation procedures may influence the type of links researchers are able to tap into and, thereby, the results of a particular study. Time for

Declarative Lexical Knowledge 31

reflection may induce learners to draw on their meta-semantic knowledge and their knowledge of the world, whereas tight time restrictions may activate strong and immediately accessible associative links between the lexical entries.

Links between L1 and L2 lexical items?
Since our research project includes data from the same informants in both their L1 and L2, it is necessary to outline the assumptions adopted in the study concerning the relations between the three levels of knowledge across two or more languages.

Level I is perceived as the primarily language neutral, universal conceptual system representing our shared background knowledge of the world (for instance, Dufour and Kroll, 1995). Probably, much of our conceptual knowledge of the natural world is cross-culturally shared; for example, the fact that the moon looks yellow and comes out at night together with the stars. Culture specific concepts and background knowledge are also developed; for example, the knowledge that the colour of road signs varies from country to country or that abstract concepts such as romance and honour may refer to different underlying cultural phenomena. Moreover, more personal, experiential knowledge is found in our memory; that is, knowledge that may only be shared by a few people or that is completely idiosyncratic in nature.

Level II, the level of lexical entries, is perceived as having primarily language specific elements. Cognates are the lexical items that have a shared representation at the formal and semantic level, whereas other informational features (grammatical and pragmatic) will most probably be language specific. The degree of overlap in the two language systems is naturally dependent on the relative closeness of the languages. In the present study, in which the languages investigated are two closely related Germanic languages, the degree of overlap between the lexical entries is relatively large compared, for example, with the overlap between English and Chinese.

Level III is also perceived as having a language neutral, common core of meta-semantic knowledge. Meta-knowledge of specific paradigmatic relations and knowledge of which types of semantic relations can be found between lexical items are probably universally shared (Murphy, 2003). Language specific meta-semantic knowledge is most likely to be knowledge of certain collocational restrictions (syntagmatic knowledge specifying that specific lexical items co-occur; for instance, 'tall man' and 'high/tall building') and pragmatic restrictions connected to the different lexical items (for instance, stylistic knowledge specifying that

32 *Vocabulary and Writing in L1 and L2*

the English lexical items 'guy', 'boy' and 'bloke' are near synonyms with different usage restrictions).

2.3 Different ways of investigating lexical network knowledge

In the following, we will focus on research that has been carried out on network knowledge, with an emphasis on the types of studies that have influenced and informed the procedures used in our own empirical research. Network knowledge can be described both in terms of the types of links found in the word web and in terms of the number of links in the word web. Some studies have looked at informants' ability to produce words that are related to a number of stimulus words, while others have focused on the informants' ability to recognize and select links between lexical items. These different research perspectives on lexical relations will be dealt with below.

2.3.1 Productive word association studies

The most well-known elicitation tool used to investigate lexical relations is the free word association task (Entwistle, 1966; Palermo, 1971; Meara, 1978; Politzer, 1978; Söderman, 1993; Singleton, 1999; Wolter, 2001; Namei, 2002, 2004). L1 or L2 informants are most often asked to provide the first word that springs to mind in response to a stimulus word (cf. Table 2.1). The word association format, which gives the informants little time for reflection, operates on the assumption that the learners must have immediate access to the associative links in questions. The network links described on the basis of word association responses are understood to be the strongest and most immediately accessible relations in the word web. Unfortunately, few of the researchers directly address the question of which level of representation is accessed in the word association studies, but the underlying assumption seems to be that the technique primarily taps into the associative links between lexical items defined as Level II links above (Section 2.2.2).

Differences in network knowledge are described on the basis of the response types given, development being reflected as shifts in the response patterns found; for example, from form to semantically related associations or from syntagmatic to paradigmatic responses. Others have viewed the ability to supply canonical links (that is, the responses most frequently given by native speakers) or low frequent semantically related responses as a hallmark of advanced network knowledge (see Table 2.2 and the presentation below).

Declarative Lexical Knowledge 33

Table 2.2 Response types identified in word association research

Stimulus word	Form-related response	Semantically related response		
		Syntagmatic	Paradigmatic	Canonical
black	back	bird	colour	night
hand	land	shake	nail	finger

Form-related or semantically related responses
Studies have shown that both young children speaking their L1 and L2
beginners tend to give more form-related – that is, clang – responses
('cheese' – 'chair'; 'bed' – 'bird'; 'sour' – 'hour'), whereas older, more
advanced learners predominantly give meaning-based – that is, semantically related – associations ('cheese' – 'bread'; 'bed' – 'pillow'; 'sour' –
'bitter'). This has been seen as an indication that the mental lexicon in
the early stages of learning is structured on the basis of formal features
of lexical items, whereas the more advanced lexicon is meaning-driven
(Singleton, 1999).

Syntagmatic or paradigmatic responses
If we look more closely at the semantically related links, many word
association studies have shown that learners at the earlier stages (in both
L1 and L2) tend to supply a syntagmatically related link; that is, a
collocational structure (the word 'bird' as a response to 'black', or the
word 'shake' as a response to 'hand'). Later, the paradigmatic links pre-
dominate; that is, more hierarchical associations such as hyponyms,
meronyms, synonyms and antonyms are given (the word 'colour' as a
response to 'black', and 'nail' as a response to 'hand'). Other researchers
(Entwistle, 1966; Namei 2002, 2004) have shown that the response
patterns of very advanced L2 learners or adult native speakers reflect a
shift back to more syntagmatically related responses.

Canonical responses
Many native speakers tend to give identical responses to the same
stimulus words. Words such as 'ice', 'hot', 'freezing' and 'blue' are, not
surprisingly, very frequently given as responses to the word 'cold'. These
more stable, frequently given associations can therefore be characterized
as more prototypical or canonical (Schmitt, 1998; Singleton, 1999;

34 *Vocabulary and Writing in L1 and L2*

Murphy, 2003; Wilks and Meara, 2002) than other more infrequently given responses (for example, 'shoulder', 'hankie', 'dreary' as associations to 'cold'). Canonical responses can either be paradigmatically ('cold'– 'hot') or syntagmatically ('cold'– 'freezing') related to the stimulus word. It could be hypothesized that canonical associative links – for example, the connections between the lexical entries 'dark' and 'night', and 'slow' and 'snail' – play a central role in the structuring of the mental lexicon, perhaps functioning as bridges or pointers between different parts of the lexical net.

Even if canonical responses are defined as the links most often given by native speakers, it is, however, important to stress that lexical items differ in their tendency to trigger prototypical associations. The stimulus word 'white' is more likely to lead to the response 'black' than the word 'bread' is likely to trigger 'butter'. Nevertheless, both 'black' and 'butter' are the most frequently given associations to the two stimulus words and are thus canonical response types to these lexical items. Moreover, it is important to note that the variation in the different lexical items supplied by native speakers as responses to a stimulus word is extremely high. In the English native speaker baseline data collected in our study (see 2.4.2), 61 different lexical items were given as responses to the stimulus word 'dark', whereas 77 different lexical items were given as associations to the stimulus word 'sweet'. The two most frequent associations to 'sweet' were 'sugar' and 'sour', supplied by 40 and 22 of the 127 native speakers, respectively, whereas the two most frequent associations to 'dark' were 'night' and 'black', given by 62 and 37 of the baseline informants, respectively.

High frequent and low frequent responses

Namei (2002; 2004) worked with cross-sectional data from a large number of bilingual informants and native speakers. She looked not only at the formal and semantic properties of the responses, but also analyzed her data in relation to word frequency of the responses given. It was found that more advanced learners tended to supply more abstract and low frequent lexical associations. Her results showed a tendency to give more low frequent and abstract associations to high frequent and concrete words; that is, to the lexical items that are expected to be acquired early and therefore have a deeper knowledge base.

It is in no way surprising that the tendency to supply low frequent associations is linked with proficiency level and degree of word knowledge. Low frequent items are most often found in written texts and

Declarative Lexical Knowledge 35

knowledge of these items is known to develop late (Arnaud, 1997), primarily in connection with literacy training and more formal, academic schooling. More low frequent semantic responses can therefore be hypothesized to be a defining or distinguishing feature of the fairly advanced mental lexicon. Or phrased differently, the more advanced learner or the native speaker will be more likely to supply not only more canonical responses, but also more low frequent, non-canonical responses than the less advanced L2 language learner.

Factors affecting response patterns
Numerous studies (L1 study: Entwistle, 1966; L2 studies: Söderman, 1993; Singleton, 1999; Wolter, 2001; Namei, 2002, 2004) have documented that the whole lexicon as such cannot be described as either form-driven versus meaning-driven or syntagmatically versus paradigmatically structured. The structural properties of the lexicon will rather be determined by the language learner's degree of knowledge of the individual lexical item. In the initial phases of learning, the semantic specifications in the lexical entry are relatively weak, and we thus find that formal factors play a significant role. When dealing with less familiar vocabulary items with weaker semantic specifications mapped onto the word, the more advanced learner may still rely more on the form-driven, phonological information in the lexical entry. With increased word knowledge, the words become more and more meaning-driven. Paradigmatic or syntagmatic response types will be given, but the response type will be related to the degree of word knowledge. Namei (2002, 2004) also found an increased tendency to give more prototypical or canonical responses as a function of degree of word knowledge.

Both form-related and different types of meaning-related responses (paradigmatic, syntagmatic, canonical) may be given by learners from all proficiency levels; however, a shift in the relative distribution of the response types is found, not only in relation to the learners' proficiency level, but also in relation to the frequency of the lexical items used as stimulus words. Moreover, it is likely that the relative recency of retrieval of a lexical item may influence the likelihood of this word being triggered in a word association task. As discussed above, the connections between the lexical items are continuously changing, and some may weaken or even become dormant. This does not necessarily mean that the more advanced students cannot supply the type of links found in the response patterns of less proficient learners, but rather that other, additional links may have developed and are now also potential candidates as associations to a stimulus word.

36 *Vocabulary and Writing in L1 and L2*

Finally, it is important to note that L1 studies (Ervin, 1961; Deese, 1965) and the L1–L2 study by Nissen (Bagger Nissen, 2002; Bagger Nissen and Henriksen, 2006) have documented that the response patterns given are also highly affected by the word classes tested; that is, more paradigmatic responses are given to nouns than, for example, verbs. Moreover, it has been shown that the use of concrete versus abstract stimuli (for instance, concrete versus abstract verbs) will influence the response patterns given (Namei, 2002, 2004; Hartmann, 2004).

2.3.2 Receptive task types

The word associates format

The research reviewed so far has been based on a productive version of the word association task. Read (1993) has developed a receptive version of the word association format, the so-called 'word associates test'. In the first version of this task type (Figure 2.2), informants were asked to select four potential links to each stimulus word. The relations between the lexical items are either syntagmatic, paradigmatic or analytic. The four other words included in the task format are distractors; that is, words that are not related to the stimulus word. The number of associative links that the test taker is able to identify correctly determines the learner's level of network knowledge. The test format was later changed (Read, 1998, 2000) in order to minimize the guessing element.

The word associates test was developed to find a reliable task format to measure learners' receptive network knowledge, and the test has been further explored and changed by other researchers (for example Greidanus and Nienhuis, 2001; Greidanus et al. 2004; Greidanus et al. 2005). These tests differ from the original word associates format by only including words that are potential relational links to the target item and excluding unrelated distractors. The difficulty level of the test is markedly increased because test takers are forced to consider the relative relatedness of the options given. This makes it a far more sensitive elicitation tool, enabling the researcher to tap deeper into the learners' network knowledge.

Edit	arithmetic	film	pole	publishing
	revise	risk	surface	text

Figure 2.2 The word associates format

Lexical quality is assessed on the basis of the number of 'correct' associational links identified by the test taker. Not surprisingly, the results showed that 'very advanced' foreign language learners identified more links than 'advanced' students (Greidanus and Nienhuis, 2001; Greidanus et al., 2004). In the 2001 study, which targeted vocabulary across five frequency ranges (all between 1000 and 5000), the results were higher for more high frequent words compared to less frequent vocabulary items included in the tasks. The network knowledge was assessed to be dependent on degree of word knowledge, and it was argued that vocabulary grows in depth more slowly than it grows in breadth (Greidanus and Nienhuis, 2001). In a more recent study, Greidanus, Beks and Wakely (2005) tested low frequent items on both 'advanced' and 'very advanced' native and non-native speakers of French. It was found that native speakers were able to identify more correct links than non-native speakers, and that 'very advanced' informants could identify more than 'advanced' informants. The results show that both native and non-native speakers continue to develop their depth of lexical knowledge. Not surprisingly, the non-native speakers in the 2005 study did not do as well as the learners in the 2001 study, which targeted more high frequent words.

Graph theory and other receptive task types
The receptive studies reviewed above looked at the number of items in the net. Other researchers (Wilks and Meara, 2002; Meara and Wolter, 2004; Skriver, 2005) have looked at the density of lexical links in semantic memory; that is, the degree of inter-connectivity between the lexical items. Based on the principles of graph theory, Wilks and Meara (2002) and Skriver (2005), for example, employed a receptive test format, presenting random chains of very high frequent words. The informants were not asked to identify a specific number of 'correct' links, but were free to decide which links could be found between the lexical items in a given chain of words, the aim being to establish the relative density of the lexical networks for the informant groups studied.[2]

A basic premise of graph theory is that the network structure will become denser as more items are connected. Two implicit assumptions underlying the network metaphor were explored: that high network density is a positive quality of the lexicon, and that the L1 lexicon is denser than the L2 lexicon. The first assumption is interesting in relation to communicative effectiveness. A denser network may be assumed to increase and thereby facilitate the route of access to an item, based on the assumption that the route between lexical items will become shorter. This is the

38 *Vocabulary and Writing in L1 and L2*

premise behind the assumption stated earlier that not only vocabulary size but also the structural qualities of the lexicon would be a significant factor for efficient language use. The second assumption is based on the premise that the density of the lexicon increases with repeated language exposure, a factor that correlates with an increase in either age and/or language proficiency. This assumption was directly tested and confirmed by Wilks and Meara (2002), who found that L1 informants could identify more lexical relations than L2 informants. Moreover, it was shown that the density level for both L1 and L2 learners was higher than initially expected. As pointed out, differences between these research findings and the initial expectations based on previous productive word association research may reflect a difference between a productive and a receptive task; that is, the fact that it is much easier to recognize an associative link than to produce one. In our research project, it was decided to include both a receptive and a productive network knowledge task, so this point will be taken up in relation to a comparison between the two tasks used.

Another interesting point raised by these findings is that some lexical items (at least in the initial stages of learning) may be isolated; that is, have no linkages to other items. This is probably the reason why weaker informants often are not able to supply a response under time constraint in productive word association tasks or may simply resort to giving a formal response in order to live up to the task requirements. Finally, the number of links 'radiating' from an individual item differs, so some lexical items may have many connections, while others will have fewer. It could be hypothesized that canonical responses reflect lexical items with many links; that is, words with more retrieval paths and, therefore, words more frequently given as associations.

Receptive network knowledge in L1 and L2

As discussed above, a number of studies have looked at the difference between receptive network knowledge in the L1 and the L2 (Schoonen and Verhallen, 1998; Verhallen et al., 1999; Greidanus et al., 2005; Wilks and Meara, 2002; Skriver, 2005). The learners' level of network knowledge was assessed on the basis of their ability to identify potential network links. The findings of all these studies confirm the expectation that native speakers are able to identify a significantly higher proportion of network links than are L2 learners. In other words, the results indicate that the mental lexicon of a language learner is qualitatively different; that is, less dense than that of the native speaker. An implication of this may be that an L2 learner's retrieval paths are different as to the number of paths and their length; a fact that may well affect his ability to access words effectively in L2 reception. The results from some of these studies, however, also showed that a progression towards native speaker response behaviour did take place across time for the different L2 informant groups; that is, the more advanced learners could identify more links than the less experienced informants could.

2.4 Investigating the learners' network knowledge

We decided to include the measures of both lexical network knowledge and vocabulary size in the project design. The first sections below, 2.4.1 and 2.4.2, deal with the elicitation tools used for measuring the informants' network knowledge and the collected native speaker baseline data. In 2.4.3 to 2.4.5, the procedures of analysis employed and the actual results of the network study are reported and discussed. In 2.5, we will describe the L1 and L2 vocabulary size tests used and the results obtained in these measures.

As will be outlined in more detail below, the network knowledge of the informants' L1 and L2 lexicon was investigated both through the use of a receptive word connection task and by means of a productive word association task. General research questions were addressed in relation to differences between the learners' L1 and L2 network knowledge (R1) and in relation to cross-sectional differences in the English (R2) and the Danish data (R3).

R1   Is there a significant difference between the informants' L1 and L2 network knowledge of a number of high frequent nouns and adjectives measured in a receptive word connection task and a productive word association task? If yes, will the expected difference be found across all three educational levels and across both task types?

R2   Is there a significant difference in the informants' L2 network knowledge of a number of high frequent nouns and adjectives measured in a receptive word connection task and a productive word association task across all three educational levels; that is, can a progression be found from Grade 7 to Grade 10 to Grade 13?

R3   Is there a significant difference in the informants' L1 network knowledge of a number of high frequent nouns and adjectives measured in a word connection and a word association task across all three educational levels; that is, can a progression be found from Grade 7 to Grade 10 to Grade 13?

40   *Vocabulary and Writing in L1 and L2*

2.4.1   The elicitation instruments – two different types of network tasks

Two types of tasks were used to investigate our informants' level of network knowledge: a traditional, productive word association task and a receptive word connection task that was developed specifically for this project. Both tasks were given in English and in Danish; the Danish tasks being translated versions of the English task. The informants were first asked to do the tasks as ordinary pen-and-paper tasks without concurrent think-aloud. After the completion of each task, retrospective data, during which the informants explained and qualified the choices made in the pen-and-paper task, was collected.[3] The tasks were counter-balanced as to language, and data were collected with a week's interval between the Danish and English versions of the same task. The productive word association task in a given language was always carried out before the receptive word connection task in the same language (see Table 1.2, p. 12).

The word association task

In the word association task (from now on referred to as WAT), 48 high frequent nouns and adjectives taken from the Kent–Rosanoff 1910 list (see Postman and Keppel, 1970) were read out to the informants at 15 second intervals. When a word had been read out, the informants had to write down the first two words that came to mind in response to the stimulus word. As can be seen from the example of a task sheet in Figure 2.3, adjectives were listed alternately, and word classes were denoted by including an indefinite article in front of the nouns.

In the instructions, the informants were told that only one word could be written on each line; that both words should be associations to the stimulus word; that they need not worry about spelling mistakes; that there were no right or wrong answers; and that they had to cross

1	a moon	___lait_____	_____nat_____
2	cold	___snow_____	___vinter_____
3	a child	___happy_____	___EMPTY ___
4	beautiful	___moon_____	___EMPTY ___

Figure 2.3   Example of a task sheet from Grade 7

out the stimulus words that they did not know. Finally, they were instructed not to go back and fill in blanks or change anything already written on the task sheet. In order to ensure that the restrictions on the time allotted for each item were followed, the informants were given coloured sheets of paper to cover the stimulus words and were told not to move the coloured paper down to the next stimulus word before this word had been read aloud. Four additional stimulus words ('flower', 'happy', 'bird', 'thin') were used in a short trial session, and time was allowed for questions concerning the task format. Time on task for the retrospective session was 20 minutes.

The 24 nouns included in the WAT are all concrete nouns. In order to tap associations to words from a representative range of semantic topics, an equal number of nouns were chosen from six semantic fields with which the younger informants were expected to be familiar (people, body, animals, house, food, geography). The choice of the 24 adjectives turned out to be more difficult, with the final list representing some typical antonym pairs (for instance, 'soft' – 'hard'), some three word sets ('long' – 'short' – 'high'; 'bitter' – 'sour' – 'sweet') and a range of colour terms. The selection of the words, especially the adjectives, was primarily based on results from field tests involving two grade 6 classes, in order to ensure that the majority of the stimulus words would be known to our informants.[4]

Table 2.3 Stimulus words included in the word association task

Nouns	Adjectives
moon, child, fruit, house, woman, chair, hand, bread, head, spider, river, lion, eagle, ocean, soldier, butter, window, sheep, bed, stomach, cheese, mountain, doctor, foot	cold, beautiful, afraid, hungry, slow, sweet, dark, deep, soft, short, quiet, bitter, yellow, long, high, hard, blue, thirsty, white, black, red, sour, heavy, green

The word connection task

In the word connection task (from now on referred to as the WCT), 24 target words (the first 12 nouns and the first 12 adjectives from the WAT, listed first in Table 2.3) were presented again to the informants. An equal number of cognate and non-cognate words were included among the target words.

Five out of the ten words listed with each target item represent the five most frequent associations from a number of native speaker norming

42 Vocabulary and Writing in L1 and L2

| COLD: | war ☐ | water ☐ | frost ☐ | hand ☐ | hot ☐ |
| | warm ☐ | snow ☐ | pain ☐ | winter ☐ | ice ☐ |

Figure 2.4 The word connection task

lists.[5] The five other words are semantically related, but infrequent responses given by only one native speaker in the norming lists; that is, these words represent potential but clearly more peripheral links in the lexical net. The informants were instructed to select the five words they considered to be most strongly connected to the stimulus word. The test format thus resembles the more sensitive Dutch receptive word associates tests discussed above (Greidanus and Nienhuis, 2001; Greidanus et al., 2004; Greidanus et al., 2005).[6] However, our test format was based on potential links taken from native speaker baseline data, and most of the links are in the form of high frequent words. The instruction to this task was rather long, giving various examples of possible relations between three target words ('happy', 'flower' and 'clever') and a number of potential links. This procedure was intended to prevent the informants from feeling that some links were automatically regarded by us to be more valid choices than others were. They were told to spend time on each of the potential links and to indicate in each of the boxes next to the words whether the word was judged to represent a strong (S) or a weak link (W) to the target word. If a potential link was unknown, the box had to be marked (N). Each box had to be filled out and five strong links – no more or no less – had to be identified. An example sheet with a learner task solution to the example items 'flower' and 'clever' was also presented. Finally, the learners were given the opportunity to fill out a task sheet for the stimulus word 'white' and were given time to ask questions. In the actual pen and paper task, with 20 minutes time on task, they were allowed to go back and make changes in the decisions made. In the subsequent retrospective session, with 30 minutes time on task, they were, however, not able to correct or add to their previous answers.

A comparison of the two network tasks

The two tasks included the same 24 very high frequent nouns and adjectives, but they differ in a number of respects. In the productive word association task, a strict time limit was imposed, so the informants were placed under considerable time constraint to supply immediate associations to the stimulus words. The stimulus words were presented in both an oral and written form, and the informants had to write down their responses. The pressure to supply an immediate, productive response was intended to tap into the strongest and most accessible lexical associations between lexical items in their mental lexicon. The task is, however, fairly open and free, so the informants were given the opportunity to supply the associations they wanted, both with regard to relational type and word frequency. In the receptive word connection task, they were limited by pre-set options in the form of high frequent words. The stimulus words were not read aloud, but were presented with the potential links to the target words; that is, the informants only had to identify (decode) and select between the lexical items presented with each target word. Field testing sessions with grade 6 learners had shown that 20 minutes would give most informants ample time to work carefully through the task and to reflect on the choices made, so the conditions of the WCT format did not place the informants under the same time pressure as the WAT.

The substantial differences in the two elicitation tasks employed probably enable us to tap into different types of relational knowledge. However, we cannot substantiate which constructs of network knowledge are being operationalized, but it is hypothesized that the WAT taps more directly into the associative links between lexical items described in Level II in the discussion of representational knowledge outlined above (Figure 2.1). The WCT with time for reflection probably gives the informants a greater opportunity to draw on both their conceptual knowledge (Level I, Figure 2.1) and their meta-semantic knowledge (Level III, Figure 2.1).

2.4.2 Native speaker baseline data

In order to identify which responses could be classified as canonical links in the WAT and to identify the five strongest links to the target words in the WCT, native speaker norming data were needed. Baseline data from 127 native speakers of English from the Department of English Language at the University of Glasgow and 108 native speakers of Danish from the Department of Scandinavian Studies, Nordic Philology Section at the University of Copenhagen, carrying out the same network tasks, were therefore also collected.[7] The informants in both norming groups were first-year students in their twenties who were paid for their participation. The WAT and the WCT data were collected with a week's interval under the same

44 *Vocabulary and Writing in L1 and L2*

pen and paper task conditions given to our own informants, but without retrospection.

In the analysis of our learner data, we were expecting to find a gradual approximation across the three learner groups to the native speaker response patterns in relation to the learners' ability to identify the strongest links to a target word (in the WCT) and to supply canonical links (in the WAT). One could ask why the ability to identify or supply a native-like response is seen as a hallmark of a well-developed mental lexicon. The underlying assumption is that native-like associational patterns will reflect the types of conventional access routes or lexical pathways in the mental network available to a fully competent language user in communicative situations.

2.4.3   Results from the receptive word connection task

The informants were asked to identify the five strongest links to each of the 24 stimulus words included in the WCT, which, in principle, would generate a maximum score of 120 for each language. However, the results from our two native speaker baseline groups revealed that more strong links were actually identified by the English native speaker informants (126 strong links) compared with the Danish baseline informants (120 strong links). The results from the two languages are therefore reported in percentages of the maximum possible scores for each task (Table 2.4).

The same procedure for reporting will be followed for the results of both network tasks and for the L1 and the L2 vocabulary size tests (see Section 2.5). First, a comparison will be made between the L1 and L2 scores (research question R1). Then, the scores across educational levels for the L2 data will be given (research question R2). Finally, the scores across educational levels for the L1 data will be presented (research question R3). All the results are based on data from 29 informants from each grade level. Addressing the research questions, the data were

Table 2.4   WCT scores

		G.7	G.10	G.13
L2	M	64.89%	71.29%	70.60%
	SD	8.15	4.6	5.36
L1	M	71.09%	74.83%	74.46%
	SD	6.89	3.44	5.04

subjected to one-way (three levels: G.7, G.10 and G.13) between-subjects analyses of variance (ANOVAs). For the data that lived up to this type of analysis, the Tukey post hoc measure could be applied. However, for most of the scores the non-parametric Kruskal–Wallis procedure and the Tamhane post hoc measure had to be used (see Appendix A.1.1 for a description of the statistical procedures).

To determine whether there was an overall difference between the two languages in relation to the WCT scores, an ANOVA was performed. A statistically significant difference was found between the two languages for all three grade levels (ANOVA: $p < .001$; levels (G.7: $F (1, 28) = 22.963$; G.10: $F (1, 28) = 18.187$; G.13: $F (1, 28) = 24.674$); that is, the informants identified more canonical relations in the Danish task compared with the English task, irrespective of educational level.[8] As to the L2 data, a difference was found between G.7 and G.10 (Tamhane: $p < .002$) and between G.7 and G.13 (Tamhane: $p < .008$), whereas no differences were found between the G.10 and G.13 informants. Turning to the L1 WCT scores, significant differences were found between G.7 and G.10 (Tamhane: $p < .037$), whereas no differences were found between the G.10 and the G.13 informants or between G.7 and G.13. The findings from the word connection task will be discussed below in connection with a discussion of the word association results; however, it is clear that the results found here mirror findings from previous studies using receptive tasks. Native speakers identify more 'correct' links than non-native speakers, and intermediate and advanced L2 learners identify more links than less proficient learners.

2.4.4 Results from the productive word association task

The coding procedure: different response types
Based on the findings of earlier word association research, a coding system with ten mutually exclusive response types was developed to analyze and describe the response patterns given by the informants in the WAT (Figure 2.5 and Appendix A.2).

Most researchers using the word association format have drawn a distinction between form-related and semantically related responses, arguing that development in the lexical net can be described as a shift from a form-driven to a meaning-driven organizational structure. The criteria for identifying the two response types are clear and straightforward, and potential coding problems that might arise could easily be resolved by consulting the retrospective data. The distinction between form-related and semantically related responses was included in our coding system.

46 *Vocabulary and Writing in L1 and L2*

Most studies have also operated with a distinction between paradigmatic, syntagmatic and idiosyncratic response types. It is, however, extremely difficult to find clear and objective criteria for characterizing a specific response as belonging to any of these three categories. Some researchers have also argued that a shift back to syntagmatic responses can be detected for more advanced language users, but it is impossible to find any reliable way of distinguishing between an early or a late syntagmatic association. One can also question the criteria for distinguishing between responses that are semantically related to the stimulus word in a clear and recognizable way (the paradigmatic and syntagmatic responses) and the more idiosyncratic associations, which may only make sense to one or just a few people. Even our native speaker baseline data contain a number of associations that, on sight, seem difficult to understand or immediately recognize as being meaningfully related to a stimulus word ('moon' triggers 'child'; 'green' triggers 'day'). A quick Internet search, however, reveals that most of the associations that initially seem odd or extremely idiosyncratic turn out to be lexical combinations that are used widely as creative collocations; for instance, in the form of names of a musical group, titles of songs, lines in poems or simply as brand names for different types of products. Due to these extensive coding problems, it was decided not to operate with a distinction between paradigmatic, syntagmatic and idiosyncratic response types.

Some semantically related responses occur so frequently in word association data from native speakers that they have been described as prototypical or canonical associations. Moreover, a number of researchers have reported an increased tendency to supply canonical links as proficiency develops (see Namei, 2002, 2004). Canonical response types were therefore included in the coding scheme. Based on the native speaker norming data collected for this study, it was possible to develop objective criteria for identifying the most frequent – that is, canonical – responses to each stimulus word. As discussed in 2.3.1, several responses can be described as canonical in relation to a given stimulus word, but the number of frequently occurring responses varies from stimulus word to stimulus word. In order to operate with the same number of canonical responses across the different word classes, across the two languages and in the receptive and the productive task, it was decided that the five most frequent responses from the baseline data to each target word would ideally be regarded as canonical links. Some of the stimulus words, however, gave rise to so many different associations that it was decided that only responses given by roughly ten per cent or more of the

Declarative Lexical Knowledge 47

informants from the norming groups could meaningfully be classified as canonical links. This procedure generated an almost equal number of canonical links in the two data sets (English = 183 and Danish = 184).

Namei (2002, 2004) found that her advanced informants supplied more low frequent, semantically related responses than the less advanced informants did. As discussed in 2.3.1, the ability to supply low frequent responses could be viewed as a hallmark of advanced organizational structure. This distinction was therefore included in the taxonomy of response types, using the 5000 word level as a cut-off point between high frequent and low frequent responses. According to Nation and Waring (Nation, 2001; Waring and Nation, 2004), the first 5000 words will give text coverage of approximately 90 per cent for any text type. Moreover, many researchers have mentioned the 5000-word level as a vocabulary threshold for language use, arguing that language users with an L2 vocabulary size under this level cannot transfer important L1 higher order skills – for instance, reading or writing strategies – to an L2 task. Lastly, the Danish frequency dictionary (Bergenholz, 1992), which had been used for the development of the L1 vocabulary size test (see 2.5.1 below), only ranked the first 5000 words in the corpus. Ideally, similar frequency lists should be used in the coding procedure for the two data sets. It was therefore decided to base the coding of the L2 data on the frequency indications from the web based list found at: ftp://ftp.itri.bton.ac.uk/bnc/lemma.alfind. The English frequency indications were double-checked with the indications in Leech et al. (2001), and Bergenholz (1992) was used for the coding of the Danish data.

Based on the distinctions discussed above, a final coding scheme with ten response types was developed (Figure 2.5 and Appendix A.2). The abbreviations printed in bold indicate the ten response types included in the task analysis. The response types are mutually exclusive, in that only one code could be given to each of the valid responses elicited from each informant on each task.[9] The first four response types ('empty' (E), 'repetition' (R), 'translation' (T) and 'ragbag' (RB)) were regarded as 'unqualified' response types; that is, instances where the informants failed to provide a form-related or semantically related response. The analysis of the other responses included six central response types: one form-related response type and five subcategories of semantically related responses. The chaining responses (CH) are semantically related associations to the informant's first association (see Appendix A.2); that is, not direct associations to the stimulus word.

The retrospective data were used extensively in the coding procedure to support the actual decisions made by the researchers. High interscorer

48 *Vocabulary and Writing in L1 and L2*

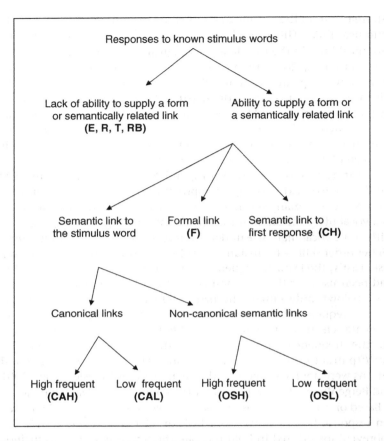

Figure 2.5 Response types identified in the word association data

reliability, based on a coding of 12 (13.79 per cent) of the word association tests from each language by two independent researchers, was established (Cohen's Kappa: L2 data: 0.876; L1 data: 0.833).

Since some of the target words turned out to be unknown or were misheard by some of the informants, the results are only given for the valid responses for each individual informant and are reported in percentages.

Need for an overall word association score

A central research aim in the lexical study has been to find a method of describing the overall network quality of the informants' lexicon that would enable us to make comparisons between the learners' level of productive network knowledge across the two languages. Moreover, the findings from an overall productive network score could be compared with some of the other lexical measures included in the study: the receptive word connection task score, the vocabulary size and the various lexical inferencing measures.

Development in the lexical network may be envisaged as a shifting pattern of response behaviour, reflecting changes in the relative distribution of the same general response types. The focus in much word association research, as discussed in detail above, has been on describing these general shifts in response behaviour across learner groups; for instance, between L1 and the L2 informants or between L2 learners from different proficiency levels. Unfortunately, very few endeavours have been made to use word association results in a way that would enable the researcher to transpose these patterns into a word association measure, which would allow direct comparisons across individual learners in the form of a ranking of the relative structural properties of their mental lexicon.

Schmitt (1998) and Wolter (2002) have developed methods for calculating a general word association score, suggesting a procedure of identifying the canonical responses and using weighted stereotypy scores awarded in relation to the relative canonicity of the responses given; that is, giving higher scores to more frequent native speaker responses. Many canonical links are, unsurprisingly, high frequent lexical items. For example, only 28 out of the 183 canonical links in our English norming data are low frequent links and many of these links are only just above the 5000-word level. As documented by Namei (2002, 2004), advanced learners are more likely to supply low frequent responses than less proficient learners are. If canonical associations (for instance, the response 'glass' to the stimulus word 'window') were awarded higher scores as a hallmark of advanced network structure than non-canonical, low frequent semantically related links (for instance, the response 'sill' or 'glazing' to 'window'), the potential shift in response behaviour towards more low frequent semantic responses documented by Namei would, in effect, lead to a decrease in word association scores for more advanced learners. It was therefore decided not to use a scoring system based on response stereotypy.

Due to the problems discussed above, a scoring system was developed, based on the findings in previous word association studies, which have described various developmental shifts in response behaviour across

50   *Vocabulary and Writing in L1 and L2*

Table 2.5   Scores awarded to different response types

Response type	Examples from L2 with the stimulus word 'bread'	Score
Inability to supply an L1 or L2 response ('unqualified')	*brød* (L1 translation) bread (repetition of stimulus)	0
Form-related	red	1
Chaining	table	1
High frequent non-canonical, but semantically related	white, birds	2
High frequent canonical	food, water	3
Low frequent canonical	toast, loaf	4
Low frequent non-canonical, but semantically related	grainy, flour	5

proficiency levels: (1) a shift from form-related to meaning-based responses; (2) increase in the number of canonical responses; (3) increase in the number of low frequent responses. Each of the valid responses given by an informant was then categorized and awarded a separate response type score according to the taxonomy of response types developed (Table 2.5).

A response type score was calculated for each informant by dividing the total score with the number of valid items. Unsurprisingly, some of the weaker informants would often give the same response to a number of different stimulus words. To minimize the effect of such mere repetition across the data set, the response type score was then multiplied with a lexical variation score that had been calculated on the basis of the individual informant's semantic responses.[10] This scoring procedure generated an overall word association score for each informant, both for their L1 and their L2.

The overall score is seen as a measure of the individual learner's productive network knowledge of a number of high frequent nouns and adjectives. However, it must be pointed out that the score can only give an estimate of network knowledge for a certain stratum of the lexicon, based on lexical items from two word classes taken from a limited frequency range. The results based on the overall word association score are presented in Table 2.6 below.

Table 2.6 Overall word association score

		G.7	G.10	G.13
	M	151.83	208.65	221.77
L2	SD	49.76	25.26	28.95
	M	217.89	238.65	239.17
L1	SD	24.23	19.82	31.85

Results for the overall word association score

To determine whether there was an overall difference between the two languages in relation to the overall word association score, an ANOVA was performed. The results showed significant language differences across the grade levels; that is, for all three educational levels, the L1 scores were higher than the L2 scores (ANOVA: $p <$ .001 (G.7: $F (1, 28) = 56.282$; G.10: $F (1, 28) = 37.065$; G.13: $F (1, 28) = 22.659$).

Looking at the differences across the three educational levels on the L2 WAT scores, significant differences were found between G.7 and G.10 and between G.7 and G.13 (Tamhane: $p < .001$), but no differences were found between the G.10 and the G.13 informants. The same results were found for the L1 scores across the three educational levels; that is, significant differences could be detected between G.7 and G.10 (Tukey: $p <. 010$) and between G.7 and G.13 (Tukey: $p < .006$), whereas we found no differences between G.10 and G.13.

In the previous section, we have presented the results on the overall word association score. Clearly, all three learner groups did better in their native language compared with the foreign language. The cross-sectional results for both languages showed that the intermediate and advanced learners outperformed the younger pupils, whereas the task failed to discriminate between the informants from G.10 and G.13. These findings will be discussed later in connection with a more general discussion of the results found for both network tasks. We will now look at the WAT data more qualitatively, exploring whether differences can be found for the various response types given in the word association task (Table 2.7). This analysis may give us a better understanding of the underlying differences in the informants' network knowledge.

52   *Vocabulary and Writing in L1 and L2*

Table 2.7   Differences in response types in L1 and L2

Type of response	L1/L2		G.7	G.10	G.13
		M	21.42%	6.23%	4.28%
	L2	SD	22.16	7.41	5.20
Unqualified responses		M	5.54%	1.76 %	2.23%
	L1	SD	6.96	2.67	2.62
		M	27.40%	33.90%	32.55%
	L2	SD	12.43	9.89	11.72
Canonical responses		M	37.49%	39.62%	36.97%
	L1	SD	10.94	10.97	11.54
		M	5.05%	9.8%	12.8%
	L2	SD	3.55	3.51	5.75
Low frequent responses		M	13.29%	14.93%	16.15%
	L1	SD	5.73	5.44	6.82

'Unqualified' responses

The question of the relative number of links in the mental lexicon is touched upon indirectly in the first step of our analysis of the different WAT responses. The four 'unqualified' response categories (responses coded as empty, repetition, translation or ragbag) can be interpreted as the informants' lack of ability to provide a form- related or a semantically related association. In other words, the number of 'unqualified' response categories reveals the extent to which the informants did not have immediately accessible links in their mental lexicon.

The L1 scores for the 'unqualified' responses were significantly lower than the L2 scores for all three educational levels (ANOVA: G.7: $F (1, 28) = 16.258$, $p < .001$; G.10: $F (1, 28) = 11.029$, $p < .003$; G.3: $F (1, 28) = 7.949$, $p < .009$); that is, the informants found it much more difficult to supply an associative response in the L2 than in their L1. Looking at the L2 scores for the three educational levels, significant differences were found between G.7 and G.10 (Tamhane: $p < .004$) and between G.7 and G.13 (Tamhane: $p < .001$), whereas no differences were found between the G.10 and the G.13 informants. Regarding the Danish data, a significant difference was also established between the G.7 and G.10 (Tamhane: $p < .029$), whereas no difference was found between the scores for the G.7 and G.13 informants and the G.10 and the G.13 learners.

In the model of lexical representation presented above, it was envisaged that associative links between the L1 and the L2 lexical items exist.

Declarative Lexical Knowledge 53

The weaker informants who do not have easy access to an L2 association would therefore be expected to resort to a Danish response in the foreign language task. The results for the translation types in the L2 data are, however, unexpectedly low for all three informant groups (G.7: 1.97 per cent > G.10: 1.29 per cent > G.13: 0.54 per cent).

Form-related and semantically related responses
As discussed above, research has shown that the more advanced lexicon is primarily meaning driven, and it has been established that the organizational structure of the mental lexicon is highly affected by degree of knowledge of the individual word (Söderman, 1993; Wolter, 2001). Since we are dealing with very high frequent stimulus words, it was expected that if the informants were able to give a response, it would be in the form of semantically related responses, and that even the low level informants would only supply very few form-related responses. This prediction was clearly confirmed by the data. Most of the associations given by learners from any of the grade levels are, indeed, in the form of lexical items that are semantically related, either to the stimulus word (response types: OSH, OSL, CAH and CAL) or to the first response given (CH). Only a very limited number of the L2 responses were form-driven (G.7: 1.29 per cent; G.10: 0.29 per cent; G.13: 0.75 per cent). The same picture emerges for the L1 data (G.7: 0.63 per cent; G.10: 0.60 per cent; G.13: 0.67 per cent). The form-related responses found in the data from the university students are given by very few informants.

Canonical responses and low frequent responses
In the discussion above, we focused on the informants' ability to supply semantically related links. Let us now look in more detail at the meaning-based responses, focusing more specifically on the results for the canonical and the low frequent, semantically related responses.

As can be seen from the figures in Table 2.7, only about 27 to almost 40 per cent of the associations given were canonical links; that is, responses mirroring the five most frequent associations to each stimulus word given by the native speakers from the norming groups. To determine whether there was an overall difference between the number of canonical links in the L1 and the L2, an ANOVA was performed. A statistically significant difference was found for all three educational levels; that is, the L2 scores were significantly lower than the L1 scores (ANOVA: G.7: $F (1, 28) = 16.048$, $p < .001$; G.10: $F (1, 28) = 8.200$, $p < .008$; G.13: $F (1, 28) = 6.554$, $p < .016$). Looking at the L2 or the L1 data, no significant differences were found between any of the three

54 *Vocabulary and Writing in L1 and L2*

educational levels in relation to the number of canonical responses given in any of the languages.

If we look more closely at the actual figures, it is evident that the percentages of canonical links increase from G.7 to G.10 and then decrease again for the G.13 informants in both data sets, even if this trend does not reach statistical significance. For the L1 data, the G.13 informants even supply fewer canonical links than the G.7 informants. This result tallies with the expectations voiced previously: that the canonical responses reflect links that become well established in the net as experience with the target language increases. With increasing proficiency, the more advanced informants are also able to supply other associations; for example, in the form of low frequent, non-canonical links to which the younger learners with smaller vocabularies are less likely to have access.

Both the canonical responses and the 'other semantically related' responses were coded in relation to frequency. Based on the results reported by Namei (2002, 2004), the expectation was that more low frequent responses (CAL and OSL) would be found in the Danish data compared with the English data. Moreover, one would expect a significant increase in the number of low frequent responses across the three educational levels for the English WAT.

As predicted, the analysis revealed significant language differences for all three educational levels; that is, more low frequent responses were given in the L1 data compared with the L2 task (ANOVA: $p < .001$ (G.7: $F (1, 28) = 53.928$; G.10: $F (1, 28) = 26.825$; G.13: $F (1, 28) = 12.619$). Looking at the L2 data, Tamhane tests showed significant differences between G.7 and G.10 ($p < .001$) and between G.7 and G.13 ($p < .001$). A difference was also found between G.10 and G.13, but this difference did not reach statistical significance ($p < .060$). For the Danish data, no significant differences were found between any of the three educational levels; that is, the informants tended to give the same number of low frequent links when operating in L1, irrespective of grade level.

The findings are in line with the results that will be reported later in relation to the vocabulary size data. Here, it was found that all the informants reached the 5000-word frequency level in their native language, whereas only four G.10 informants and ten G.13 informants reached the cut-off point for this word level in the L2 data. In other words, many of the informants do not seem to have a vocabulary in the foreign language that is sufficiently large to enable them to respond with low frequent lexical items in the productive word association task. In the L1, the learners' vocabulary is sufficiently large to enable them to create links to low frequent words, words that are therefore available as potential responses in the WAT.

2.4.5 Summary and discussion of the findings related to network knowledge

Looking at the within-subject results first, differences between the two languages were found for the receptive word connection task across all three educational groups; that is, the informants identified a larger number of strong (= canonical) links in the L1 task compared with the L2 task. These results mirror the research findings reported in previous studies on receptive network knowledge. For the overall productive word association score, the L1 scores were also higher than the L2 scores across all three grade levels. When looking more closely at the different response types given on the word association task, it was found that the informants from all three educational levels gave fewer 'unqualified' responses, but more canonical and low frequent responses in the L1 compared with the L2. In other words, the learners' L2 network knowledge was found to be significantly different from their L1 network knowledge, both receptively and productively.

Turning to the between-subject results, significant differences in the L2 ratings were found between G.7 and the two other educational levels on both network tasks, whereas no differences could be detected between the G.10 and G.13 informants. The analysis of L2 response types showed that G.7 pupils gave more 'unqualified' responses than G.10 and G.13 informants who, in turn, were able to supply more low frequent semantically related responses than were the informants from G.7. No statistical differences were found across any of the educational levels in relation to the number of canonical links supplied. The results for the L1 data were more mixed. On the WCT scores, significant differences were found between G.7 and G.10, whereas no significant differences were found between G.10 and G.13 or between G.7 and G.13. For the overall WAT scores in L1, we found significant differences again between G.7 and the two other educational levels, whereas no significant differences were found between G.10 and G.13. Looking more closely at the response types in the word association task, no differences were found across the three grade levels on the Danish task; that is, we could not identify the source of difference found between the younger and the more advanced informants.

The results on both network tasks indicate that the learners operate differently in the two languages both receptively and productively, irrespective of educational level. In other words, the organizational

56 *Vocabulary and Writing in L1 and L2*

structure of the L1 and the L2 mental lexicon is both quantitatively and qualitatively different, not only for the younger beginners from G.7, but also for the more intermediate learners from sixth-form colleges as well as our more advanced informants who study English at university level. The results are rather surprising, considering the fact that we are tapping into not only productive but also receptive network knowledge of very high frequent nouns and adjectives – lexical items that would be expected to be fairly well established in the mental lexicon of at least the intermediate or the advanced informants. It could be hypothesized that the differences found between L1 and L2 would have been even more pronounced had we tapped into their network knowledge of high frequent verbs or more low frequent vocabulary items across all the major word classes.

Even if the cross-sectional results for L2 indicate that some development in relation to network knowledge has taken place for the G.10 and G.13 informants, the within-subject results clearly show that the L2 lexicon seems to 'lag behind' in respect of organizational properties. In the present study, we operate with very high frequent stimulus words that are expected to be well-known by the more advanced learners but, even for the university students, a difference could be detected between L1 and L2. This is a clear indication of the 'tortoise-like' slowness of the acquisition of network knowledge which has earlier been described by Aitchison (1987) for the L1 lexicon and which was pointed out by Greidanus and Nienhuis (2001) for L2 learners. It is likely that development of native-like L2 network knowledge requires large amounts of repeated exposure to authentic target language input in varying contexts. Even if the availability of un-dubbed and authentic English language input is extremely high in Denmark, the amount of repeated exposure in the form of varied oral and written input afforded in a foreign language environment may still not be enough to develop the same organizational properties of the mental lexicon in the target language compared with the native language.

If we focus on L1 development, it is interesting to note that Greidanus et al., (2005) found a difference between advanced and very advanced native speakers when testing low frequent items above the 5000-word level. This was seen as an indication of the continuous growth of depth of vocabulary knowledge, not only for L2 learners, but also for native speakers. Our tasks did not discriminate in the same way for L1, which may be explained by the fact that we are dealing with very high frequent items.

2.5 Looking at the informants' vocabulary size

In the previous sections, we have focused on the informants' receptive and productive network knowledge. Let us now turn to the investigation of their vocabulary size in L1 and L2.

2.5.1 The test formats

Nation's 'Vocabulary Levels Test' was used as an elicitation tool to measure our informants' L2 (English) vocabulary size (see Nation, 2001: 416–24 for a complete version of the test used). In this test format, which measures receptive knowledge of word meaning, the informants are asked to match lexical items with synonyms or short definitions in a multiple choice format. The version chosen was the updated form of the test, developed by Schmitt et al., (2001). The Levels Test has the advantage of being well described: it has been validated, and it has often been used as a general measure of vocabulary size in vocabulary acquisition research and in a number of pedagogical studies. Another advantage of the test format is that it tests vocabulary across a number of frequency bands, so it is well suited to test informant groups such as ours, which span large age differences and proficiency ranges. However, the Academic Word Level, which is one of the five frequency bands in the original test format, includes academic words across a range of different frequency bands. For our research purposes, it was decided to exclude this band of more specialized vocabulary; a procedure which left us with a final vocabulary size test with 120 test items across four frequency bands (2000-, 3000-, 5000- and 10,000-word level).

It was not possible for us to find an existing Danish vocabulary size elicitation tool that was comparable with the Levels Test, and which would fit our research purposes. A parallel L1 vocabulary size test was therefore developed specifically for the project. The validation of the task was carried out in close collaboration with Dr Norbert Schmitt from the University of Nottingham, who had validated the original L2 version of the Levels Test.[11] The L1 task follows the L2 test format as closely as possible, with 120 test items across four frequency bands. However, because it had been developed to measure the vocabulary of our informants' native language, and with the purpose of being suitable for discriminating between native speakers from three educational groups, it was decided to choose four frequency levels that included more low frequent items than Nation's L2 test. This procedure was

58 *Vocabulary and Writing in L1 and L2*

necessary in order ensure that the Danish L1 version was well-suited to test advanced native speakers; that is, challenging enough for our university students.

Few updated Danish frequency lists exist, and none of the Danish corpora lists all the vocabulary items in broad frequency bands similar to the levels adopted in the English test. The best option was a Danish frequency dictionary (Bergenholz, 1992), which was used to establish the relative frequency of both the target items and the distractors included in the test. Each of the four frequency levels in the Danish test reflects the number of overall instances of the words in the dictionary database: Level 1 = 60 instances in the corpus (approximately equivalent to the 5000-word level), Level 2 = 25 instances; Level 3 = 10 instances and Level 4 = between 1 to 5 instances. As can be seen, Levels 2 to 4 include fairly or extremely low frequent vocabulary items from the Danish corpus.

The two tests target different frequency bands but, in relation to word classes tested, the number of test items included, the procedure used and the instructions given, the two tasks were designed to be as parallel in design as possible.

2.5.2 Predictions about vocabulary size

We know that the size of our vocabularies continues to expand throughout our lives, influenced by the amount and type of language to which we are exposed. Unsurprisingly, high frequent lexical items are most often acquired first due to the frequent and varied exposure we get to these items in all types of language input. Low frequent items are often acquired and established in our mental lexicon through reading input, and the acquisition of these words is often related to our educational experience in a more formal school setting and our widening literacy training and mastery. All our informants will naturally have had earlier and far more input and interaction in their L1 than in their L2. On the basis of the differences in age, in the numbers of years being exposed to English and in general educational experience between our grade level groups, it was therefore predicted that a substantial difference in vocabulary scores would be found both across the two languages as well as across the three educational levels when looking at each language separately. Moreover, one would expect to find a significant difference in relation to the frequency levels acquired across the two languages, as well as across the three informant groups.

Overall scores

The two vocabulary size tests were scored in relation to both the overall number of correct items (maximum score 120) and the informants'

Table 2.8 L2 and L1 vocabulary size scores

		G.7	G.10	G.13
L2	M	33.79	71.86	94.79
	SD	22.44	20.59	14.71
L1	M	50.24	83.52	102.10
	SD	18.4	18.74	10.12

mastery of the different frequency bands. The overall results from the English and Danish vocabulary size tests are reported in Table 2.8. Again, it is important to stress that the Danish test includes more low frequent items than the English test.

As could be predicted, the vocabulary size scores for the English test were significantly lower than the Danish test scores for all three educational levels (ANOVA: G.7: $F_{(1, 28)} = 27.874$, $p < .001$; G.10: $F_{(1, 28)} = 13.525$, $p < .001$; G.13: $F_{(1, 28)} = 10.667$, $p < .003$). Looking at the English or the Danish data separately, significant differences across the three educational levels were found in both data sets (Tamhane: L2: $p < .001$; L1 $p < .001$).

It is evident that the informants managed to do far better on the L1 vocabulary test compared with the L2 task, irrespective of the fact that the L1 test targets lexical knowledge of more low frequent items than the L2 test. It had been our hope that the L1 test format, with more low frequent items, would be sensitive enough to enable us to discriminate between the informants, even in their native language. The results for both vocabulary tests did, in fact, reveal significant differences between the three grade levels and showed the expected linear development: G.7 < G.10 < G.13.

Results in relation to the four frequency bands

An overall test score can only give us a rough estimate of the informants' vocabulary size, but the score does not tell us which range of lexical items is mastered by the individual test taker. Does the learner know a range of lexical items across the whole vocabulary, or is it that less advanced informants primarily score correctly on the high frequent items included in the test and know only a few infrequent words?

The levels test format, spanning four different frequency levels, enables us to establish which frequency bands have been acquired by the informants. In the test format, the maximum score for each frequency band is 30. Some researchers have argued that a score of

60   *Vocabulary and Writing in L1 and L2*

26 out of 30 items on a specific frequency band in Nation's Levels Test reflects that the test taker masters the frequency level in question. Thus, a score of 26 or above on Level 1 on this L2 test signifies that the language learner has a vocabulary of approximately 2000 words. This cut-off point for establishing a vocabulary threshold for each frequency level was adopted in the present study.

Table 2.9 lists the number of informants who have reached a certain frequency level, bold print marking where the results tend to cluster for each grade level (again: N = 29 at each level). Level 1 of the Danish test roughly reflects a mastery of the 5000-word frequency band.

It is unsurprising that all the informants, irrespective of grade level, have mastered Level 1 in their native language. Many of the informants have reached Levels 2 and 3, and a few university students even managed to reach Level 4, which represents knowledge of extremely infrequent vocabulary items.

Looking at the scores for the English test, only 14 out of the 87 informants have a vocabulary corresponding to or above the 5000-word frequency level. Of the informants, 35 – most of them, unsurprisingly, from G.7 – are even below the 2000-word level. Some of these G.7 informants have obtained a general vocabulary score as high as 66 and yet still do not manage to reach the cut-off point established for the 2000-word level. In other words, they seem to know a fair number of

Table 2.9   Informants' acquisition level on the vocabulary size test

The Danish Levels Test				The English Levels Test			
	G7	G10	G13		G7	G10	G13
				Level 0	24	11	0
Level 0	0	0	0	Level 1 2000 words	5	12	8
				Level 2 3000 words	0	2	11
Level 1 60 times	22	11	2	Level 3 5000 words	0	4	5
Level 2 25 times	7	13	8				
Level 3 10 times	0	5	15	Level 4 10,000 words	0	0	5
Level 4 1–5 times	0	0	4				

English words, but do not exhibit stability within the frequency bands containing high frequent items to reach the cut-off points for these levels. The same can be said for the surprisingly many G.10 and G.13 informants who fall below the 5000-word level cut-off point. Some of these informants do not even meet the Level 1 or Level 2 test score requirements, disregarding the fact that many of them score correctly on half or even more of the items on the overall test results and almost reach the cut-off point for one or even two of the levels above.

A statistically significant difference was found in the informants' vocabulary size both across languages and across the three educational levels; that is, all the groups obtained higher scores on the Danish test compared with the English test, irrespective of the fact that the L1 task targeted more low frequent vocabulary items. Moreover, it was established that most of the learners failed to reach the cut-off point for mastering the 5000-word level in L2. By contrast, all learners were on or above this level in their L1. Research literature has emphasized the importance of having a well-established sight vocabulary base of at least 5000 words to be able to operate in an L2 (Laufer, 1997a; see Section 2.1.1). As will be discussed below, the lack of ability to reach this threshold level is likely to have an impact on these learners' ability to operate efficiently in the L2.

2.6 Correlations between the lexical measures

In the previous sections, the results from the different lexical measures (receptive and productive network knowledge and vocabulary size) have been presented. We also looked at possible correlations between the three lexical measures. First, we investigated whether correlations could be found between the Danish and English versions of the WAT, the WCT and the size scores. The only correlation found in the Danish data was between the Danish WAT and the Danish size test for the G.7 informants ($.526^{**}$, $p < 0.01$). For the English data, no correlations were found between the WCT and the WAT, or between the WCT and the size test for the G.10 and G.13 informants. High correlations were, however, found between the English WAT and the English size test across all educational levels (G.7: $.852^{**}$; G.10: $.689^{**}$; G.13: $.546^{**}$, all $p < 0.01$). Moreover, correlations were found between the English WCT and WAT ($.708^{**}$, $p < 0.01$), and between the English WCT and the size test ($.715^{**}$, $p < 0.01$) for the G.7 informants.

The fact that so few correlations were found may perhaps be explained by the differences in the 'sensitivity' of the three tasks, not

62 Vocabulary and Writing in L1 and L2

Table 2.10 Correlations between the lexical measures in L2 and L1

Comparisons	Correlated measures	G.7	G.10	G.13
The three	SIZE L1 – SIZE L2	** .754	** .615	** .631
tasks across	WCT L1 – WCT L2	** .623	** .491	** .685
L1 and L2	WAT L1 – WAT L2	* . 445	.229	** .640

Notes: Significant correlations at the 0.01 level (two-tailed) ** or 0.05 level (two-tailed) *

only in relation to the frequency levels targeted, but also in relation to other design features. Both network tasks measure knowledge of high frequent nouns and adjectives, whereas the size task targets a much larger stratum of lexical knowledge, including low frequent items across three word classes. The difference is especially pronounced for the Danish tasks. The Danish size test taps into very low frequent items on or far below the 5000-word level, whereas both the receptive and productive network tasks include words that are extremely high frequent and thus well-established in the vocabulary of native speakers. Moreover, the receptive WCT with time for reflection may be expected to be less taxing for the informants than the productive WAT with a very tight time limit for response. These differences may, as discussed before, also influence the type of network knowledge we are able to tap into.

We also looked at the correlations between the lexical scores in L2 and L1 in order to investigate whether there is a close relationship between how an individual informant fares on the same lexical task type in the two languages (Table 2.10).

In comparison with the results between the three lexical tasks, a number of correlations were found for all three tasks when comparing L1 and L2. Only the overall word association task scores for the G.10 informants do not correlate. In other words, learners with 'good', 'medium' or 'low' vocabulary knowledge in their L1 seem to be faring equally well or equally badly on the same lexical measures in their L2.

2.7 Concluding remarks

This chapter has focused on different aspects of our learners' declarative lexical knowledge, both in relation to size and network structure. Unsurprisingly, the results from the size tests show that the learners' L2 vocabulary lags behind their L1 knowledge. Moreover, significant differences could be found across all three grade levels in both languages. Research literature has emphasized the importance of having a well-established sight vocabulary base of at least 5000 words to be able to operate in an L2. Few of the G.7 and G.10 informants managed to reach the cut-off point for the 5000-word level in L2. Moreover, similar to the findings reported by Nurweni and Read (1999) for their Indonesian university students, many of our university informants have an L2 vocabulary smaller than 5000 words.

The lack of stability in the informants' L2 vocabulary knowledge with regard to vocabulary items from the high frequency bands was also reflected in the results of our productive and receptive network tasks. Greidanus, Beks and Wakely (2005) found a difference between L1 and L2, and between advanced and very advanced informants when measuring low frequent items. In the present study, however, it was surprising to find that differences could be detected between L1 and L2 for all three educational levels on both network tasks, which tap into relational knowledge of very high frequent lexical items. These differences were also reflected in the number of canonical links and low frequent links provided by the informants in the Danish and the English WAT tasks; that is, the ability to supply canonical and especially low frequent links was found to be the hallmark of the more advanced lexicon. As argued previously, the results found could be an indication that not only acquiring a large vocabulary, but also developing a 'native-like' organizational structure takes a great deal of time and may be dependent on enormous amounts of input and types of language exposure that are not readily available to the foreign language learner. It is highly likely that the results found, both in terms of the frequency bands mastered and in relation to quality of network knowledge, will have negative implications for our informants' ability to function efficiently in online communicative tasks in the foreign language.

Research perspectives and pedagogical implications

The three lexical tasks employed differ, not only in relation to the constructs operationalized, but also in relation to the vocabulary items targeted. The fact that we have been dealing with learners spanning three educational levels forced us to include high frequent items as stimulus words in the two network tasks. A research design where all three lexical tasks target the same vocabulary items across a range of frequency bands – for example, in line with the network task format developed by Greidanus and Nienhuis (2001) – would possibly have brought out more correlations between the lexical scores for productive and receptive network knowledge and vocabulary size. The Levels Size

64 *Vocabulary and Writing in L1 and L2*

Test format, which ensures that the task becomes progressively more demanding, could be used in the design of other lexical tasks, enabling the researcher to develop more comparable lexical tasks for both vocabulary breadth and depth.

Henriksen (1999) has argued that a relationship exists between different dimensions of vocabulary knowledge, hypothesizing that development in one dimension would effect development in the others. Correlations between the L2 word association task and the L2 vocabulary size test did indicate that some relationship exists between size and organizational properties of the L2 lexicon. The present research design, which includes a measure for vocabulary size and two measures for network knowledge, does not, however, enable us to throw more light on this. Greidanus and her colleagues have put valuable effort into developing a valid receptive task format in line with Read's word associates test and the receptive word connection task used here. The work on developing a method for establishing an overall word association score carried out in the present study has enabled us to quantify the productive network knowledge of the lexical items tested. Task development of this kind is a prerequisite for carrying out research that involves comparisons across learners and between different lexical measures, reflecting different underlying lexical constructs. A future study, including a vocabulary size test, a receptive network task, a productive word association task and a test format that could tap into the informants' level of word knowledge in line with the Vocabulary Knowledge Scale developed by Wesche and Paribakht (1996) could be a possible way of testing whether a relationship exists between the different dimensions of vocabulary knowledge.

The results of the present study have shown that our informants' need to develop their vocabulary knowledge further, both in terms of size and network structure. Despite the fact that English is one of the central subjects throughout the educational system, with an emphasis on reading authentic texts, and despite the availability of English language input in Denmark, learners may still benefit from more systematic and explicit vocabulary work in the classroom, including various kinds of lexical tasks focusing on words from different semantic fields; for example, mind maps, sorting and gradation tasks. Moreover, learners may benefit from reading material that is organized thematically, ensuring that related lexical items are recycled and presented in varying contexts. It may also be beneficial to include tasks that raise and strengthen learners' meta-semantic awareness of network relations. Finally, using test types that also target network knowledge in the form of word associates tests or productive association tasks may give learners a realistic picture of the quality of their lexical competence, motivating them to continue to develop their vocabulary not only in terms of size, but also in relation to quality.

Notes

1 Analytic relations can be defined as words that describe a key feature of the stimulus word and are therefore often found in a dictionary definition of the word; for instance, 'night' and 'dark' in relation to 'moon'.
2 Meara and Wolter (2004) subsequently amended the elicitation tool, and are now exploring the use of a computerized task version called V_link. In this format, ten stimulus words are presented together, and the test taker is asked to identify potential association pairs between the lexical items and to rate the relative strength of the connections found.
3 In the retrospective sessions for both network tasks, the informants were told to describe as precisely as possible why they had chosen the specific word as a strong link (in the WCT), or why the specific associations had been given (in the WAT).
4 Knowledge of the stimulus words was necessary in order for the informants to be able to carry out the receptive task. This naturally affects the results of the productive word association task; that is, fewer empty or phonologically related responses were expected compared with a task including additional low frequent stimulus words.
5 At the time of task development, our own native speaker baseline data had not yet been collected. The word association responses from four existing word association norming lists were therefore conflated to find five canonical links for each stimulus word; that is, the most frequently given responses: Jenkins (1952); Miller (1961, 1962) – English list; Miller (1957, 1958) – Australian list – reported in Postman and Keppel (1970); Edinburgh Association Thesaurus (Internet resource: http://www.eat.rl.ac.uk/).
6 The word connection task was developed and field-tested during 2001. At the time, we were not acquainted with the studies carried out by Greidanus and her colleagues, so we were unfortunately unable to lean on the valuable experience and expertise of the Dutch researchers.
7 We would like to thank staff and students from the English Department in Glasgow and the Nordic Department in Copenhagen for their participation, and for ensuring that the data collection could take place under optimal research conditions.
8 Field-testing in two grade 6 classes (one educational level below our youngest informants) had revealed a fairly good overall knowledge of all the lexical items included in the task material. However, an explanation for the difference found between L1 and L2 in the word connection task scores across the three educational levels could be that our informants did not have sufficient receptive L2 vocabulary knowledge of the potential links from they were asked to choose. The informants had been asked to indicate lack of word knowledge on the task sheet, but only a few of the strong relations (canonical links) were marked as unknown, with most of these found in the G.7 data. For

66 *Vocabulary and Writing in L1 and L2*

the G.7 informants, the significant differences between L1 and L2 could therefore, in part, be caused by insufficient L2 knowledge of potential network links.

9   The task format was field-tested in two grade 6 classes to ensure that the stimulus words would be known to most of our informants. As an additional precaution, the informants were asked to indicate lack of knowledge of the stimulus words on the task sheet or in the retrospective session. It turned out that some of the weaker informants did not know some of the stimulus words, so these words were coded as unknown and disregarded in the data analysis for the individual informant. In cases where the stimulus word has been misheard and associations were therefore given to a wrong lexical item (for instance, the Danish stimulus word 'hård' = 'hard' misheard as 'hår' = 'hair'), these words were also left out of the analysis. All other responses were regarded as valid associations and coded according to response type.

10 A lexical variation score was calculated: we divided the number of lexical types an individual informant used by the number of semantically related responses given by the same informant and multiplied this by 100.

11 Anja Knudsen, one of our MA students carried out much of the practical work involved with test development. We would like to thank Dr Norbert Schmitt for his invaluable help in relation to the validation of the Danish version of the Levels Test and Anja Knudsen for her work in the development and validation process. Any shortcomings in the development, validation and use of the test are, of course, entirely our responsibility.

3
Lexical Inferencing Procedures in Two Languages

Kirsten Haastrup

The lexical inferencing study deals with the way in which informants try to guess the meaning of unfamiliar words placed in a context that is comprehensible to them. The aim is to give a detailed account of an individual's first or early encounter with a new word. Our definition of lexical inferencing is taken from Haastrup (1991: 13).

> The process of lexical inferencing involves making informed guesses as to the meaning of a word in the light of all available linguistic cues in combination with the learner's general knowledge of the world, her awareness of the co-text and her relevant linguistic knowledge.

As pointed out in Chapter 1, a common feature of all three studies is that we have data from the same informants performing parallel tasks in their first language, Danish, and their first foreign language, English. Thus, we have a comprehensive database that, also for lexical inferencing, allows us to draw on L1 data when we attempt to interpret L2 data. Our specific research questions are therefore closely connected with the main research question concerning similarities and differences between our informants' behaviour in L1 and L2.

In order to give the reader a first impression of our approach, we quote an example from the L2 lexical inferencing task. The example is taken from a text about Africa that includes the following passage: 'The town is very dirty. All the people are hot, they have dust between their toes, and there is a strong smell of **sewage** in the air. We both fell ill, and my friend had bouts of diarrhea.' The informants' task is to verbalize all their thoughts and ideas concerning the test words (printed in bold type), ending their considerations with a guess of what the word means.

67

68 *Vocabulary and Writing in L1 and L2*

a very strong smell of sewage – in the air – sewage – age at the end – sew/su:/ – age – I would say the word diseases – there is – strong smell of diseases in the air perhaps sweat but I choose to say diseases – something about being sick or something – all sick – I think it means that there was disease in the air.

In this extract we can see a Grade 7 informant using cues from the text to help her solve the lexical problem with which she is faced: she draws on the immediate co-text of the test word 'in the air' as well as the essence of the following sentence, which is 'something about being sick'. She also looks for potential linguistic cues to meaning in that she pays attention to the second syllable of the test word -*age* and not – a strategy that would have been wiser – to the word stem *sewer*.

The lexical inferencing procedures have been analyzed from different angles. One is related to the informants' use of knowledge sources, including contextual as well as linguistic cues to meaning, as is evident from the example above. Moreover, we have studied the actual process through which informants arrive at their suggestion for word meaning and, finally, we have considered whether the outcome of the process is a good guess or not. Having given this first and very brief characterization of our conception of lexical inferencing, we shall now view it within a broader framework.

3.1 Situating the study within the field of lexical inferencing research

Since the field is very broad, we shall start by using bold strokes and distinguish between approaches to lexical inferencing that primarily take a lexical viewpoint and those that adopt or include a comprehension aspect. A description of these two approaches is attempted below, which also serves the purpose of characterizing our own study as one that integrates the two views.

The lexical perspective
Over the last few decades, many studies have investigated the degree to which lexical inferencing processes lead to an accurate word guess (for an early example, see Bensoussan and Laufer, 1984). Such studies focus on the product that is the result of the inferencing process. We have included this aspect in our study, referred to as levels of inferencing success, and paid attention to the influence that informants' lexical knowledge may have on the quality of their word guess. Closely linked

to this is the issue of whether word guessing procedures are likely to be effective and, following on from this, whether they can be recommended as word learning strategies. This perspective has interested many researchers, and a question often asked is whether learners' involvement in word guessing procedures for a specific word is likely to lead to their actual acquisition of that same word (see, for instance, Laufer and Hulstijn, 2001). We do not study this directly. We do, however, focus on the procedures underlying acquisition, since the use of verbal protocols gives us the advantage of gaining direct access to what the informants pay attention to or notice about the target words in the lexical inferencing task, such as, for instance, the word stem 'discriminate' in the target word 'indiscriminately'.

Early L2 lexical inferencing studies paid much attention to the aspect of knowledge sources, addressing, for instance, the extent to which the linguistic knowledge sources used by the learners were intralingual or interlingual. The target language used for the early studies was typically English and the informants' source language was often a fairly closely related language, such as French or Danish. However, the last ten years or so have seen an increasing interest in working with different target and source languages, including non-European languages (see, for instance, Mori, 2002). This has resulted in a number of studies that, in relation to knowledge sources, examine cross-linguistic influences between closely and distantly related languages. An important example of this is a recent study by Paribakht involving Farsi-speaking university students of English (Paribakht, 2005). Although the present study includes data on the use of knowledge sources, our findings relating to this issue will not receive much attention in this book, as we have chosen to focus on the processing aspect, as discussed below.

The comprehension perspective: inferencing processes at text and word level
Viewed from this perspective, lexical inferencing is closely linked to inferencing at text level, inspired by the research by, notably, Brown and Yule (1983) and by Kintsch's (1998) views on discourse comprehension. Common to these authors is that they see the process of inferencing as operating on all levels of comprehension, including text level and word level. Inferencing covers connections people make when attempting to reach an interpretation of what they read. Readers thus seek connections within the text and with their previous knowledge in an effort to construct a coherent mental representation of text meaning. It is our contention that just as inferencing ability is regarded as essential for text

70 *Vocabulary and Writing in L1 and L2*

comprehension and the reading process, lexical inferencing is crucial for word comprehension. Lexical inferencing is thus seen as a sub-category of text inferencing.

This was the approach used in the description of lexical inferencing processes in Haastrup's study (1991), which pursued the link between lexical inferencing and text comprehension. Taking inspiration from interactive reading models, Haastrup looked at the way in which reading processes in L1 and L2 were accounted for. The present study does the same in that we adopt key constructs used in the description of reading processes and adapt them to serve our purpose, as will be explained in Section 3.2.2.2.

To conclude, we shall refer to our view of lexical inferencing as an integrated approach, reflecting that our study integrates the comprehension perspective with the lexical perspective, and implying that we elicit and analyze learner processes as well as attend to our learners' achieved level of lexical inferencing success. Since this is an approach that is shared with and inspired by Canadian research, this plays an important role in the short literature review below.[1]

3.1.1 Previous research of particular relevance to the present study

A comparison between the same informants' lexical inferencing in L1 and L2 is a major issue addressed in this chapter. To our knowledge, there is no published study that includes the processing aspect, and compares the L1 and the L2 dimensions for the same groups of informants. Lexical inferencing studies of either the first or a foreign language appear to be fairly similar, in that they investigate many of the same aspects. What constitutes a major difference, however, is the age of the informants, in that L1 studies typically use very young children as informants. This means that the results from L1 studies are not really comparable with L2 studies such as ours, which use teenagers and adults as informants. Our primary focus will therefore be L2 lexical inferencing studies.

Three main aspects of L2 lexical inferencing have been studied: the knowledge sources that informants draw on, the processes involved when informants infer word meaning and, finally, the product of their attempts at inferencing. The empirical studies vary as to their coverage of these dimensions; that is, some look at one dimension only, others at two, but few include all three. It is therefore the latter multidimensional approach that receives most attention in the following.

We shall use Haastrup's (1991) study as an example of an L2 inferencing study that includes the processing aspect. The two informant groups in the study came from grade levels 9 and 12, and the investigation covered use of knowledge sources and types of processing, as well as inferencing success. One of the most innovative features of the project was the processing aspect, for which Haastrup proposed a tentative model of L2 comprehension, including a continuum of processing types. A second distinctive feature was the choice of target words for the task, in that Haastrup introduced the distinction between words with and without potential linguistic cues to meaning, and investigated this word-type issue systematically. Among the main findings relevant in this context are the following: informants' ability to use complex processing, including the ability to use knowledge sources, increases with their rising L2 proficiency level, as does the ability to produce precise guesses, referred to as a high level of inferencing success.

For many years, an important issue on the research agenda has been the question of which factors contribute the most to lexical inferencing success. A good deal of evidence supports the assumption that one decisive factor is the learners' L2 proficiency level in general (Haastrup, 1991; Quian, 1999). As early as 1993, Wesche and Paribakht began a decade of research investigating the interrelationship between learners' L2 reading comprehension, L2 vocabulary acquisition and L2 lexical inferencing procedures (Paribakht and Wesche, 1993; Wesche and Paribakht, 1995; Paribakht and Wesche, 1997; de Bot et al., 1997). Today, we know from these and other studies that two important predictors of lexical inferencing success are L2 vocabulary knowledge and L2 reading skills. As to the former, Laufer (1997b) demonstrated that lexical knowledge has an important role to play, witnessed by the low success rate of informants who lacked it; the importance of the reading factor has also been documented by Horst et al., (1998) and Huckin and Coady (1999). In 1999, Paribakht and Wesche published their influential study with the telling title '"Incidental" L2 vocabulary acquisition through reading: An introspective study', which emphasizes how difficult it is to predict word-learning outcomes. Based on data from adult ESL readers, they point to a multifactor explanation behind the achievement of lexical inferencing success that, in addition to text and word characteristics, includes variables such as learners' previous L2 learning experience and L1 transfer.

Little attention has been paid to the process aspect of lexical inferencing, but there is one recent Canadian study (Nassaji, 2004) in which adult intermediate ESL learners with different language backgrounds are investigated, both with regard to strategy use and lexical inferencing success, with the help of think-aloud protocols. He reports that strategies

72 Vocabulary and Writing in L1 and L2

were identified using an inductive procedure, and the three main strategy types were: identifying, evaluating and monitoring. A main focus in the study was the relationship between learners' vocabulary knowledge and their lexical inferencing procedures, and Nassaji's results indicate that a significant relationship exists between depth of vocabulary knowledge and type of strategy use, as well as between depth of vocabulary knowledge and inferencing success.

On the basis of the above findings, we decided to include research questions in our own study about the role played by L2 reading comprehension and L2 vocabulary knowledge in relation to L2 lexical inferencing success.

3.1.2 The research issues addressed in the present study

As mentioned above, our study adopts an integrated approach covering three central aspects of lexical inferencing. The focus of our presentation in this chapter will be the L1–L2 dimension in relation to lexical inferencing processes as well as to lexical inferencing success, as is evident from research questions one and two below. Research question three addresses the relationship between our informants' lexical inferencing success in the L2 on the one hand and their L2 reading skills and L2 vocabulary knowledge on the other. We shall report our findings in this area in Chapter 5, in which we bring together all the insights gained on our informants' lexical competence, including the results from Chapter 2.

The three research questions are:

R1 Is there a difference between the lexical inferencing processes used and the level of inferencing success achieved in L1 and L2 for the same students?

R2 Is there a difference between the lexical inferencing processes used and the level of inferencing success achieved for informants at the three educational levels?

R3 Can a relationship be found between informants' lexical inferencing success in L2 and their reading skills and vocabulary knowledge in L2?

After this introduction, we turn to a proper presentation of the study.

3.2 The lexical inferencing study

The presentation of the study includes the following main sections: the design of the study (Section 3.2.1), the analytical framework used for the coding of the verbal protocols (Sections 3.2.2 and 3.2.3) and, finally, a presentation of the results (Section 3.3), followed by a discussion (Section 3.4).

3.2.1 Design

Presenting the tasks

Two parallel *tasks* were devised, one in Danish and the other in English. It was crucial for the validity of the study to ensure that the Danish and the English inferencing tasks were parallel with respect to topics, types of test words and collection procedures.

The two tasks consisted of five short factual *texts*, all dealing with different topics. We included subject matter that was likely to be of interest to as many informants as possible and which would not be too cognitively demanding. In this regard, we focused chiefly on the youngest group – namely, the 13 year olds in Grade 7 – bringing in areas such as popular science and anthropology by means of, for example, texts on great explorers. The texts were based on authentic material but adapted for our particular purpose. This simplification procedure resulted in texts that were relatively easy to read but with a fairly high concentration of difficult words.[2] The ideal was to create texts that would be fully comprehensible to all informants. This was obviously a difficult requirement to meet since the informant group spanned such a wide range, and the ideal was not fully met, as will be discussed later. The English texts in particular created problems, which we tried to alleviate by providing glosses to words that were essential for comprehension.[3] In sum, every attempt was made to ensure that the English and Danish texts were comparable with respect to comprehensibility (Table 3.1).

Thirty *test words* were included in the task, the aim being to find words that would be unknown to all the participants. Although this constraint

Table 3.1 Illustration of the matching of topics in three texts

	Danish text	English text
Explorers	Columbus and America	R. Scott and the South Pole
Health	Body and movement	Health in a developing country
Animals	Dinosaurs	Apes and monkeys

74 *Vocabulary and Writing in L1 and L2*

naturally had to apply to all informants taking part, it was felt that the higher-level group – namely, the university students – was crucial in this regard. If a word were unknown to them, then it was most improbable that this would be known to the learners in Grade 7. In the selection of test words, a second criterion was essential; namely, that there had to be items representative of what we regard as the main word types. This was because different word types were expected to elicit different forms of processing. The word types are:

1   *A words* with no linguistic cues to meaning;
2   *B words* with potential linguistic cues to meaning in the form of affixes;
3   *C words* that have at least one central linguistic cue to meaning; that is, a word or a word stem, plus a prefix and/or a suffix.

The above categorization into word types was based on previous linguistic analysis combined with evidence from field-testing. Using the L2 task as our example, this implies that the target words were pre-tested on Danish informants with near-native English proficiency and, only in the cases where these highly proficient learners were able to detect and use word-internal linguistic cues, was a particular word categorized as a B or C word. Examples of the three word types are: A words: 'bouts' and 'squalor'; B words: 'permeated' and 'prevalent'; and C words: 'indiscriminately' and 'cognizance'. The task contains an equal number (that is, ten) of test words representing each of the three types, so each inferencing task has $3 \times 10 = 30$ test words.

Procedure for data collection

The three different parts of the tasks were all introduced with oral instructions, which included several examples of what the informants were expected to do.

The pre-test. The informants completed a pre-test immediately before being given the actual inferencing task in order to discover which items were familiar to them so that these words could be excluded from the analysis. At this stage, the test words were presented in alphabetical order and out of context. Time allowed for the completion of this part of the task was four minutes.

The lexical inferencing task with concurrent think aloud. The informants were then given the actual inferencing task with the 30 test words embedded in running text (for task and instruction, see Appendix A.3.1).

For each test word (which was printed in bold face), they were instructed to verbalize all their thoughts and ideas, ending their considerations with the following phrase (original in Danish) 'So I think the word means ...'. The time allowed was 32 minutes.

The retrospective task. After a brief instruction, the informants were presented with the same inferencing text, but with a slightly different layout. This time they were required to focus on what had helped them to arrive at their suggestions for word meaning in the task they had just completed. For each test word, they had to end their verbalizations with the phrase, 'What helped me arrive at my suggestion for word meaning was ...'. The time allowed on task was 20 minutes.

To summarize: in respect of design, the Danish and the English inferencing tasks were parallel with regard to types of topics and texts, types of test words and data collection procedures.

The verbal protocols
The validity of introspective methods rests on the assumption that information recently attended to by an individual is kept in short-term memory and is directly accessible for producing verbal reports, as explained in Chapter 1. For the lexical inferencing study, two methods are employed: concurrent think aloud, which is immediately followed by retrospection. In the various analyses carried out on the basis of these verbal reports, the researchers draw on think aloud (TA) and retrospection (Re) in combination. This implies that, in the coding of the protocols, the analysts take the TA protocols as their point of departure and use the Re protocols to shed light on and supplement the TA. In cases of discrepancy between the two protocols for a particular test word, TA takes priority over Re, since the concurrent procedure is believed to give the immediate and more direct access to the informants' processes.

In the following sections, many extracts from learner texts are quoted and, as an introduction to these, we would like to present a few facts about the transcriptions. Although every possible effort has been made to preserve the authenticity of these rich and very informative data, some aspects are lost from audio recording to protocol extract. In addition to the obvious shortcomings that occur when spoken language is converted to written form, there is the issue of translation. For the L1, as well as for the L2 inferencing task, informants think aloud and retrospect in their mother tongue, Danish, which requires translation into English for an international readership. Since our primary

76 *Vocabulary and Writing in L1 and L2*

purpose with the presentation of the learner texts is to make the informants' use of notably linguistic cues as transparent as possible, our translation is basically a very literal one, often word for word, which will no doubt strike the reader as sounding non-native. All protocols are presented in a translated version.

3.2.2 The analytical framework for the data analysis[4]

In connection with the coding of the verbal protocols we ask three main questions: (1) Which knowledge sources do the informants activate?; (2) Do informants make use of the activated cues by combining or even integrating them into their suggestions for word meaning?; (3) Do informants arrive at a suggestion for word meaning and, if so, is it an accurate guess, a reasonable guess that makes sense in the context, or a wild guess?

In order to answer these questions we used (1) a taxonomy of knowledge sources; (2) a taxonomy of processing types; and (3) a rating scale for inferencing success. These will be introduced below. At this point, it should be emphasized that when we – for instance, in the taxonomy for processing types – use expressions such as 'informants combine and integrate cues', we are aware that all we can actually say is what they are paying attention to. The individual informant's mental processes are not directly reflected in the TA protocols but derived through our interpretation of the comments offered by the informants.

3.2.2.1 A taxonomy of knowledge sources

The taxonomy includes three major categories: contextual, intralingual and interlingual cues, which will be introduced below. We shall deal briefly with the taxonomy here; for a more detailed description, see Haastrup (1991).

Contextual cues stem from either the co-text of the test word or from informants' knowledge of the world. With regard to the former, the subcategories distinguish between cues that are taken from the narrow versus the broad context. The term 'knowledge of the world' includes not only factual knowledge, but also everything that the informant brings to the task in the form of attitudes, beliefs, prejudice, personal experience and common sense. The two main contextual cue types typically work together, in that a reader will use her background knowledge in her interpretation of a text.

Linguistic cues refer to word-internal cues and include intralingual and interlingual cues at all levels of the linguistic system. *Intralingual cues* are taken from the language of the test word and are typically words, word stems and affixes. From the L2 inferencing task, an example of a cue from the morphological level is the English prefix 'in-' for the test word 'indiscriminately'. *Interlingual cues* include the use of other languages. Referring again to the English inferencing task, two main sub-categories were established: the use of cues from the L1, Danish, and the use of languages other than Danish and English, such as Spanish, French or Latin.

The taxonomy outlined above accounts for the way in which we categorize the informants' statements with regard to the origin of cues and the types of knowledge they build on. We shall now turn to procedural aspects of lexical inferencing, addressing the question of how learners use the different types of cues in their processing.

3.2.2.2 The coding framework for processing types

The coding framework was established in order to enable us to describe our informants' procedural knowledge (Færch and Kasper, 1983; Wolff, 1994). As discussed in Chapter 1 (Section 1.8.1), such knowledge refers to the various procedures involved in comprehending, producing and learning language, and our focus of attention here is processes in comprehension – more specifically, the way in which informants select and combine activated contextual and linguistic cues.

The source of inspiration for the framework is, at a very general level, Kintsch's (1998) views on discourse comprehension, as introduced in Chapter 1 and taken up again in this chapter in connection with a comprehension perspective on lexical inferencing (see Section 3.1). At a more specific level, our analytical framework has taken inspiration from interactive reading models and borrowed important key constructs such as top-down and bottom-up processing, which we have adopted to serve our specific purpose (see Grabe and Stoller, 2002; and Koda, 2005, for reading models).

The framework presented below is, as noted above, a further development of that established by Haastrup for her earlier L2 study (1991). Some sub-categories have been added and a few other changes have been necessary in order to accommodate L1 processing along with L2 processing. As the framework is very comprehensive and quite complex, we cannot offer a full account of it here.[5] In connection with our presentation of the major features, we have chosen to include many examples that we hope will give the reader an impression of the very rich data from the think-aloud and retrospection sessions.

78 Vocabulary and Writing in L1 and L2

Two macro types of processing

In the framework for coding, the first distinction made is between *two macro types of processing:*

- *P1 processing*: holistic processing based exclusively on contextual cues, referred to as pure top processing
- *P2 processing*: analytic processing which includes the informant's activation of linguistic word level cues.

We shall explain and illustrate these two macro types with examples taken from L2 inferencing (English).[6] The protocol below shows an example of P1 processing which is defined as follows: the informant uses contextual cues only; these include co-text cues as well as cues based on knowledge of the world.

P1 processing

Example 3.1 (From text about health) – test word 'squalor' in context: 'In the poor world people are killed by the conditions they live under, the **squalor** and the lack of food and money.'

> TA *In the poor countries people are killed by their conditions – by the conditions down there which they live under* – <the /skweilor/ and the lack of food and money> so squalor *the lack of food and money* the /skweilor/ – what would you say – what can be compared to this – what they can die from and something like that ... I think the word means infect something (giggles).
>
> (L2 protocol – G.10 informant)

In this extract, the informant translates from the context (indicated by * in the transcription), which is taken as an indication that she is paying attention to co-text cues. This translation seems to be the starting point that sparks off her use of knowledge of the world: 'the lack of food and money – what can be compared to this – what can they die from'. The rest of the protocol, not quoted here, continues this line of thought ending with the proposal for word meaning: 'infect something'. In this particular case, the use of knowledge of the world is explicitly stated, in contrast to the many cases where this source is more hidden or implicit. In fact, co-text cues can never be said to exist completely independently of knowledge of the world.

The second macro type of processing, *P2 processing*, is illustrated below.

P2 processing

Example 3.2 (From text on explorers) – test word 'undergirding' in context: 'Today, scientists are working on the **undergirding** of theories about the South Pole area.'

> **TA** <what Scott discovered – undergirding – of theories – of that knowledge – – the undergirding – – of theories> I think it is about how they – they are still working on like to support the theories – that exist about the south pole or the area ... that is undergir – in this general context – <scientists are working on the undergirding> undergirding – I think – I think the word means supporting (understøttende) – substantiating (underbyggende).

> **Re** undergirding – here it is probably both the word because – under – not to you know – to gird or girding as such – actually doesn't tell me that much – but if you look at that under – and then in that – in this context – this is why I come up with – with this then – so what helped me before was partly the word in itself – and at the same time also the context.

(L2 protocol – G.10 informant)

From the TA, it appears that the informant uses contextual cues in that she reads aloud from the context, with pauses grouping phrases of the text. Later in the protocol, she uses the expression 'in this general context', which supports this interpretation. However, in the Re it becomes clear that the informant did not arrive at her proposal for word meaning exclusively based on the use of contextual cues. The morphological cue '*under-*' played an important role, documented both by the statement 'so what helped me before was partly the word itself' and by the fact that the two synonyms given as proposals for word meaning in TA both start with '*under-*' ('*understøttende*' – '*underbyggende*'). As we have seen, this extract exemplifies the macro type for which activation of linguistic cues is included in the processing.

For the first macro type, P1 processing (see Example 3.1), the coding is simple, since pure top processing has no sub-categories. In contrast to this, the second macro type includes several sub-types, which will be presented below. Example 3.2 illustrated one of eight types. As an introduction to the coding of this second macro type, we shall account for the rationale behind establishing a hierarchy of cue levels (Figure 3.1).

At the top of the hierarchy we place contextual cues, which stem from textual cues as well as informants' knowledge of the world. In correspondence with the construct of top-down processes in reading, the

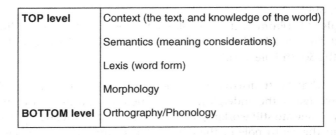

Figure 3.1 A hierarchy of cue levels

rationale is that the understanding of a text – or, in our case, a particular word – can only be achieved by conceiving of this word within the textual framework. Starting from the bottom, the levels from orthography/phonology and upwards to semantics refer to the activation of linguistic cues from the test word itself; that is, word-internal cues. These cues relate to knowledge of the language system, and the ranking order assigned to them is inspired by traditional linguistic analysis; that is, moving from smaller to larger units; in our case, from the micro level of orthography/phonology via morphology and lexis to meaning considerations (semantics). Thus, the movement from bottom towards top also reflects a movement away from exclusive attention to formal features towards an inclusion of meaning considerations.

The processing continuum

As noted above, P2 processing includes several types, some of which even involve further sub-categorization. In this context, we shall restrict ourselves to account for the main categories, which are placed on what we refer to as the processing continuum. This continuum is divided into four sections, as shown in Figure 3.2.

The criteria used when placing the processing types on the continuum are, first, the criterion of *ruling* (see below) and, second, the informants' *activation* or *integration of linguistic cues* to meaning.

The criterion of ruling. The first and primary criterion used for the placing of processing types on the continuum is the distinction between top-ruled and bottom-ruled processing. As explained in the introduction, our approach to lexical inferencing is one that includes a text comprehension view. This implies that, in order to solve the lexical inferencing task effectively, the informant has to interpret the unfamiliar words in a text in a way that fits the context. More specifically, it means that when

Section 1 of the continuum:
Top-ruled processing with integration of linguistic cues

P2.8. Top-ruled interactive processing with full integration of linguistic cues

P2.7. Top-ruled interactive processing with integration of a central linguistic cue

P2.6. Top-ruled interactive processing with integration of non-central cue(s)

Section 2 of the continuum:
Top-ruled processing with activation of linguistic cues

P2.5. Top-ruled processing with activation of linguistic cues. There is beginning or possible integration of linguistic cues.

P2.4. Top-ruled processing in the form of context-ruled processing with activation but no integration of linguistic cues.

Section 3 of the continuum:
Undecided with regard to ruling

P2.3. Undecided with regard to ruling

Section 4 of the continuum:
Bottom-ruled processing

P2.2. Bottom-ruled processing

P2.1. Pure bottom processing

Figure 3.2 The processing continuum with eight main types

the informant activates linguistic cues, these must be interpreted in a way that respects the textual framework. Thus, contextual cues, which include cues from the text as well as cues from the informants' knowledge of the world, constitute the top of the cue hierarchy. *Top-ruled processing* can be characterized as follows: the informants let top cues rule and seem to acknowledge that there is nothing over and above contextual cues. In other word, they conceive of the word within the textual framework.

For *bottom-ruled processing*, the informants' attention is focused on formal features of the test word, while ignoring the contextual cues that

82 *Vocabulary and Writing in L1 and L2*

could and should contribute to the processing. Their sole attention seems to be on linguistic cues at the micro-level, notably orthographic/phonological cues from the very bottom, resulting in a proposal for word meaning that does not make sense in the context.

We shall first exemplify *bottom-ruled processing* (see Figure 3.2, section 4, P2.2).

Bottom-ruled processing

Example 3.3 (From text on explorers) – test word 'fortitude' in context: 'the men were hit by another storm that lasted for days. With quiet **fortitude** they waited for death in the tent.'

> TA Fourtide <with quiet fourtide> fourtide – I think the word means 'past'.
>
> Re so this was fourtide – then then I thought of the Danish word *fortid* – that was it – that was what I said – I could see that there was another Danish word which resembled it.
>
> (L2 protocol – G.7 informant)

In the TA the informant activates an L1 cue, apparently triggered by similarity between the way she reads and pronounces the test word 'fortitude' and the Danish word '*fortid*'. (The informant pronounces the word 'fortitude' approximately as 'fourtide'.) Her mispronunciation of the English word makes her think of the Danish word '*fortid*' ('past'). This becomes evident during the retrospection, in which she states directly that 'there was another Danish word which resembled it'. Thus, the informant appears to be focused on the test word at the levels of orthography/phonology, and there is no indication that she considers to what extent her suggestion for word meaning makes sense in the context. The example illustrates the defining features of bottom-ruled processing; namely, that it is data-driven by bottom-level cues and that these cues are not integrated into the conceptual framework established by the text.

We shall now turn to *top-ruled processing*, illustrating it with one of the most advanced types of processing, which is referred to as top-ruled processing with integration of linguistic cues. (see Figure 3.2, section 1, P2.7).

Top-ruled processing

Example 3.4 (From text on health) – test word 'contributory' in context: 'A serious problem is malnutrition, and there are many **contributory** causes to this.'

TA there are many things that contribute – or there are many – things that – help to contribute to this – contribute perhaps – er – er – I have I can't find the word *there are* <many contributory causes to this> contributory er –*contributory* – yes – or what do you say – oh god – contribution contributory – er – – I lost it – the word in my head – there are many (breath) – contributory (whispers) many contributory (whispers) – give a contribution ... there are many – then I choose to end up saying that contributory – means – *contributory* – yes – *contributory*.

Re here I will say that contribution is like – someone who gives something – so that was what helped me a little – but it was actually the word but I also think that – that the actual co-text was important here ... What helped me before was the co-text as well as the word contribution.

(L2 protocol – G.13 informant).

The TA extract starts with the informant paraphrasing the context of the test word, which seems to trigger the linguistic cue 'contribution' and leads to the proposal for word meaning '*medvirkende*' (the Danish word for 'contributory'). In the excerpt from the retrospection, the informant very neatly sums up what she has just paid attention to during TA and what helped her arrive at her proposal for word meaning: '[it] was the co-text as well as the word contribution'. We categorize this protocol as top-ruled processing with integration of linguistic cues, since this informant integrates the meaning that she takes from the intralingual, lexico-semantic cue of 'contribution' into the textual framework. When using bottom-ruled processing, informants fail with regard to the following aspects: they locate either irrelevant or some but not all the relevant information (only linguistic bottom-level cues), and they do not combine and interrelate this information with information from contextual cues. In short, they do not build up a plausible proposal for word meaning.

We have now characterized processing from the extreme ends of the processing continuum; that is, sections 1 and 4 (see Figure 3.2). However, in order to account for what we find in the data, we have to add a grey area, which we refer to as *processing that is undecided with regard to ruling* (referred to as P2.3 processing, section 3 on the continuum) and illustrate with an example.

Processing that is undecided with regard to ruling
Example 3.5 (From text on health) – test word 'indiscriminately' in context: 'In order to help the plants to grow, families were shown how

84   *Vocabulary and Writing in L1 and L2*

to place animal dung in holes in the ground instead of spreading it **indiscriminately.'**

> **TA** well it is probably something about being discriminatory (sighs) – and I don't know what it could mean in this context – – I really don't know – perhaps something about that there is – that it discriminates someone or that it is polluting when it is just spread out (rising intonation).
>
> **Re** well it is something about being discriminatory and indiscriminatory undiscriminatory – but that doesn't fit into the context at all – so here I think I gave up ...
>
> (L2 protocol – G.10 informant)

In the TA, the informant activates a linguistic cue from her L1 'being discriminatory', which she obviously only knows in the sense of discriminating against somebody (perhaps in the form of racial discrimination). In her last utterance, the informant also activates context, in that she quotes from the immediate co-text into which she tentatively places the word 'polluting'. At the end of the retrospection (not quoted above), she sums up by saying 'I mean I am able to translate the word in one way or another but it simply does not fit in – and I – so I don't know.' Thus, for this type of processing we observe that the activated cues appear to be contradictory to the informant. In some cases, the informant seems to be pulled in different directions, often by contextual cues leading in one direction and linguistic cues in another. The result of this is either alternative proposals for word meaning or no proposal. The retrospection reveals that the informant herself is aware that she has not solved the problem. As she indicates awareness that her idea stemming from the linguistic cue makes no sense in the context, this processing type is not bottom-ruled. We therefore need a separate category reflecting the fact that the informant seems to give equal weight to contextual and linguistic cues. From a developmental perspective, this may be seen as a first step away from paying attention exclusively to micro level linguistic cues and moving in the direction of top-ruled processing.

The criterion 'integration of linguistic cues'. The second important criterion used for distinguishing the processing types on the continuum is mere activation versus integration of linguistic cues. As can be seen in Figure 3.2, this distinction becomes relevant from section 3 and upwards, and we shall start by looking at a processing type from section 2, P2.4; that is, top-ruled processing with activation of linguistic cues. The informants activate contextual cues as well as one or more linguistic cues – typically, only one – and it is characteristic that this linguistic cue seems to be an incidental association; at least, it is obvious that the informants do not make any use of it. Thus, the verbal reports point to informants who let contextual cues rule, and what is lacking in section 2 processing, compared with section 1, is an integration of the activated linguistic cue(s). Such integration is a defining feature of the top section of the continuum, to which we shall now turn.

Top-ruled processing with integration of linguistic cues includes sub-types representing either partial or full integration. We have already illustrated two of these. In Example 3.4, we saw an informant who, for the test word 'contributory', activated and integrated the related word 'contribution' into her proposal for word meaning (P2.7 processing in Figure 3.2). This example was chosen to illustrate the activation of what we refer to as central linguistic cues; that is, a word or a word stem. However, we also find sub-types from section 1 of the continuum where the informant does not find a central cue, but pays attention to morphology in the form of affixes – notably, prefixes. Such use of non-central linguistic cues was shown in Example 3.2 (P2.6 processing in Figure 3.2). We shall finally present an example of what we refer to as *top-ruled processing with full integration*, which means that the informant integrates at least two linguistic cues, of which one must be central (P2.8 processing in Figure 3.2).

Top-ruled processing with integration of linguistic cues
Example 3.6 (From text on health) – test word 'curative' in context: 'Of course doctors should be interested in the **curative** effect of medicine, but it is even more important that they analyze why people get the disease in the first place.'

> **TA** <of course ... first place> then I need to find the word curative I think that this word means healing so the sentence reads *doctors should be interested in the healing effect in medicine* yes I think that's it – the word means healing.

> **Re** here I definitely thought of the word 'cure' which means well a rescuing a well something that could cure you and then I thought that curative had to be the healing effect that's what I thought 'tive' is the same as 'e-n-d-e' in Danish which means that it was the healing and then it also said medicine – the curing or healing effect of medicine seemed to fit well together.
>
> (L2 protocol – G.13)

86   *Vocabulary and Writing in L1 and L2*

In this TA protocol, we see clear evidence of the informant's use of contextual cues in that she tries out whether her word proposal 'healing' fits into her translation of a long passage from the text. From the retrospection, however, it appears that the word 'cure' (a central cue) and the ending '-ive' (non-central cue) contribute to her suggestion for word meaning. In our combined analysis the fact that the same synonyms 'curing' ('*kurerende*') and 'healing' ('*helbredende*') are used in both the TA and the Re is seen as evidence of the activation of linguistic cues right from the outset. The informant completes the retrospection by stating that her proposal appears to fit the context. This extract meets the criterion of integrating two linguistic cues to meaning into the framework of the text and thus represents top-ruled processing with full integration of linguistic cues, the most advanced type of processing on the continuum.

Overview of the coding framework for processing types

We can summarize the processing types as follows: in our framework for coding, we distinguish between two macro types of processing: (1) P1 processing – that is, holistic processing in the form of pure top processing based exclusively on contextual cues; and (2) P2 processing – that is analytic processing that includes the informant's activation of word internal linguistic cues. The latter macro type has eight main types that are placed on a processing continuum (Figure 3.2).

In Figure 3.2, the processing types were placed on a continuum (from section 4 towards section 1) in a way that, in more than one respect, was intended to reflect an upward movement. First, from bottom-rule towards top-rule, we here imply a movement from a micro level with focus on form to a macro level with a meaning focus. Secondly, zooming in on the upper part of the continuum, we find an upward movement with respect to the use of linguistic cues: from the mere activation to the integration of such cues into the conceptual framework established by the text. As one moves up the continuum, it is characteristic that a variety of cue types from different levels in the hierarchy are brought into play. From the very top of section 1, P2.8 processing constitutes the optimal degree of interaction, not only between contextual and linguistic cues, but also internally between linguistic cues from more than one level in the hierarchy (see Figure 3.1, showing the hierarchy of cue levels). For the above reasons, complex processing from the top section of the continuum will be referred to as *advanced processing*.

3.2.3 The quality of lexical inferencing

In the previous section, we have detailed the procedural aspect of lexical inferencing, paying most attention to analytic processing on the processing continuum. The intention with this section is to highlight the relationship between the quality of the process and the quality of the product by asking which type of process is likely to lead to a good result.

In order to address this question we shall begin by introducing the distinction between potentially effective processing and ineffective processing, and define effectiveness in relation to informants' chances of making a qualified guess or, at least, a guess that makes sense in the context. From this definition, it follows that potentially effective processing types must be top-ruled, so that P1 processing – that is, pure top processing – as well as P2 processing from sections 1 and 2 on the continuum belong to this category. This omits sections 3 and 4 on the continuum. These two sections constitute the second category; namely, that of ineffective processing. Let us add that our reason for referring to 'potentially effective', rather than simply 'effective', is that effectiveness depends on the informants' declarative lexical knowledge as well as their procedural knowledge. This implies that if the relevant vocabulary knowledge is missing, effective processing alone cannot guarantee a good outcome in the form of a high quality guess.

At this point, we shall make explicit our assumptions of what makes an informant a good word processor with respect to process as well as product. In her study of L2 lexical inferencing, Haastrup (1991) found that a good word processor is one who: (1) has a processing repertoire that includes the full range of potentially effective processing types; (2) is flexible in her processing; and (3) achieves a high level of lexical inferencing success. Inspired by this, we selected three hallmarks of good lexical inferencing for the present study that will constitute the basis for our analyses and results: *advanced processing, adaptability of processing* and *lexical inferencing success*.

3.2.3.1 First hallmark: advanced processing

From the broad category of potentially effective processing types, we singled out *advanced processing*; that is, top-ruled processing with integration of linguistic cues. This complex type poses a challenge to the informant, as it requires analysis as well as synthesis skills: word analysis to identify relevant word-internal linguistic cues such as word stems, prefixes and suffixes; and synthesis, understood as the ability to integrate these cues into a coherent whole at word level. The result of this process

88 *Vocabulary and Writing in L1 and L2*

must, furthermore, be integrated into the conceptual framework of the text. Synthesis and integration skills are thus required from a lexical perspective as well as from a text comprehension perspective, implying that the informant has to master a double integration process. Another way of explaining the same phenomenon is to say that advanced processing places heavy demands on an informant's procedural as well as declarative knowledge. The former includes the individual's mastery of top-ruled processing and good word analysis skills, which enable him or her to identify and select relevant components of the target word; and, as for the declarative aspect, lexical knowledge of these components must be added. In sum, advanced processing is a case of maximum interaction between an informant's declarative and procedural knowledge.

To measure an informant's advanced processing, the following procedure was used. For each informant, the verbal protocol for each test word was categorized and the number of instances of her use of processing types P2.6, P2.7 and P2.8 was added up. With regard to the connection between the quality of the inferencing process and the inferencing product, we note already at this point that when an informant masters advanced processing, she stands a good chance of achieving a high level of inferencing success. This issue will be elaborated upon below.

3.2.3.2 Second hallmark: adaptability of processing

In order to capture another characteristic feature of good word processing, we created the construct of *adaptability*, which assesses the extent to which informants adapt their processing to word type, and thus make the best use of a word's processing potential. We see this construct as a specification of what was earlier referred to as *flexibility* (Haastrup, 1991) and regard it as a hallmark of high quality processing.

As mentioned in Section 3.2.1, the 30 predefined target words in the lexical inferencing tasks include ten words from each of the three categories: words without linguistic cues (A words) and words with linguistic cues to meaning (B and C words). Let us now envisage an informant who is to infer the meaning of a word with potential linguistic cues to meaning, such as the target word 'abysmal', classified as a C word. This word looks extremely difficult to him, so instead of attempting analytic processing he resorts to pure top processing, which is both simpler and, in his experience, often works. Below, this might be what is happening.

Example 3.7 (From text on savants) – test word 'abysmal' in context: 'Not so long ago, the future for savants was **abysmal**. Today many savants have a good life.'

TA ... so it was impossible – that you could not get a decent life – in that sense – but then today you can have a decent life because we have realized that even though they have a handicap you can still give them a normal life – so what I am trying to say is that I think the word means something about – about well – well it was impossible to have a – well that you couldn't have that back then ...

Re ... they say that *a long time ago* – and then they tell us that – back then – back then their lives were different – we don't know how ... so I would say that back then they could not live normally – I was thinking along those lines.

(L2 protocol – G.10 informant)

In both protocols, we see quite extensive use of contextual cues, in the form of cues from different parts of the co-text, as well as from the informant's knowledge of the world ('even though they have a handicap you can still give them a normal life'). However, there is no trace of the activation of linguistic cues from the informant. The point we want to make is that, in some of his other verbal protocols, this particular informant has shown that he actually does have advanced processing in his repertoire. However, he fails to apply it for 'abysmal', for which it is the ideal type of processing. The example shows a low degree of adaptability, and the explanation behind this could be that the informant lacks the relevant declarative lexical knowledge, which prevents him from making optimal use of the word's processing potential.

The construct of adaptability is operationalized by means of an *adaptability index*. For each of the three word types, a number of the potentially most effective processing types has been identified:

- For **A words**: pure top processing
- For **B words**: processing types from *section 2 on the continuum*; from section 1 on the continuum only the least demanding type; that is, P2.6 processing
- For **C words**: processing types from *section 1 on the continuum*, restricted to the two most demanding types; that is, P2.7 and P2.8 processing.

The adaptability index is worked out using the following procedure: one point is given each time an informant uses one of the potentially most effective processing types for the word type in question. If the processing type chosen by the informant is not one of the potentially most effective, a zero score is awarded. The maximum score for an informant who processes the 30 test words is therefore 30 points.

90   *Vocabulary and Writing in L1 and L2*

In sum, the purpose of using the adaptability index is to capture the extent to which an informant makes the best use of a word's processing potential; it thus reflects the way in which the informant's choice of processing type is adapted to word type.

3.2.3.3   Third hallmark: levels of inferencing success

Inferencing success refers to the quality of the informants' proposals for word meaning; that is, how successful they are in inferring the meaning of the 30 test words. The success measure thus focuses on the outcome of the informants' problem solving efforts, in contrast to the two other measures introduced above, which focused on the processes.

Inferencing success is a conveniently short term that in reality covers 'levels of lexical inferencing success'. We differentiate on a 4-point scale between accurate guesses, approximate guesses, wrong guesses that could logically fit the context and, finally, wrong and wild guesses. We shall give an example of four different proposals for word meaning that achieved a score of either 0, 1, 2 or 3 points (Table 3.2). The test word is 'shaggy' appearing in the context: 'The orangutan has a **shaggy** coat of reddish-brown hair.'

The accurate guess obviously emphasizes the lexico-semantic perspective, in that the informant has identified the correct meaning of the word so, viewed in a vocabulary acquisition perspective, this successful guess constitutes a promising start. As to the 'wrong but logical guess', we decided, in a rather unorthodox way, to give the informant credit for conceiving of the target word within the textual framework by rewarding it with one point. From the above example, it is evident that the proposal 'protective' reflects no understanding of the actual meaning of 'shaggy'. However, in the verbal protocol the informant reveals that his reason for suggesting 'protective' is that 'the orangutan spends time

Table 3.2   Levels of lexical inferencing success

Level of success		Proposal for word meaning
Accurate guess	3 points	*uglet* ('tousled')
Approximate guess	2 points	*rodet* ('untidy')
Wrong, but logical guess in context	1 point	*beskyttende* ('protective')
Wrong and 'wild' guess	0 points	*pelset* ('coated')

way up in the trees where it is cold and windy'. So, his suggestion makes sense. Based on examples such as this, we argue that it is appropriate to reward a guess that clearly is not 'wrong and wild' and, moreover, that it is in line with our approach to lexical inferencing that not only adopts a lexical but also a comprehension perspective.

The scores for each of the 30 test words are added up, so the maximum possible score for an informant is 30 words × 3 points = 90 points.

In conclusion to this section, we would emphasize that we regard the three hallmarks of advanced processing, adaptability of processing and lexical inferencing success as interrelated. When an informant adapts her processing to word type by choosing the optimal type of processing, this has the best chance of leading to a high level of lexical inferencing success. In the following, these hallmarks of lexical inferencing quality will constitute the focus of our presentation.

3.3 Results

This section will present the statistical analyses, which will be followed by a summary of the main results. As an introduction to the analyses, we shall account for the distinction made between *valid* and *invalid items* for analysis. An item refers to one informant's protocols for a particular test word. Items are categorized as invalid for two reasons: (1) the item is known; or (2) the item is empty. In connection with the first factor, we could quickly and reliably identify the known items by referring to the pre-test results. From this, it was evident whether, from the outset, an informant had a precise, or sufficiently close to precise, knowledge of the test word that the item should be categorized as 'known'. Very few items had to be rejected for analysis on this account. More items were lost due to the fact that the protocols were empty for a particular test word. There turned out to be many unattempted test words, especially towards the end of the task so, for some informants, it was clearly lack of time that was the main reason for the many empty items.[7] As the number of empty items was considered a potential threat to the reliability of the statistical analyses, a separate calculation was carried out, which fortunately proved that our concern was largely unwarranted.[8] Although the problem with invalid items turned out to be smaller than feared, we still had to deal with the fact that our 90 informants did not have the same number of valid items. This means that in the analyses all figures are presented as percentages of valid items. In order to illustrate the adopted procedure, we use the analysis of advanced processing. For each informant, the verbal protocol for a test word was categorized as

92 *Vocabulary and Writing in L1 and L2*

one of the nine processing types (P1 processing + P2 processing with eight types). For each individual informant, a calculation was made of the proportion of advanced processing in relation to total processing; that is, the informant's number of valid attempts. In Table 3.3, the figures for advanced processing indicate the means for each of the three educational groups in percentage out of total valid items for the group.

Pertaining to the reliability of the coding work, three coders (A, B and C) worked on the data, (A + B on knowledge sources and processing types and A + C on lexical inferencing success). When a fair level of agreement had been reached, the analysis of the data was carried out. Interscorer reliability was calculated on the basis of data from nine informants; that is, 10 per cent of the informant population (see Appendix A.3.3). This included nine L1 protocols (three from each grade level) and nine L2 protocols (three from each grade level). For knowledge sources, the agreement was 82 per cent (L1 and L2 protocols). As to processing types, the agreement was 0.87 Cohen's Kappa (L1 protocols) and 0.91 (L2 protocols) and, for lexical inferencing success, 0.80 Cohen's Kappa (L1 protocols) and 0.74 (L2 protocols).

3.3.1 Results of the statistical analyses

In accordance with the main research questions, the following analyses were carried out. First, for the within-subjects data, the analysis applied focused on whether or not a difference was found between lexical inferencing procedures in L1 and L2 for the same students. Second, with regard to the between-subjects data, results were compared across the three educational levels. In both cases, all three hallmarks of quality lexical inferencing were analyzed: advanced processing, adaptability of processing and lexical inferencing success.

3.3.1.1 Advanced processing

The construct of advanced processing indicates top-ruled processing with integration of linguistic cues. As described above, advanced processing is operationalized as the use of the processing types P2.6 + P2.7 + P2.8 from section 1 of the processing continuum.

The research questions addressed: (1) Is there a difference between the use of advanced processing in L1 and L2 for the same students?; (2) Is there a difference between the use of advanced processing by informants at the three educational levels?

Addressing the research questions, the data were subjected to one-way (three levels: G.7 and G.10 and G.13) between-subjects analyses of variance (ANOVAs). For the data that lived up to this type of analysis, the Tukey post hoc measure could be applied. However, for many of the

Lexical Inferencing Procedures in Two Languages   93

scores, the non-parametric Kruskal–Wallis procedure and the Tamhane post hoc measure had to be used (see Appendix A.1.1 for a description of the statistical procedures).

The table below presents the results that constitute the basis for analysis. Figures refer to group means in percentage out of total valid attempts.

First, with regard to the *within-subjects results* (research question R1), comparing the use of advanced processing in L1 and L2 within each grade level, we use the G.10 column as an example. We can see that the use of advanced processing is higher for L1 (34.53 per cent) than for L2 (9.17 per cent). The same is the case for the other two groups, with the magnitude of the difference being particularly large for G.7 (16.23 versus 1.53 per cent). For the whole informant population, the use of advanced processing in L1 was three times that of advanced processing in L2 (91 versus 31 per cent). To determine whether there was an overall difference between the two languages, an ANOVA was performed, which confirmed that the differences between L1 and L2 results were statistically significant for each of the three educational levels (ANOVA: $p < .001$: G.7: $F_{(1,29)} = 48.827$; G.10: $F_{(1,29)} = 174.890$; G.13: $F_{(1,29)} = 49.526$). Second, addressing the *between-subjects* data (research question R2), we first note that, overall, the use of advanced processing increases with rising educational level. However, an ANOVA revealed a difference between the L1 and the L2 data. In L2, statistically significant differences were found between all three grade levels, whereas this was not the case for L1. The pattern for L2 (Tamhane: $p < .001$) is that the G.10 group is better than the G.7 group, and the G.13 group is better than the G.10 group: G.7 < G.10 < G.13. For the L1, significant differences were found between G.7 and G.10 and between G.7 and G.13 (Tukey: $p < .001$), but the difference between the G.10 and the G.13 group did not reach statistical significance, so the pattern is G.7 < G.10 and G.13. In answer to the research questions, we conclude, first, that irrespective of grade level, informants use a significantly higher

Table 3.3 Advanced processing across languages and educational levels

		G.7 (n = 30)	G.10 (n = 30)	G.13 (n = 30)
L2	M	1.53%	9.17%	21.23%
	SD	2.85	7.15	2.35
L1	M	16.23%	34.53%	41.03%
	SD	12.43	11.99	11.29

94 *Vocabulary and Writing in L1 and L2*

percentage of advanced processing in their L1 than in their L2 and, second, that the use of advanced processing increases with a rising educational level.

3.3.1.2 Adaptability of processing

The construct of adaptability indicates the extent to which an informant adapts her processing to word type. This is operationalized by means of an adaptability index, as described above. The purpose of using the adaptability index is to capture the extent to which an informant makes the best use of a word's processing potential. The measure of adaptability is a highly sensitive measure in that it not only indicates whether an informant has the full range of processing types at her disposal, but also whether she applies them in the appropriate places.

The research questions addressed: (1) Is there a difference between adaptability of processing in L1 and L2 for the same students?; (2) Is there a difference between adaptability of processing by informants at the three educational levels?

The results presented in Table 3.4 provide the basis for answering these questions. Figures are based on group means in percentage out of total valid attempts.

With regard to question 1 – that is, the *within-subjects* results – we see that for the G.13 group, for instance, figures are higher for L1 (60.9 per cent) than for L2 (45.63 per cent), as is the case for the other two groups. To determine whether there was an overall difference between the two languages, an ANOVA was performed, which confirmed that the differences between L1 and L2 results were statistically significant for all three educational levels (ANOVA: $p < 0.001$: G.7: $F_{(1,29)} = 78.940$; G.10: $F_{(1,29)} = 80.678$; G.13: $F_{(1,29)} = 51.038$). Addressing the *between-subjects* data (research question R2), we note that the G.10 group has higher figures than the G.7 group, and that the G.13 group has higher figures than the G.10 group: G.7 < G.10 < G.13, and add that for both L1 and L2,

Table 3.4 Adaptability across languages and educational levels

		G.7 (n = 30)	G.10 (n = 30)	G.13 (n = 30)
L2	M	17.87%	32.93%	45.63%
	SD	9.27	83.17	11.82
L1	M	37.93%	53.57%	60.93%
	SD	14.38	11.86	9.13

differences between grade levels were found to be statistically significant (L1: Tamhane p < .001; L2 Tukey: p < .001). Based on this analysis, it is concluded that, at all grade levels, informants have higher adaptability rates in their first rather than in their second language and that, in both L1 and L2, adaptability of processing increases with a rising educational level.

3.3.1.3   Lexical inferencing success

Levels of lexical inferencing success refers to the informants' solving of the inferencing task; that is, how successful they are in inferring the meaning of the 30 test words. The success measure thus focuses on the end product of the informants' efforts at problem solving. As described above, the total score for an informant was calculated, and this was then converted into a percentage of his/her valid attempts.

The research questions addressed: (1) Is there a difference between the levels of lexical inferencing success achieved in L1 and L2 for the same students?; (2) Is there a difference between the achieved level of lexical inferencing success by informants at the three educational levels? Table 3.5 provides the basis for answering these questions.

First, for the *within-subjects* results, we compare the levels of inferencing success achieved in L1 and L2 within each grade level. Using the G.7 column as an example, we see that the rate of inferencing success is higher in L1 (28.93 per cent) than in L2 (16.83 per cent), as is the case for the other two groups. In the L1, the range is from 28 to 58 per cent, and in L2 from 16 to 48 per cent. To determine whether there was an overall difference between the two languages, an ANOVA was performed, which confirmed that the difference between L1 and L2 results is statistically significant (ANOVA: p < .001:G.7: F $(1,29)$ = 96.739; G.10: F $(1,29)$ = 59.621; G.13: F $(1,29)$ = 33.602). Second, addressing the *between-subjects data*, figures indicate that, with a rising educational level, the pattern is one of increasingly better results: the G.10 group is

Table 3.5   Inferencing success across languages and educational levels

		G.7 (n = 30)	G.10 (n = 30)	G.13 (n = 30)
L2	M	16.83%	37.27%	48.10%
	SD	11.72	10.10	8.74
L1	M	28.93%	50.07%	58.80%
	SD	14.58	11.30	8.16

96 Vocabulary and Writing in L1 and L2

better than the G.7 group, and the G.13 group is better than the G.10 group: G.7 < G.10 < G.13. For the L2 data, the differences between the three groups were significant (Tukey: p < .001). The same was found for the L1 data (Tamhane: p < .001). In conclusion, when comparing levels of lexical inferencing success, the overall pattern found was that, at all grade levels, informants achieved significantly higher success rates in their L1 than in their L2, and that the success rate increased significantly with a rising educational level.

3.3.2   Summary of main findings from the statistical analyses

We shall start by focusing on the L1–L2 dimension (within-subjects data), followed by a closer look at the grade level perspective (between-subjects data).

Comparing lexical inferencing in L1 and L2 for the whole informant population. Pertaining to the two measures that reflect high quality processing, it was found that the population as a whole used more advanced processing in their L1 than in their L2, and that this difference was statistically significant. The magnitude of the difference was large, in that the use of advanced processing in the L1 was three times that of advanced processing in the L2. As for the adaptability measure, we found that our population also had a significantly higher level of adaptability in L1 than in L2. Finally, turning to the product measure of inferencing success, the result was that, for the population as a whole, lexical inferencing success was higher for the L1 than for the L2, with statistically significant differences. All in all, when comparing the informant groups' lexical inferencing behaviour by including both the process and product measures, we found that their results in L1 were clearly superior to those in L2.

Comparing lexical inferencing across grade levels in both languages. Adopting a grade level perspective and starting with the processing dimension, we found that the use of advanced processing increased with grade level in both languages. The same was the case for adaptability of processing. However, when we look for statistically significant differences between the three grade levels, the patterns are not the same across languages. Whereas the L2 pattern is Grade 7 < Grade 10 < Grade 13 for both processing measures, the L1 patterns vary. For adaptability, it is Grade 7 < Grade 10 < Grade 13 and, for advanced processing, Grade 7 < Grade 10 and Grade 13. As to the product measure, the result was that lexical inferencing success increased with educational level, and that there were statistically significant differences between all three levels for both languages. All in all, when viewed from a grade level perspective, we found that for all three hallmarks the quality of lexical inferencing increased with a rising educational level in both languages. With one exception (advanced processing in L1), all the differences found were statistically significant.

3.4 Discussion

For a discussion of the results, we return to a more qualitatively oriented approach that will help us to interpret and elaborate on the findings from the statistical analyses. We start by highlighting processing characteristics of the mature, the intermediate and the immature inferencers, which is followed by a section that addresses the question of whether the processing continuum can also be regarded as a developmental continuum. Finally, results from the present study are compared to those of previous studies.

3.4.1 Processing characteristics of the mature, the immature and the intermediate inferencer

The aim of the following is to give a qualitative description of lexical inferencing behaviour based on the quantitative findings presented earlier. Few explicit references to tables will be made, but the reader can relate our descriptions below to the figures in Tables 3.3, 3.4 and 3.5. The description of the mature inferencer is based on the group results from Grade 13, and the intermediate and immature inferencers are linked to results from the Grade 10 and Grade 7 groups. We would note that the shift from grade level terms to terms referring to maturity level is intentional. The term mature emphasizes the fact that a rising educational level also reflects a higher level of cognitive development of the informants.

In the characterization of the three types of inferencers, we do not refer to their use of pure top processing; this holistic processing, based exclusively on contextual cues, is used by immature and mature inferencers alike. We have chosen to base our description on informants' use of analytic processing on the following line of argument: when learners make use of potential linguistic cues to meaning, where these are available, this enhances their chances of arriving at a precise rather than an approximate guess, since linguistic cues can add to what contextual cues can give. We have argued above that advanced processing is the optimal processing type for words with linguistic cues and, at the same time, it

98   *Vocabulary and Writing in L1 and L2*

is also a demanding type of processing, because it requires maximal interaction between procedural and declarative lexical knowledge. We therefore let learners' frequent and appropriate use of advanced processing set the ultimate goal for high quality processing.

We shall base our characterization of the three types of inferencers on their L2 processing of the target word 'curative', belonging to the group of test words with potential linguistic cues to meaning.

The mature inferencer

In connection with our characterization of the mature inferencer's processing of the test word 'curative', we will start with an example, for which the reader is referred to Example 3.6 (Section 3.2.2.2). Here, we see an informant using advanced processing – one of the potentially most effective processing types for a word with linguistic cues – which helps him produce an accurate guess. This example serves to illustrate the procedures used by the prototypical mature inferencer, who makes relatively frequent use of advanced processing and has relatively high figures for adaptability, which can only be achieved if one has command of the full repertoire of processing types. In sum, the pattern underlying the relatively high level of inferencing success is: (1) frequent use of advanced processing; (2) hardly any use of bottom-ruled processing; (3) high adaptability of processing.

The intermediate inferencer

For this inferencer, we shall begin by showing a prototypical example of her processing based on the target word 'curative' appearing in the context: 'Of course doctors should be interested in the **curative** effect of medicine.'

> #### Extract 3.1   L2 protocol: Grade 10 informant
>
> TA *the doctors should be interested in* – – <the curative effect> *of medicine* – – curative – is there a word which is similar to it in Danish (rising intonation) – /kurativ/ – no that – it could be similar to you know currence – so the /curren/ effect – <should be interested in the curative effect of medicine> – I think – I think the word means – the effect that it gives – well I can't really explain it.
>
> Re Here I read the c – context like – before – and that was what made me – think that was it – the effect you know ...

Our interpretation of the TA protocol, strongly supported by the retrospection, is that the informant's processing is top-ruled and mainly based on contextual cues with activation, but not integration, of linguistic cues into her proposal for word meaning (Figure 3.2, type P2.4). Based on the contextual cues only, she does not arrive at a proposal for word meaning other than the paraphrase 'the effect that it gives', which is void of meaning. First, as compared to the mature inferencer, this intermediate informant uses only half as much advanced processing, and her adaptability figures are lower. For the intermediate inferencer, the most frequently used processing is top-ruled with activation, but no integration, of linguistic cues (section 2 on the continuum), as seen in the extract above. So, although this informant has advanced processing in her repertoire, she does not apply it in this case, and since her proposal for word meaning lacks the contribution of linguistic cues, the informant has little chance of producing an accurate word guess. If she is lucky, she gets two points for an approximate guess on the scale for inferencing success. Second, as compared with the immature inferencer, the intermediate informant uses much less bottom-ruled processing, which indicates that she has moved upwards on the continuum to potentially effective top-ruled processing. This clearly distinguishes her from the immature inferencer.

Using the Grade 10 group as our prototype for the intermediate inferencer, we have found that, for all three hallmarks, this group occupies a middle position between the Grade 13 and the Grade 7 group, which comes as no surprise. The pattern underlying an intermediate level of inferencing success is: (1) much less use of advanced processing and a lower level of adaptability, as compared with the mature inferencer; (2) much more use of top-ruled processing and less use of bottom-ruled processing, as compared with the immature inferencer; (3) as to adaptability of processing, the intermediate inferencer takes up an exact middle position between the other two groups.

The immature inferencer

We shall start by looking at a prototypical example of the immature inferencer's processing using the target word 'curative'. (For context, see Extract 3.1 above.)

> **Extract 3.2 L2 protocol: Grade 7 informant**
> TA Well – curative – well there is a thing called cultured right – the modern ways of – so I think the word means something like the cultured – yes.
>
> Re That was a little bit the word it is a little similar to that thing to cultured right ... but that was very much because it looked like a Danish word.

100   *Vocabulary and Writing in L1 and L2*

Both protocols indicate that the informant pays attention to a perceived similarity between the English word 'curative' and the Danish word '*kultiveret*' (cultured). This is clearly expressed in the retrospection, where the informant uses the expressions 'this is similar to' and 'it looked like a Danish word'. In our interpretation both these terms, not least the latter, signal a focus on formal features of the word. We therefore see this extract as illustrating bottom-ruled processing, a decision supported by the fact that the informant's proposal for word meaning does not fit into the framework of the text. With regard to the success scale, she scores zero for this item.

As a general characterization in relation to the other groups, we note that the immature inferencer has a restricted processing repertoire, applied with low adaptability and resulting in a low level of inferencing success. For this immature group, however, we wish to add a positive comment to the disheartening description given above. This group actually uses a fair amount of potentially effective processing in the form of pure top processing, and some of the informants in the group even get as far as producing approximate guesses based on holistic processing. However, our summing up – which reflects only their use of the processing continuum – paints a rather discouraging picture of the immature group. The pattern underlying the less successful product is thus: (1) very infrequent use (if any) of advanced processing; (2) frequent use of bottom-ruled processing; (3) low adaptability of processing.

To sum up: as expected, the use or non-use of advanced processing clearly distinguishes between the three groups. This demanding type of processing requires procedural knowledge, at text level in the form of reading ability and top-ruled processing and, at word level, declarative lexical knowledge of words, word stems and affixes. Moreover, to initially identify such linguistic cues and then to integrate them is dependent on both analysis and synthesis skills; in other words, interaction between procedural and declarative knowledge. Many of these abilities are dependent on a high level of foreign language proficiency, notably reading skills and vocabulary knowledge; so, it comes as no surprise that advanced processing in the foreign language is way beyond the capacity of most informants in the immature group, not least in the L2 context. That L2 reading and L2 lexical knowledge are, indeed, strong predictors of L2 lexical inferencing success has been confirmed by the present study, as will be discussed in Chapter 5.

Finally, we shall turn to *the L1–L2 dimension*. According to the quantitative results, L1 inferencing is of a higher quality than L2 inferencing, at all grade levels. Since the greatest difference between processing in the

Lexical Inferencing Procedures in Two Languages   101

two languages has been found for the immature inferencer – that is, the Grade 7 group – we shall complete this section by looking at a typical example of how an informant from this level processes two comparable test words in L1 and L2. The test word from L1 is *'akvatiske'* ('aquatic') and, from L2, 'contributory'. They are both test words with linguistic cues to meaning and with relatively strong contextual support.

L1 inferencing
The example is taken from the text on dinosaurs and is based on the test word *'akvatiske'* appearing in the context (translated from Danish): 'Finally there are the ictosaura which are **aquatic** reptiles whose body made them perfectly adapted to catch fast swimming prey.'

> **Extract 3.3   L1 protocol: Grade 7 informant**
> TA aqua – tic – atic – uatic – quatic – that could be something to do with water – a type that can stand up to water or swims in water or something like that – I think it means swims in water.
>
> Re ... something like they were able to swim or something like that.

In the TA extract, the informant starts out by activating intralingual cues at the orthographic level, experimenting with various ways of dividing up the word. Soon, however, she seems to give up the word analysis approach and turn to the co-text, where she finds contextual cues such as 'swims in water'. This becomes her proposal for word meaning. In our interpretation, the processing type used is top-ruled processing with activation, but no integration, of linguistic cues (see Figure 3.2, type P2.4 from Section 2 on the processing continuum).

L2 inferencing
In connection with the L2 task, the target word 'contributory' was used, taken from the text on health and appearing in the following context: 'A serious health problem is malnutrition, and there are many **contributory** causes to this.'

> **Extract 3.4   L2 protocol: Grade 7 informant**
> TA /kontri'buti/ contri that's something like town so – /but/ – /buteri/ – <causes to this> – – *there are many* </kontri – 'buteri/ – causes to this> – cause – there are many – oh – I think it is – town – town-fights – cause – causes that – yes.
>
> Re What helped me was contri – that is because it is a town – and then – butory – that – I thought that came a little from – from battle

102 *Vocabulary and Writing in L1 and L2*

or fight ... it sounds a lot like that each town fight – is the explanation to this – so that was what helped me before.

The TA protocol in Extract 3.4 starts with word analysis of the kind that was seen in Extract 3.3. There is activation of linguistic cues such as 'contri', which the informant translates as *'by'* (meaning 'town'). How she arrives at *'kamp'* (meaning 'fight' in Danish) is difficult to say, although it is clear from both protocols that /butory/ plays a role. That the proposal for word meaning is *'bykampe'* ('town fights') is confirmed by the retrospective protocol. So, although the informant pays attention to the word 'cause' from the immediate co-text, this seems to have no impact on her proposal for word meaning, which is not incorporated into the conceptual framework of the text. The processing is thus characterized as bottom-ruled (see Figure 3.2, P2.2 processing from section 4 on the continuum).

Comparing the two examples above, we emphasize that, in the L2, the informant uses bottom-ruled processing, whereas in the L1 she uses top-ruled processing with activation of linguistic cues: the distinctive feature here is the shift from bottom-rule to top-rule and, in processing terms, this is crucial. In L2, the Grade 7 informant uses an ineffective processing type whereas, in L1, she demonstrates an ability to carry out potentially effective processing. We look at this shift to top rule as a great step forward with respect to procedural knowledge and as an illustration of the finding that an immature inferencer's processing in L1 is of a much higher quality than her L2 processing. Now, the obvious question to ask is why an informant who uses top-ruled processing in her L1 does not transfer such potentially effective processing to her L2. While this is a question that we cannot answer definitively, we can say with certainty that differences found between L1 and L2 inferencing for the same informant cannot be due to factors pertaining to the informant's maturity level, including his or her general cognitive development. The main explanatory factors behind L2 inferencing being inferior to L1 inferencing are believed to be those relating to overall second language proficiency and, in particular, to L2 reading skills and L2 lexical knowledge. All in all, operating in an L2 context is more demanding than functioning in a similar context in L1. The next section will look into the degree to which L1 lexical inferencing can be said to be ahead of L2 inferencing.

3.4.2 The processing continuum viewed as a developmental continuum

On the basis of her 1991 study, Haastrup formulated the proposal that the processing continuum could also be seen as a developmental continuum;

implying that when an immature learner of a foreign language starts using analytic processing, she tends to make frequent use of the lower part of the continuum, whereas the mature learner makes frequent use of the top part. Haastrup's proposal was based on a cross-sectional study of L2 inferencing. We shall now consider this proposal in the light of our substantial database, which includes lexical inferencing in two languages and from three educational levels.

As argued above, the reason for focusing on P2 processing, to the exclusion of holistic P1 processing, is that mastery of advanced processing from the top of the continuum is the primary hallmark of high quality lexical inferencing. Thus, reaching the top of the continuum is viewed as the ultimate goal for learner development. We have previously accounted for the way in which the grouping of processing types into four sections reflects an upward movement from bottom-rule towards top-rule, as well as from the mere activation of linguistic cues to full integration of all potential linguistic cues (see Figure 3.2).

We now tentatively propose that learners on their way up through the educational system move from the bottom to the top of the processing continuum. Just as the grouping of processing types on the continuum reflects an upward movement towards advanced processing, learners' increased use of this type of processing over time is believed to follow the same route. This developmental perspective is what we shall now pursue. Using the metaphor of a ladder, we envisage a Grade 7 learner who stands on the bottom rung, a Grade 10 learner who has moved higher up the ladder, and a Grade 13 learner who has moved very close to the top. We therefore use the same metaphor of 'climbing a ladder' for the educational levels, as well as for the way in which the processing types are placed on the continuum. For our description of how far up the continuum a particular informant group has reached, we apply the measure of relative frequency of use. In concrete terms, this means that, for each informant, we calculate which percentage of her processing falls into each of the four sections of the continuum out of her total processing on the continuum. It is important to note that the percentages quoted below are therefore internal to P2 processing. We shall start by looking at processing in relation to the four sections on the continuum, as presented in Table 3.6.

Let us begin by looking at the top level; that is, advanced processing from *section 1*. As we know already from the statistical analyses, there is a gradual increase in the frequency of use of section 1 on the continuum with a rising educational level. Furthermore, at each grade level figures are higher for L1 than for L2 (see Table 3.3). This confirmed the figures in Table 3.6. Turning to the bottom of the continuum and looking at *section 4*, we expect to find a gradual *de*crease in the use of this section

104   *Vocabulary and Writing in L1 and L2*

Table 3.6   Distribution of processing in relation to sections on the continuum

Sections		G.7		G.10		G.13	
		L1 (%)	L2 (%)	L1 (%)	L2 (%)	L1 (%)	L2 (%)
Top	1	31.2	5.0	51.7	20.5	65.3	41.1
	2	30.3	32.0	31.8	52.9	26.4	44.0
	3	10.3	9.7	4.9	11.6	4.1	7.6
Bottom	4	28.1	53.3	11.7	14.9	4.2	7.3

with a rising educational level, since section 4 processing involves ineffective bottom-ruled processing; this expectation is confirmed. For both L1 and L2, there is a gradual decrease from G.7 to G.10 to G.13, in L1 (28 per cent > 11 per cent > 4 per cent) and in L2 (53 per cent > 14 per cent > 7 per cent) – a fall that is clearly dramatic.

The results did, in fact, meet our expectations in relation to the extreme ends of the continuum. We shall now take a brief look at *sections 3 and 4*, neither of which received any attention in the statistical analyses. The relation between processing in sections 4 and 3 is that the former is bottom-ruled whereas the latter is undecided with regard to ruling. Such indecision we see as the beginning of an awareness that bottom-ruled processing is inefficient or 'wrong', and that a good guess must fit into the textual framework; that is, be top-ruled. Looking at the figures for section 3 in Table 3.6, we see that whereas G.7 learners have almost the same amount of undecided processing in the L1 and L2 (10.3 per cent versus 9.7 per cent), there is more of a difference for G.10 (4.9 per cent versus 11.6 per cent). It would therefore seem that, for the G.10 informants, an incipient awareness of the expediency in 'getting upwards' towards top-ruled processing sets in earlier in the L1 than in the L2. This shift from undecided ruling to top rule is a major one, as it implies that the informant crosses the borderline between ineffective and potentially effective processing, and moves upwards into new territory.

Let us finally concentrate on the *grade level view* and observe how the three groups differ with regard to the frequency with which they use the different sections of the continuum. Starting with *Grade 7*, we see that, in L1, the highest percentages are found in sections 1 and 2 (31 per cent and 30 per cent) – interestingly, in perfect balance and, together, accounting for 61 per cent of the processing. As for L2, however, the same group has its highest figure of 53 per cent in section 4, which illustrates a dramatic difference between L1 and L2 processing for these immature inferencers. Turning to the *Grade 10* group, we note that the high figures are found in sections 1 and 2; for L1, it is 51 per cent in section 1 and, for L2, it is 52 per cent in section 2. Whereas it is evident that the Grade 10 group has climbed upwards in both languages, it also appears that in L2 the last move upwards from section 2 into section 1 has not yet been accomplished (in the L2, section 1 processing is relatively very low). Turning finally to *Grade 13*, we see that, in L1, this group has its highest figure in section 1 (65 per cent) and, in L2, an even balance is found between sections 1 and 2, which together account for 85 per cent (41 per cent + 44 per cent) of the processing. In sum, looking at differences between the three groups, the youngest group stands out by its extensive use of the bottom section of the continuum, especially in L2. In comparison, the processing of the two other groups is concentrated on the two upper sections of the continuum in both languages, with very little use of the lower part. The main difference between Grades 10 and 13 is the latter group's more extensive use of section 1 processing in L2.

We have found that, for both L1 and L2 inferencing, there is a gradual increase in the relative frequency of the use of the upper half of the continuum with a rising educational level. Regarding our comparison of L1 and L2 inferencing, we have furthermore observed the tendency that L1 inferencing is ahead of L2 inferencing, with the most striking feature being the large gap found for the Grade 7 group. Applying the metaphor of the ladder, we can say that our top educational level, the Grade 13 group, stands on the top-most rung of the ladder in the L1 as well as in the L2 context. In contrast, our lowest educational level, the Grade 7 group, has climbed quite far up the ladder in the L1 context, but not nearly as far in the L2 context.

Finally, we conclude that the above analysis lends support to Haastrup's earlier proposal (Haastrup, 1991) that the processing continuum could be envisaged as a developmental continuum for L2 inferencing. Moreover, based on the present findings, this proposal can be extended so as to include L1 inferencing and, since our study has a longitudinal dimension to it, we have data that make it possible to trace the development of the individual informants over time. Only by using these data can the proposal be properly validated.

3.4.3 Discussion of results in relation to previous studies

With the aim of putting our findings into a broader research perspective, we turn to studies of L2 inferencing, since this is the area

106 *Vocabulary and Writing in L1 and L2*

of lexical inferencing research that can offer results comparable to our own.

We shall start with studies that include the processing aspect, and a natural choice is Haastrup's earlier study of Danish learners of English from two educational levels (Haastrup, 1991). The results of the present study confirm Haastrup's findings from the early study: that the quality of lexical inferencing, including both process and product, increases with the educational level of the informants. Moreover, the validity of this finding has been put to the test by the addition of a third group of learners in the present study; that is, the more advanced university group. Although Haastrup's earlier study included an analysis of both the lexical inferencing process and the quality of the guess, the interconnection between these two aspects did not receive much attention. The present study has highlighted the link between process and product by introducing the construct of adaptability. By doing so, we have shown that it is essential for lexical inferencing research to observe a distinction between word types and not just treat unfamiliar words as one unspecified group.

In a more recent study, Nassaji (2004) investigated the relationship between strategy use (*processing type*, in our terminology), lexical inferencing success and the role played by vocabulary knowledge. Nassaji adopts an integrated approach to lexical inferencing, and his understanding of lexical inferencing as a meaning construction process influenced by the richness of the learner's pre-existing semantic system is much in accordance with our own. It thus makes sense to compare his results with ours. Using adult intermediate learners of English with different language backgrounds, Nassaji found that learners' depth of vocabulary knowledge was a stronger predictor of lexical inferencing success than their strategy use. The fact that he chose depth of vocabulary knowledge rather than breadth is a point that makes his results particularly relevant to ours, as will be discussed in Chapter 5, where we bring together all the aspects of our informants' lexical competence that have been investigated. At this point, we wish to emphasize that, by choosing vocabulary knowledge as a predictor of lexical inferencing success, Nassaji has taken up a main theme in the literature; that is, the search for factors that can account for a high level of inferencing success.

As detailed earlier, the main predictors of lexical inferencing success revealed so far in the many studies of adult learners have been L2 vocabulary knowledge and L2 reading skills (see Section 3.1.1 above). Both Laufer (1997b) and Paribakht (2005) found that lexical knowledge has an important role to play and, with regard to reading, Bengeleil and Paribakht (2004) found that reading level seems to influence guessing ability, and report that many studies have found high correlations between these two factors. Based on our study of Danish informants, in Chapter 5 we shall report on the relations found between the following L2 measures: lexical inferencing (process and product), reading ability and lexical competence (see Tables 5.1–5.8). Suffice it to say, at this point, that moderate and high correlations were found between vocabulary size and lexical inferencing success, as well as between reading ability and lexical inferencing success, at all grade levels. These results thus corroborate previous findings and also add to them, since our study spans a wide informant range including three educational levels.

Finally, we wish to address the question of which rate of inferencing success one can expect when investigating L1 and L2 inferencing for the same learners using parallel tasks, such as we have done. Focusing on our top group – the university students – we found that, in the L1, their success rate was 58 per cent. As we have not found a relevant point of comparison, all we can say is that we had expected a better result for mature students' first language use, and add that this may well be due to the nature of the inferencing task, with its high concentration of difficult words in short texts (see Section 3.2.1 above and the discussion below). For the L2, the same group's success rate was 48 per cent and, in this case, there are previous studies that point to our results as being at the low end. However, relevant as it may be to compare results across studies, it is also risky, since informants represent different proficiency levels and language backgrounds. When we compare the university groups used, for instance, by Wesche and Paribahkt (personal communication), their informants have typically studied for a longer period than ours, who are only one month into their university courses. Finally, we wish to emphasize that a very important factor is undoubtedly the relationship between the informants' L1 and L2, and the degree to which these languages are closely or distantly related. So, let us end these considerations with a question related to this factor: Is the observed difference of 10 per cent between the success rates in Danish and English, which are both Germanic languages, large or small? The best way to address this question, we believe, is to carry out more multilingual investigations that include both closely and distantly related languages within the same study, and thus allow for a more valid analysis of the role played by cross-lingual factors.

3.5 Perspectives on research design and teaching

Beginning with *research design*, we wish to point out what were found to be the main advantages and shortcomings of the approach used in this study of a student's first encounter with an unfamiliar word. First, we have experienced that there may be a problem with the five short texts, because they include a high concentration of low frequent and difficult target words that the informants may never meet in the real world. Especially our youngest informants have told us that these words looked so weird that they felt tempted to give up on guessing them. As regards successful guessing, even our top group – the university students – did not have a high degree of inferencing success in their first language, and we must consider whether this could be an artefact of the task. However, on the positive side, we find that using a task that throws light on 30 instances of lexical problem solving within two pages of text is a good research tool. Moreover, by its very nature, the lexical inferencing task forces the process of noticing, and the verbal protocols freeze the picture and tell us – if not all – then much of what informants pay attention to.

Second, we want to compare our lexical inferencing task with an actual reading task. In an authentic reading task, readers focus on text comprehension and, when they encounter unfamiliar words during the reading process, they will not automatically engage in lexical inferencing procedures. If they find that a particular word appears to be a keyword in the text, they will probably try to find the precise meaning of that word, perhaps by trying to infer its meaning, possibly followed by a dictionary check. If, on the other hand, the same word is considered less important for the understanding of the text, the readers may well decide to simply skip the word or settle for an approximate guess; that is, a here-and-now comprehension of what the word might mean in that particular context. Thus, their reading goal is likely to influence the degree to which they invest time and effort in the processing of the word in question. This point emphasizes a major difference between the lexical inferencing task with predefined word problems that the informants have to solve, and a more true-to-life reading task, in which readers themselves choose which unfamiliar words they want to deal with, and in which way.

These observations have been added because, throughout the chapter, we have emphasized the close link between reading and lexical inferencing. There is, however, a difference that is brought out in the definition of the task that we have given our informants. They are asked to guess the meaning of unfamiliar words in a written text, which makes it different from saying that the task is a reading task. Thus, we claim validity for our task while acknowledging that it is not a natural reading task.

Moving on to the lexical perspective, we wish to put forward a hypothesis concerning lexical inferencing viewed as a first phase of vocabulary acquisition. We propose that individuals have the best chance of actually acquiring a word with potential linguistic cues to meaning if they, at the first or early encounter with the word, get involved in successful analytic processing. The hypothesis rests on two assumptions: first, that the nature of the processing on this occasion influences the following phases in the acquisition process; and, second, that analytic processing invites task-induced involvement and can be compared to depth of processing, which is known to enhance retention (Laufer and Hulstijn, 2001). So, although we know that, in most cases, the acquisition of a particular word is a long process that requires at least authoritative feedback on the word guess and, typically, several additional encounters with the word, preferably in different contexts (Gass, 1999; Van Daalen-Kapteijns et al., 2001), it is our contention that analytic processing, for which the informant makes the best use of the word's processing potential by utilizing linguistic cues to meaning, will enhance the acquisition process. However, let us conclude by emphasizing that this is a hypothesis that has to be tested in a different research design.

Turning to *teaching perspectives*; findings from the present study emphasize the crucial, and expected, role played by declarative lexical knowledge for lexical inferencing, and it is suggested that learners' problems, especially in L2 inferencing, are partly due to their lack of L2 vocabulary knowledge. This insight thus supports the importance of developing students' vocabulary knowledge and calls for vocabulary enhancement activities in language teaching (see the discussion in Chapter 6).

A prevalent theme in this chapter has been the development of the informants' procedural knowledge in comprehension and, since their L2 procedural skills have been found to lag behind their L1 skills, we propose that teachers should take account of this by focusing their students' attention on the potential transferability of effective processing types from L1 to L2. Moreover, as lexical inferencing processes are closely related to reading processes, we recommend that reading strategies and word guessing strategies are taught in combination, and that the development of both is supported by awareness-raising activities.

110 *Vocabulary and Writing in L1 and L2*

Such activities should find a place in both mother tongue teaching and foreign language teaching.

In this brief discussion of teaching perspectives, we have dealt with declarative and procedural knowledge separately. However, since the two are very much related, we wish to conclude the chapter by underlining the finding that the quality of lexical inferencing procedures is dependent on interaction between declarative and procedural knowledge. Just as our study has highlighted the importance of maximal interaction between the two, as witnessed by advanced processing, it is our contention that, if students in the classroom are made aware of the fact that the quality of their guess depends on the processes they use, this insight will help them develop their strategic competence in comprehension. As we believe that this is an aspect of students' communicative competence that is of equal importance in the mother tongue and the foreign language, we recommend intensified cooperation between language teachers on this issue. We will elaborate on this in Chapter 6.

Notes

1 I would like to thank Marjorie Wesche and Sima Paribakht for valuable comments on an earlier draft of this chapter. Any shortcomings remain, of course, entirely the author's responsibility. Moreover, I want to thank them both for sharing with us the current version of their comprehensive literature review on lexical inferencing, which has been an important source of inspiration for us.

2 Many of the texts originated from reference books. In relation to the topic of dinosaurs, for instance, the starting point would be the entry in a Danish encyclopedia, which would supply text passages including a number of suitable test words in context. In the next phase, we would rewrite the co-text around these test words, taking inspiration from parallel texts in books on dinosaurs for children and young people. Another text source was magazines on popular science.

3 The comprehensibility of the English texts – that is, the co-text of the test words – was tested on two groups of Grade 7 students. Such field-testing helped us to decide which co-text words should be glossed.

4 I would like to thank my research assistants, Hanne Lindegaard Svensson and Kim Pedersen, who worked on the coding of the lexical inferencing data. They helped me develop and refine the analytical framework for lexical inferencing success and processing types, and also carried out the actual coding of a large number of verbal protocols. Without their talent and dedication, the coding work would not have been completed.

5 Readers who are interested in obtaining the detailed description of the coding framework for processing types are welcome to contact the authors.

6 Conventions used in the protocol extracts:

<xxx>	Refers to the informants' reading aloud from the printed text
xxx	(For the L2 inferencing task) refers to the informants' translation of the printed text into Danish
/xxx/	Crude indication of pronunciation of the test word
–	Rough indication of length of pauses
– –	
– – –	
...	Marks where passages have been left out from within the individual protocol extract: these can indicate either that this is not the beginning or the end of the verbal protocol for this test word, or that part of the verbalisation has been omitted (since it does not contribute to the interpretation of the protocol that follows the extract).

7 We did foresee that lack of time might become a problem. As expected, field-testing indicated that informants, in general, needed more time for the L2 than for the L1 task. However, in order to meet the criterion of having parallel tasks, time on task had to be the same for the L1 and the L2 tasks. Moreover, there was considerable variation within the Grade 7 group used for the field-testing; some of the students rushed through the task whereas others, who were slow readers, required much more time to complete the task. The allocated time on task can thus be seen as a compromise.

8 The purpose of this calculation was to test whether invalid items had upset the planned balance between word types; therefore, two data sets were established. Data set A was based on all 30 test words. Data set B was a post hoc established set based on the 20 most valid test words; that is, omitting the test words with the highest number of invalid items. As the two data sets turned out to yield results that were very much alike on selected measures, data set A was chosen, since this was based on the largest number of test words and had the planned balance between word types.

4
Writing in Two Languages

Dorte Albrechtsen

I'am disagree with the following statement!.

It is not right a television has destroyed communication amon friends and family, actual a this quite opposite. If we take that seres about without leaving a trace. Ther can man find his friends and familly and that's good.

So I mene that's television it is real good.

and a you actor can your friend and family see you.

(Essay written by a Grade 7 student)

On seeing the essay quoted here, the off-hand reaction of most teachers would be annoyance. This fourteen year-old teenager – who does not normally do well – has again demonstrated that she is lazy, and that she does not put much effort into her schoolwork. Her essay is only 65 words long, although she had 90 minutes to complete the task. However, since the essay was produced in the context of a research project, requiring students to verbalize concurrently while writing their essays, we know from her verbal protocol that this student actually worked hard on her essay, and that she spent the full 90 minutes. So, what did she do during all this time? At first, she spent a lot of time trying to understand the writing prompt, which was in English. In fact, throughout the writing process, she struggled with language. Although she worked hard trying to solve her problems, she was clearly bogged down by having to write in a foreign language. For her, this task turned out to be more of a jigsaw puzzle than a writing task. The research context opens a valuable window on the hard work that some of the less able students actually put into a meagre product, a luxury not often afforded to teachers.

In this chapter, we shall describe how such verbal protocols were analyzed and report on the results of these analyses. In doing so, we aim to answer the following two main research questions:

R1 Is there a difference between writing in L1 and L2 for the same students?

R2 Is there a difference in learner writing as a function of grade level for both L1 and L2 writing?

To address the first question, we investigated the actual writing processes of individual learners when writing in a foreign language and in their mother tongue. Such a within-subjects design allows us to assess the degree to which individual students operate in the same way in the two languages, which is an issue that is central to the teaching of writing in a foreign language. If learners experience difficulties writing in a foreign language, this may well be due to problems with writing in the mother tongue. Our investigation provides information on the extent to which the ability to write in L2 depends on L1 writing skills.

With regard to the second question, we investigated this in a between-subjects design by comparing the writing processes of learners at three very different grade levels: learners in Grade 7 who attend ordinary Danish schools; learners from Grade 10 who are in the first year of the three-year Danish sixth-form college, which prepares students for university level studies; and, finally, Grade 13 learners who are university students in their first year of English studies.

The chapter opens with a brief review of research on issues pertinent to the present investigation of the informants' writing processes – more specifically, previous research investigating students' writing processes in L1 and L2. The chapter proceeds with a section on the theoretical background of the study, detailing the writing process models that have inspired our investigation. Furthermore, we shall address the issue of investigating learners' writing processes through verbal protocols. This is followed by information on the study itself, including the informants, tasks, procedures and the analytical approach adopted in this study. As to the outcome of our investigation, the results of the statistical analyses will be presented and discussed. Furthermore, a section is devoted to a qualitative analysis of three informants, and we end the chapter with discussions and implications of the findings.

114   *Vocabulary and Writing in L1 and L2*

4.1   Previous research

This section is devoted to a brief review of previous research most pertinent to the design and results of our study. First, our focus is on studies investigating the relationship between writing in L1 and L2. The design of these studies is addressed, followed by a brief outline of the main findings of the studies and, finally, a study of formulation processes will be described in some detail. Second, the section is devoted to research on the relationship between process and product, and on the effects of L2 proficiency and L1 writing skills on L2 composition.

4.1.1   Research comparing writing processes in L1 and L2

A large body of research has investigated the writing processes of non-native speakers. For recent surveys of L2 writing studies, see Cumming, 1998, 2001; Roca de Larios et al., 2002; Leki et al., 2006. Some studies have focused on the L2 process, correlating the findings with measures of L1 writing skills, with L2 language proficiency and with essay quality. Cumming's groundbreaking study (1989) is a case in point, establishing a close connection between L1 writing skills and the quality of the L2 writing process.

Pertinent in connection with our study is the research on the relationship between writing in L1 and L2. This relationship has been the subject of a number of very different types of investigations (such as Sasaki and Hirose, 1996; Schoonen et al., 2003). The studies that we shall briefly deal with here have looked into the exact nature of the relationship between L1 and L2 writing skills by investigating the actual writing processes in both languages for the same learners; that is, in within-subject designs. Some studies investigated the writing processes of their subjects through verbal protocols, produced online (for instance, Arndt, 1987; Jones and Tetroe, 1987; Skibniewski, 1988; Krings, 1989; Cumming et al., 1989; Wong, 1993; Whalen and Ménard, 1995; Uzawa, 1996; Akyel and Kamisli, 1997; Albrechtsen, 1997; Chenoweth and Hayes, 2001; Roca de Larios et al., 2001, 2006). Other studies looked into writing processes via observations of their subjects while writing, often combined with the subjects' retrospective accounts of their writing processes or with other methods of data collection, such as computerized tracking (for instance, Skibniewski and Skibniewska, 1986; Fagan and Hayden, 1988; Hall, 1990; Pennington and So, 1993; Thorson, 2000).

Most of these studies investigate the writing process of university students, although the studies by Fagan and Hayden (1988) and Wong

(1993) deal with younger learners. The languages investigated in the studies are Chinese, English, French, German, Italian, Japanese, Polish and Spanish as L1 and English, German and French as L2. In other words, most studies deal with subjects at university level, and none of the studies have compared Danish L1 to English L2, apart from Albrechtsen's (1997) case study of one learner in grade 8. Due to the time-consuming analysis required for investigating processes, most studies operate with a limited number of subjects. Typically, the number of informants in these studies ranges from six to fourteen, the exceptions being Uzawa (1996), Roca de Larios et al. (2001, 2006) and Wong (1993) with 22, 21 and 43 subjects, respectively. To the best of our knowledge, very few studies exist that investigate the writing processes in L1 and L2 in a within-subjects design *across grade levels*. Of the studies mentioned here, only those by Roca de Larios et al. used such a design for their investigations of formulation processes. Their 21 Spanish EFL learners were equally divided between three educational levels: sixth-form college students (age 16 to 17), university students studying education (age 19–20) and postgraduate students of English (23–24).

The present study differs from previous studies with respect to: (1) the number of informants investigated (60 in both languages); (2) the languages compared (Danish L1 to English L2); and (3) the range of educational levels included (cross-sectional data from rather young learners to university students).

Turning to a brief account of the findings, the majority of the studies referred to above found more similarities than differences between the writing process in L1 and L2. The similarities are mainly seen with regard to composing strategies – such as planning, goal setting and revision, whereas differences are more likely to occur with regard to online problem solving (see Manchón, 2001, for this distinction). Compared with writing in L1, the general findings for composing strategies have been that the quantity but not the quality of, say, planning is affected by writing in L2. For online problem solving compared with L1, writing in L2 results in more problem solving, mainly due to the problems writers have in expressing their intended meaning in L2. In addition to this, fluency was found to be lower in L2 than in L1, measured either as the number of words verbalized while transcribing without interruption by other composing processes or as the time spent on problem-free formulation.

For younger groups of writers, the two studies we have been able to identify arrive at results similar to those for university level students. Fagan and Hayden's (1988) observational study of the composing strategies used

116   *Vocabulary and Writing in L1 and L2*

by grade 5 French immersion students revealed that, for planning, the students behaved similarly in their two languages whereas, with regard to editing, they edited more in English than in French. Wong (1993) investigated secondary school students (aged about 15), using think aloud and found that the quality of meaning-constructing strategies was similar in the two languages (English and Chinese).

With regard to formulation processes, the cross-sectional studies by Roca de Larios et al. (2001, 2006) focused on two main issues. In the first study, the focus was on fluency in the form of non-problematic formulation and, in the second study, on problematic formulation. For formulation in general, the students spent the same total amount of time on formulation in L1 (Spanish) and L2 (English). Cross-sectionally, the youngest group (16–17 year old sixth-form students) devoted significantly more time to formulation than the university students and the postgraduate students. With regard to fluency, all three groups taken together had a significantly higher level of fluent formulation in L1 than in L2.

When analyzing the problem-solving formulation processes, a distinction was made between compensatory and upgrading formulation processes. Whereas *compensatory* refers to instances in which students have difficulties accessing the linguistic means for expressing their intended meaning, *upgrading* covers situations in which students make an effort to find a better word or expression for their intended meaning. For problem-solving formulation, regardless of type, a statistically significant difference was found between L1 and L2: the students spent more time on problem solving in L2. When taking the two types of formulation processes into account, it turned out that no time was devoted to compensatory formulation in L1 whereas, in L2, the students spent almost equal amounts of time on compensatory and upgrading formulation. Looking at the data cross-sectionally, the almost equal distribution of the two types of formulation processes in L2 turned out to cover interesting differences between the three groups of writers. The sixth-form college students spent about three times as much time on compensatory formulation as on upgrading and, for the postgraduate students, it was the other way round. The university students, representing the mid-level, spent almost the same amount of time on the two types of formulation processes but slightly more on compensatory formulation processes. The study does not report whether or not these differences between the groups were statistically significant. These findings are interesting; they demonstrate the qualitative differences that problem solving might cover. We shall refer to these issues in the interpretation of our own results.

4.1.2 Process versus product and the effect of L2 proficiency and L1 writing skills

When studying the writing process, naturally, the expectation is that there will be some kind of correspondence between the process and the result of that process – the essay. However, this issue is only explicitly addressed in a few studies and the results are conflicting. Cumming (1989) and Cumming et al. (1989) found close relationships between the quality of the writing processes and the quality of the essays produced and, in the study by Jones and Tetroe (1987), the quality of planning corresponded to essay quality. However, Pennington and So (1993) found no relationship between process and product. These different findings might be due to differences in the number of subjects used in the investigations but might also be attributed to other variables that vary from study to study. Since our own differs from other studies on a number of parameters, we shall deal with this issue in the discussion section of this chapter (Section 4.5).

The question of the contribution of L2 language proficiency and L1 writing skills to L2 writing success is also addressed in studies of the L2 writing process. Cumming (1989) found that both variables have a bearing on L2 writing performance but, judging from the results of his study of university level students, the two variables contribute differently. L1 writing skills were found to relate significantly to the quality of the L2 writing process. In other words, expert writers in L1 demonstrated an expert process in L2 and basic writers in L1 used a basic process in L2, regardless of the fact that some of the writers in each group had intermediate level L2 language proficiency and others had advanced level L2 language proficiency. Thus, L2 language proficiency did not seem to affect the quality of the L2 writing process. In other words, if students are good writers in L1, the chances are that they operate a skilled process in L2 and vice versa. However, L2 language proficiency coincided with essay quality; informants with advanced levels of L2 proficiency obtained better ratings on their essays than those with intermediate level proficiency. These issues will also be addressed in this study.

4.2 Theoretical background

The enterprise of investigating learner processes is not only time consuming, but also tricky. Since we do not have direct access to what goes on in people's minds, we have to rely on indirect evidence of learner processes. Whether this indirect evidence is obtained via think-aloud procedures or via computer programmes tracking the subjects' every

118 *Vocabulary and Writing in L1 and L2*

move and action, the data elicited have to be interpreted. By its very nature, such interpretation is highly subjective, and all researchers can do is try to avoid idiosyncratic interpretations by respecting a set of rules that has emerged over time for this kind of enquiry. First, adopting a theory of the writing process ensures that researchers can explicate the kinds of phenomena they are looking for in the data. Second, the underlying theory of the writing process that guides the study has implications for the type of data collection used for the study. Finally, the analysis of the data must be carried out by at least two analysts who, ideally speaking, would arrive at the exact same interpretation of the same piece of data.

4.2.1 A model of the writing process

The two most quoted models of writing processes are those created by Flower and Hayes (1984) and Bereiter and Scardamalia (1987) for writing in L1. Even though attempts have been made to devise models that specifically address writing in L2, these attempts are preliminary in nature, descriptive rather than predictive, and have not been tested empirically to the same degree as the L1 models (see, for instance, Grabe, 2001). Most L2 writing research still refers to L1 models of the writing process, and our study is no exception. Flower and Hayes' model highlights the recurring processes of planning, transcribing and revision. However, the model describes one process and is thus not very explicit with respect to writing development (see Grabe and Kaplan, 1996). Hence, according to the model, poor writers operate the same process as good writers but in a less qualified manner. Bereiter and Scardamalia's theory of the writing process takes its point of departure in the assumption that poor and good writers behave very differently when writing. This difference is so substantial that two separate models are needed for capturing the way in which these two types of writers handle a writing task. Thus, the two models are more explicit than the Flower and Hayes model with regard to writing development and are therefore suitable models in our context.

As mentioned, Bereiter and Scardamalia's two main models are meant to capture differences between immature and mature writers. The main difference between these two types of writers is how they bring content and discourse knowledge to bear on the writing task. *Immature writers* are seen as operating via a knowledge-telling process that involves very little reflection. While writing, these writers proceed in a local manner via associations, drawing on their knowledge through spreading activation. Their writing does not include any sort of planning. In contrast to this, the *mature writers* use a knowledge-transforming process, which involves initial goal setting and planning. This is a much more reflective process, in which two problem-solving spaces are assumed to operate: one for handling problems related to content knowledge and one for problems related to discourse knowledge. Throughout composing, dialectical processing is in operation; this translates discourse problems to the content problem space and vice versa. The assumption is that this dialectical process results in the transformation of knowledge and hence accounts for the fact that mature writers learn something new or gain new insights when composing. On the other hand, the immature writers do not, in this way, benefit from their writing process in that they merely tell the knowledge they already have (see Galbraith, 1999, for a different view of what leads to learning through writing, as dealt with in Chapter 1). The knowledge-telling approach to writing is described by Bereiter and Scardamalia as an efficient way for immature writers to handle a complex task that exceeds their abilities.

The two models describe extreme ends of a continuum of processing when writing. Parts of the process of a mature writer will also proceed as knowledge-telling or unattended processing, and immature writers will naturally now and again experience problems to which they must attend. However, in their case, the chances are that this will lead to break downs in their process. Finally, we would like to stress that mature writers, when faced with a routine task, are likely to operate in accordance with the knowledge-telling model simply because, due to the writer's familiarity with the task, it will pose fewer problems and hence can be handled successfully by a more associative approach.

The two models give us an indication of what to look for in judging the quality of the processes revealed by our informants in their verbal protocols and serve as guidelines for the use of analytical categories and their interpretation.

4.2.2 Introspective methods

Since the models we have chosen emphasize mature writing as a problem-solving process, we are naturally focusing on attended processing and not on the automatic type of processing described by Galbraith (1999), as dealt with in Chapter 1. The most common, but also highly controversial, way of investigating attended processes is by asking informants to verbalize everything that comes to mind while they are writing. The writer will, of course, be conscious of many things while composing, and we must realize that the verbal protocols will only cover some of all the thinking that goes on while writing. To alleviate this

120 *Vocabulary and Writing in L1 and L2*

problem, some studies use retrospection as a supplementary method, as we have done for the lexical inferencing task described in Chapter 3. Retrospection normally requires close contact between researcher and informant to ensure that the retrospective data give information that can be compared across subjects. With a large number of informants, this is normally not a feasible procedure and was only possible for the lexical inferencing task because, in that task, the problems our informants had to address were predefined. In the more open task of essay writing, we assessed that the data we would gain from using immediately consecutive retrospection would not be worth the extra time and effort.

In addition to the drawbacks already mentioned, other points of criticism have been raised against the method. One such point is that, by asking learners to write and verbalize at the same time, we are in fact studying a situation that is very different from normal writing. A number of studies have investigated the issue of reactivity: whether or not having to verbalize changes the writing process, as compared with composing silently. Although the findings are conflicting, there is no doubt that having to verbalize imposes an extra task on writers, which affects, for instance, the number of revisions carried out, and it is definitely more time consuming for the writers (for instance, Stratman and Hamp-Lyons, 1994; Janssen et al., 1996). To get around the problem of reactivity, researchers have started using keystroke-logging computer programs. Although this method provides true online recording of where and when writers pause during the process, investigators still end up asking themselves: What happens during the pause? Hence, some researchers now recommend using a combination of keystroke logging and concurrent verbalization (for instance, Stevenson et al., 2006).

Finally, the possibility of a negative effect of the interaction between subject and researcher has been considered in the literature (for instance, Smagorinsky, 1994). The concern is that writers will verbalize on issues they believe will please the researcher. This is probably more of a problem in studies in which the subjects meet on an individual basis with the researcher for their think-aloud sessions, but it is, of course, a variable that is difficult to control and assess regardless of the data collection procedure. Despite all these limitations, concurrent verbalization is probably still the best option we have for tapping into learners' writing processes.

4.3 The study

In the account of our investigation of the informants' writing processes, we address the design, the analytical framework and the statistical analyses of the data. For a description of the overall project design, see Chapter 1.

4.3.1 Design

For the writing part of our project, we analyzed the verbal protocols of 20 informants from each of the three educational levels included in our study: Grade 7 (G.7), Grade 10 (G.10) and university level students (G.13).[1] The L2 language proficiency, as measured on Nation's Levels Test, was significantly different for all the three grade levels (means: G.7: 34.50, G.10: 73.95 and G.13: 95.85).

All informants were asked to write an essay in their L1 (Danish) and in their L2 (English). There were four writing prompts altogether, and each writing prompt had a Danish and an English version. The informants wrote the two essays with a week's interval (see Chapter 1). The order of presentation of the Danish and English prompts and of the topics was counterbalanced. The actual prompts (see Appendix A.4.1) were selected from the TOEFL list of writing prompts. The decision as to which prompts to use was based on field-testing. All prompts asked for an argumentative essay, and additional instructions were added to the prompts to make this clear to the informants, as seen in this example:

Do you agree or disagree with the following statement? Telephones and email have made communication between people less personal.

You are writing to somebody who disagrees with you. Try to win the reader over to your point of view. Use specific reasons and examples to support your opinion.

Argumentative essays were chosen since this genre is generally agreed to be cognitively demanding, and the aim was to ensure that the prompts would pose a challenge, even to the university students. In this way, we hoped to avoid giving the older informants a task that, to them, was a routine task. Such a task would invite a knowledge-telling process and thus would not reveal the kind of writing process they were capable of using. Since all informants were given the exact same writing prompts, the drawback was that the tasks might be too challenging for the young informants.

As mentioned in Chapter 1, at the outset, the informants were screened to ensure that those who were enrolled to take part in the study had the ability to use think-aloud procedures. This screening also served as a form of training in these techniques for the participants. In addition, all informants watched video extracts of a student verbalizing

122 *Vocabulary and Writing in L1 and L2*

while writing an essay in Danish and English. We made sure that the video recording contained verbalization in English as well as in Danish for the extracts from the English essay. In addition, the participants were explicitly told that the choice of L1 or L2 for verbalizing was entirely up to them.

As described in Chapter 1, for the collection of verbal protocols, the informants were seated in booths in a language laboratory. This set-up meant that several informants could be tested simultaneously, thus minimizing the subject/researcher interaction. In our case, the sole prompting given to the informants during the tasks was merely for research assistants to point unobtrusively to a sign reminding participants to verbalize. The informants had dictionaries at their disposal and could turn to the research assistants for help, but only for questions pertaining to understanding the actual task.

The audio-taped verbalizations were transcribed by student research assistants, who had received training prior to transcribing. The tapes were transcribed verbatim, and a transcription system was used to distinguish between three main types of verbalizations: (1) verbalizations of actual writing; (2) verbalizations of reading the prompt or the text produced up to a point; (3) verbalizations of what the informants attended to when they were neither writing nor reading. (See Appendix A.4.2, for details of the transcription scheme.)

4.3.2 Analytical framework[2]

The aim of the analyses of the protocols was to capture possible differences between processing in L1 and L2, and possible differences in processing between the grade levels. Two main approaches to analyzing verbal protocols were considered. Whalen and Ménard's system (1995) had been applied in a study of the relationship between writing in L1 and L2 in a within-subjects design dealing with university level informants. Cumming's (1989) coding scheme, inspired by Scardamalia and Bereiter (1983) and Scardamalia and Paris (1985), was used for a study of verbalizations with regard to writing in L2. The informants in Cumming's study were also university level students, but a developmental aspect was introduced by grouping the informants according to their writing abilities in L1. There was quite a range of abilities in the group of informants, enabling the forming of three groups of writers: intermediate writers, advanced writers and expert writers. The latter group consisted of professional writers, and including this group enabled a characterization of the expert process – a feature not often seen in studies of this kind.

Although the study by Whalen and Ménard (1995) had the advantage of comparing verbal protocols in L1 and L2, the developmental aspect was not in focus in the study. Therefore, the method of analysis used by Cumming (1989) was chosen for this study as it had been demonstrated that it could capture differences between three somewhat different groups of writers. Although all writers in Cumming's study were much older than most of our informants, the assumption was that this system of analysis would also be able to capture differences between the groups analyzed here – an assumption that was confirmed in a small pilot study.

The aim of the analysis is to establish qualitative differences in the processes of our informants, both when operating in L1 and in L2, and across the grade levels. As mentioned before, the knowledge-telling process is, by and large, a non-reflective process whereas the knowledge-transforming process involves reflection throughout most of the act of composing. The latter involves planning and goal setting not only initially, but also while writing. In addition, reflection happens when the writer runs into problems related to either content or discourse, and problems are often solved in a dialectic interaction between the two. As described below, Cumming's method of analysis captures not only the problem-solving aspect of the process, but also what writers attend to in the two problem spaces.

For the analyses of the protocols, the verbalizations were divided into episodes. The core of each episode was the verbalizations of what the informants attended to, and the verbalizations of their reading and of the transcription of their ideas served as context. Using Cumming's method of analysis meant that, for each episode, the core of the verbalization was coded for the type of problem-solving behaviour demonstrated by the informants and for what the informants focused their attention on in connection with their problem solving. This meant that each episode was coded for two main features: (1) attention to aspects of writing; and (2) the types of problem solving revealed in each episode. For attention to aspects of writing, the informants might attend to anything from one to four aspects of writing in each episode. For type of problem solving, only one category was allotted to each episode.

Below, we shall give examples of *attention to aspects of writing*. In reading these and other extracts from the protocols, the reader is referred to the transcription scheme in Appendix A.4.2. The main distinctions are pointed brackets indicating reading sequences, asterisks denoting transcribing sequences and hyphens showing sequences in which the

124 *Vocabulary and Writing in L1 and L2*

students reflect on or sound out their formulations. The categories listed show that informants might attend to how to phrase their ideas (attention to language use), how to structure their essays (attention to discourse organization) and which ideas to include (attention to ideas). In addition, they might verbalize on the procedures they are performing, such as announcing that they are going to read the text produced up to a point (attention to procedure).

1 **Attention to language use**

> **Example:** <people has a more stressful> *weekday* – ...... *now we need to figure out* ... people have has ... had ... people ... have ... *I'm just going to say* – *have*
> (L2: G.7 – italic text translated from Danish).

2 **Attention to discourse organization**

> **Example:** – yea goody so I have like three arguments now [looks through her papers] but erm –
> (L2: G.13).

3 **Attention to ideas**

> **Example:** – *then I could ... take something from my everyday life or something like that* –
> (L2: G.10 – translated from Danish).

4 **Attention to procedure**

> **Example:** – yes *we'll take it from the top* [turns page and clears his throat] *I am going to read it aloud* –
> (L2: G.10 – italic text translated from Danish).

As mentioned above, writers often attend to more than one aspect of writing in a given episode. The number of aspects attended to ranges from the typical combination of two aspects to the rare co-occurrence of four aspects.

5 **Concurrent attention to aspects of writing**

> This might, for instance, cover attention to language and ideas, as in:

> **Example:** <the one cheaper than the ones we> – *I have written* keep *but that can't be right damn it* [crosses out 'keep'] – <this group often has an economical advantage since the unknown brands are cheaper than the ones we> *hear of* <in the adver advertisements>
> (L2: G.13 – italic text translated from Danish).

Or it might cover attention to ideas and discourse as in:

> **Example:** *driving a bus or train or reading reading a magazine ... commercials are everywhere* – that's quite general I guess so that's alright and then I can I can specify by asking maybe a rhetorical question ... like erm –
>
> (L2: G.13).

For aspects of writing, the measures used for the statistical analysis were percentages of the number of occurrences of a given aspect (see 1–4 above) in relation to the total number of episodes of protocols in both languages. For concurrent attention to several aspects of writing (see 5), percentages were calculated of the number of episodes with attention to two or more aspects of writing in relation to the total number of episodes.

Having dealt with the categories that capture what writers attend to while writing, we shall now turn to the categories that are meant to capture the type of *problem solving* writers apply to the issues they attend to. These are exemplified below and cover different kinds of problem solving, ranging from no problem solving through mere identification of a problem to more complex problem solving. Resolution of a problem in this taxonomy is always from the point of view of the writer. Thus, there is no implication that the solution is adequate with respect to an external norm.

1 **No problem** (no problem solving apparent)

> **Example:** <make it much easier for the family to communicate exchange ideas knowledge etc with each other ...> – and form new ideas ... and form – <with each other> *and form new ideas and form new ideas new ideas*
>
> (L2: G.13).

2 **Problem identification** (problem identified but not solved)

> **Example:** *it's it is it is easy to to eh to turn it on* – I don't know if it's called that turn it on – *and then just sit down enjoy the the the ride*
>
> (L2: G.10).

3 **Problem solved quickly** (problem identified and solved but no elaboration is provided as to the nature of the problem solved)

> **Example:** *ehm eh the channels* – is they – *are filled up ehm with ehm reality shows and bad movies ehm which is a a good a good eh trap*
>
> (L2: G.10).

126 *Vocabulary and Writing in L1 and L2*

4 Heuristic searches[3] (problem addressed and either solved or not solved by elaborating the nature of the problem). Here, we distinguish two categories: *heuristic searches without resolution* and *heuristic searches with resolution*. In these categories, *heuristic searches* cover activities such as goal setting, assessing alternatives, using search routines and evaluations with respect to a criterion or rule.

Example – goal setting: – I don't really know what I agree with erm ... I guess ... I guess a little bit of both erm ... I don't think really that advertizing makes us buy things that we really do not need cause there is always this choice you ... it's not something that they make us do ... erm ... so I'm I'm probably gonna agree with the second one that new products that may make our lives better ... so erm ... yes ... erm ... I'm just gonna make some notes –

(L2: G.13).

Example – assessing alternatives: – *yes* compensate that's the word I want to use counterbalance is too neat or formal but compensate yes ... –

(L2: G.13 – italic text translated from Danish).

Example – search routine: <nice to hear the voice of> – *yes* ... err [whispers] a forgotten friend a not a ff not forgotten friend *yes that has to be it* a not for got I forget ... eh I forgot I have forgotten [whispers the following] I had forgotten I have forget forgotten orh forgot whatever – <nice to hear the voice of a not> *forgotten [sighs] friend*

(L2: G.10 – italic text translated from Danish).

Example – evaluation according to a criterion: – but why do commercials you can't start a sentence with a but ahm one can ask yourself *it sounds wrong maybe it'll sound better as I go along* –

(L2: G.13 – italic text translated from Danish).

For problem solving, the measures used for the statistical analysis were percentages of each of the categories (see 1–4 above) in relation to the total number of episodes.

Previously, we drew attention to the fact that the models of knowledge telling and knowledge transforming cover extreme ends of a continuum of writing development. When studying learners, we are likely to see a mixture of the two processing approaches, in which some writers will show more features of knowledge telling than knowledge transforming, and for other writers it will be the other way round. The question is, of course, how we decide what constitutes knowledge telling and what constitutes knowledge transforming. In studying revision processes, Bereiter and Scardamalia (1987) refer to the so-called CDO process, which stands for compare, diagnose and operate. If all three operations are applied to a given problem, this is seen as indicative of a more mature process. If, on the other hand, only the compare part of the process is in operation, this is a sign of a more immature process.

The taxonomy for problem solving was developed by Cumming (1989) for his study, and was partly inspired by a set of instructional procedures used in an investigation of the CDO process to help children to improve their revision processes (Scardamalia and Bereiter, 1983). We shall attempt an interpretation of the taxonomy used for analyzing the problem solving revealed in the verbal protocols in relation to the CDO process. The category *no problem* indicates that the CDO process is not appealed to at all. For *problem identification*, only the compare part of the CDO process is activated, as implicitly reflected in the fact that a problem is identified. However, the problem is left unsolved probably because the writer has not been able to diagnose the problem or, at any rate, does not verbalize any such diagnosis and definitely does not act or operate with regard to the problem in question. For problem solving without heuristic searches (*quick problem solving*), writers encounter a problem and solve it to their own satisfaction. In this case, the verbal protocol clearly reveals that the operating part of the CDO process happens and the compare part of the process is implicitly activated, but whether or not a diagnosis of the problem has been addressed is not revealed in the verbal protocol. In other words, diagnosing the problem does not seem to be what the writer is attending to in such cases. According to Ericsson and Simon (1993), verbal protocols reveal what writers are processing in short-term memory, and informants' verbalizations are verbal encodings of the information in short-term memory. Finally, when it comes to *heuristic searches*, we distinguish between heuristic searches without resolution and those with resolution. In both cases, the compare and diagnose parts of the CDO process are explicitly verbalized, whereas the operate part of the process is activated only for the latter type of problem solving. As mentioned above, resolution here is seen from the point of view of the writer. Only with regard to problem solving involving heuristic searches do the protocols give clear-cut evidence of the type of processing associated with mature writing.

Finally, we would like to draw attention to the fact that, in using the taxonomies of attention to aspects of writing and of problem solving for the analyses of verbal protocols, Cumming (1989) was able to establish the following characteristics of writing expertise in L2: extensive use of

128　*Vocabulary and Writing in L1 and L2*

heuristic searches with resolution and *concurrent attention to several aspects of writing*. We, therefore, expect the measures *heuristic searches with resolution* and *concurrent attention* to distinguish between our informants from the three grade levels. (For interscorer reliability with regard to the analyses of the verbal protocols, see Appendix A.4.3.)

4.3.3　Assessment of the essays

The essays were assessed using a number of scoring systems. The TOEFL scoring guide was used for a holistic rating of the essays (TOEFL, 2001). The Michigan Writing Assessment Scoring Guide (Hamp-Lyons, 1992) was applied for multiple traits scoring of the essays. In this connection, the essays were assessed with regard to three features: (1) ideas and arguments; (2) rhetorical features; (3) language control.

The TOEFL assessment and the Michigan Writing Assessment operate with a 7- and a 6-point scale, respectively. In the present study, these scales were extended to 11 points, allowing for more differentiated assessments.[4] The hope was that this would give a better spread of the results, in view of the fact that the assessment guides were to be applied to students with a wide age range and to texts written in the mother tongue as well as in a foreign language. (For interscorer reliability for the assessment of the essays, see Appendix A.4.3.)

4.3.4　Results of the statistical analyses

Having reported on the research design and analytical framework of our study, we turn to the results of the statistical analyses of the data. First, we address results based on our within-subjects data, comparing our informants' process and product results in L1 and L2. Second, we deal with our between-subjects data, comparing our informants across grade levels with regard to process and product results in the two languages separately. Third, we report on correlations between process and product results. Fourth, we address the issue of how L2 language proficiency and L1 writing skills relate to writing in L2. Finally, we sum up the main findings, also drawing attention to results that do not tally with those of other studies. Some readers might want to proceed directly to this summary of the results in Section 4.3.4.5.

4.3.4.1　Comparing results for the two languages

For the within-subjects data comparing L1 and L2 writing, we posed two questions:

1　Is there a difference between writing in L1 and L2 for the same students?

Writing in Two Languages 129

2   Is there a difference between the assessment of essays written in L1 and L2 for the same students?

To answer these questions: first, repeated-measures analyses of variance (ANOVAs) were applied to each of the variables for all grade levels combined; subsequently, repeated-measures ANOVAs were used separately for each of the variables for each grade level (see Appendix A.1.1).

Comparing processes in L1 versus L2

When comparing processing in L1 and L2 within each grade level, we find no differences at any of the grade levels with regard to two of the variables: *attention to ideas* and *problem solving with the use of heuristic searches with no resolution* (see Appendix A.1.2). These variables are, therefore, not included in the tables in this section. The differences established in the analyses will be addressed in this chapter.

For attention to **aspects of writing**, Table 4.1 shows that, for the G.13 informants, no significant differences for the first three variables listed in Table 4.1 were found. However, for G.7, we found significant differences with regard to the first three variables and, for G.10, with regard to the variables attention to *language* and to *discourse* only. In addition, for *concurrent attention*, we also found significant differences between L1 and L2 for G.7 and G.10, but not for G.13. In other words, only the G.13 students are able to transfer their attention pattern from L1 to L2, whereas the other grade levels seem to be restrained by the more demanding task of writing in L2. Their greater *attention to language* is at the cost of *attention to discourse* and, for G.7, also of *procedure*, in that the percentages are lower for the latter variables in L2.

Table 4.1   Attention to aspects of writing in L1 and L2

	Grade 7		Grade 10		Grade 13	
	Mean	Sig.	Mean	Sig.	Mean	Sig.
Language L1	26.35	.001	27.90	.001	27.50	ns
Language L2	34.40		34.20		29.55	
Discourse L1	8.75	.010	12.10	.001	13.45	ns
Discourse L2	5.40		8.70		11.25	
Procedure L1	33.75	.018	25.35	ns	21.20	ns
Procedure L2	27.75		23.45		21.50	
Concurrent attention L1	36.88	.001	48.96	.036	53.13	ns
Concurrent attention L2	50.56		53.76		55.03	

130 *Vocabulary and Writing in L1 and L2*

Table 4.2 Problem solving in L1 and L2

	Grade 7		Grade 10		Grade 13	
	Mean	Sig.	Mean	Sig.	Mean	Sig.
No problem L1	43.05	.001	31.85	.002	28.05	ns
No problem L2	30.90		26.15		26.55	
P. Identification L1	9.85	.001	7.50	.002	5.40	.001
P. Identification L2	17.20		11.95		7.95	
P. solved quickly L1	34.40	.003	37.40	.006	40.20	ns
P. solved quickly L2	40.75		42.85		40.70	
Heuristic searches with resolution L1	9.20	ns	19.5	.004	22.45	ns
Heuristic searches with resolution L2	7.80		14.40		20.35	

When it comes to *problem solving*, for the G.13 informants, the processing pattern is, by and large, the same in the two languages, as seen in Table 4.2. The only variable with a significant difference is *problem identification*, with an increase of this type for the L2 task. For the other two grade levels, Table 4.2 reveals that writing in L2 gives rise to more problem solving for G.7 and G.10. This is reflected in the fact that there is a decrease in instances of verbalizations with no problem solving (*no problem*) and an increase with regard to two of the problem-solving variables for G.7 and G.10. We should stress that the results for *heuristic searches with resolution* are similar for G.7 and G.13 in that, in both cases, no difference could be established between L1 and L2. However, the lack of difference for G.7 indicates that the informants use this type of problem solving to the same limited extent in both languages, whereas the G.13 informants use this type of processing to the same extensive degree in both languages. The G.10 students seem to have acquired the ability to use this type of processing in their L1 almost to the same degree as the G.13 students, but are not yet in a position to apply this to their L2 writing.

The answer to the research question as to whether or not there is a difference between the two languages is therefore both yes and no. For G.13, there is no difference between the two languages for the variables in Tables 4.1 and 4.2, apart from the variable *problem identification*. For G.7, there is a significant difference between the two languages with regard to all the variables, except for the variable *heuristic searches with resolution*. For G.10, there is a significant difference between the two languages for all variables, except for the variable *procedure*. In sum, only the university students demonstrate the same attention pattern and almost the same problem-solving pattern in the two languages.

Comparing products in L1 and L2

In comparing the product results in L1 and L2, Table 4.3 gives the results for the different types of assessments applied to the essays. It seems that the results of the process analysis correspond to the results of the assessment of the essays on the multiple traits measures (see (1), (2) and (3) in Table 4.3). For G.13, there is only a significant difference between the L1 and L2 assessments with regard to (3) *language control*. Thus, for G.13, the equal attention to ideas and to discourse during the process tallies with an equal rating in both languages with regard to (1) *ideas and arguments* and (2) *rhetorical features*. Unsurprisingly, when it comes to an assessment of their language, the G.13 students get a significantly lower rating for the L2 than the L1 essays. The significant difference found for the TOEFL rating is probably affected by these students' lower command of language in L2. For the other two grade levels, significant differences are established for all four types of assessment. In other words, these students perform better in their L1.

Thus, the answer to our research question is affirmative for G.7 and G.10 but, for G.13, the only difference found was for the language assessment, and we argued that their lower level of proficiency in L2 probably explains the difference found with respect to the TOEFL assessments.

Table 4.3 Essay assessment results for L1 and L2 for each grade level

	Grade 7		Grade 10		Grade 13	
	Mean	Sig.	Mean	Sig.	Mean	Sig.
TOEFL L1	5.35	.001	8.10	.001	9.05	.006
TOEFL L2	2.65		6.50		7.40	
(1) Ideas/arguments L1	5.45	.001	8.30	.002	8.95	ns
(1) Ideas/arguments L2	3.35		6.95		7.95	
(2) Rhetorical features L1	5.00	.001	7.80	.020	8.30	ns
(2) Rhetorical features L2	3.35		6.60		7.45	
(3) Language control L1	6.70	.001	8.70	.001	8.95	.004
(3) Language control L2	3.10		6.00		7.55	

132 *Vocabulary and Writing in L1 and L2*

4.3.4.2 Comparing results across grade levels

Comparing the results across grade levels for the between-subjects data, we asked the following two questions:

1 Is there a difference in processing as a function of grade level in what the informants attend to and in how they process the issues to which they attend?
2 Is there a difference between the essay assessment results as a function of grade level?

Addressing these questions, the data were subjected to one-way (three levels: G.7 and G.10 and G.13) between-subjects ANOVAs. The data lived up to this type of analysis, except for the variable *problem identification* in L2, in relation to which the non-parametric Kruskal–Wallis procedure and the Tamhane post hoc test had to be used; for all other variables, the Tukey post hoc test could be applied. For details, see Appendix A.1.2. Note that the variable *heuristic searches without resolution* is not included in the tables below since no significant differences were found between any of the levels.

Comparing process results across grade levels

At the outset, we would like to stress that the results reported below are counterintuitive, in that, for all variables for the Danish data and all variables except one for the English data, we generally only find significant differences between G.7, on the one hand, and the other two grade levels, on the other hand. In other words, no significant differences exist on most variables between G.10 and G.13.

Attention to aspects of writing in the Danish data. For the Danish data, Table 4.4 indicates the means and standard deviations for each grade

Table 4.4 Attention to aspects of writing: means and standard deviations for the *Danish* data

L1	Grade 7		Grade 10		Grade 13	
	Mean	SD	Mean	SD	Mean	SD
Language	26.35	7.50	27.90	5.20	27.50	5.20
Discourse	8.75	6.30	12.10	5.00	13.45	5.60
Ideas	31.40	9.40	34.45	6.10	37.95	5.40
Procedure	33.75	10.60	25.35	6.80	21.20	6.60
Concurrent attention	36.88	11.00	48.96	9.10	53.13	8.60

Writing in Two Languages 133

level. As can be seen from the table, the means for attention to *language* are very similar for all grade levels. For attention to *discourse, ideas* and for *concurrent attention*, we see an increase in means from G.7 via G.10 to G.13, whereas for *procedure*, as would be expected, there is a decrease in means from G.7 via G.10 to G.13.

However, the rank order of means for the variables is insufficiently pronounced to be evident in a statistical analysis. The results of the ANOVAs and the post hoc tests only reveal significant differences at $p < .05$ between some of the groups. There are no significant differences between the three groups with regard to attention to *language*. For attention to *discourse* and to *ideas*, we find a significant difference between G.7 and G.13 only, which means that G.10 is different from neither G.7 nor G.13. For attention to *procedure* and for *concurrent attention*, we find significant differences for G.7 versus G.10 and G.13, but not for G.10 versus G.13. (See Appendix A.1.2 for details).

Problem solving in the Danish data. Looking at the means for the three grade levels in Table 4.5, a pattern emerges of less problem solving for G.7 and more problem solving for the other two grade levels. This is seen in a decrease in the means for the variable covering verbalization with no problem solving (*no problem*) from G.7 via G.10 to G.13 and an increase in the means for *problem solved quickly* and for *heuristic searches with resolution* from G.7 via G.10 to G.13. However, when it comes to *problem identification*, there is a decrease in means from G.7 via G.10 to G.13. This indicates that the G.7 students are more likely to come across problems that they are unable to solve than the other two groups.

As was the case for attention to aspects of writing, we find that the rank order of means for the variables is not reflected in the results of the ANOVAs, in that the post hoc tests only reveal significant differences at $p < .05$ between some of the groups. For the Danish data, the statistical

Table 4.5 Problem solving: means and standard deviations for the *Danish* data

L1	Grade 7		Grade 10		Grade 13	
	Mean	SD	Mean	SD	Mean	SD
No problem	43.05	12.50	31.85	7.40	28.05	9.30
Problem identification	9.85	5.00	7.50	2.80	5.40	4.20
Problem solved quickly	34.40	9.70	37.40	7.70	40.20	7.40
Heuristic searches with resolution	9.20	6.90	19.50	8.60	22.45	8.20

134 *Vocabulary and Writing in L1 and L2*

analysis reveals no differences between any of the three grade levels for the variable *problem solved quickly*. For the variables *no problem* and *heuristic searches with resolution*, we find significant differences for G.7, on the one hand, and G.10 and G.13, on the other hand, but no significant difference for G.10 versus G.13. For *problem identification*, there is only a significant difference for G.7 versus G.13.

In the Danish data, the G.10 informants form an intermediate group for attention to aspects of writing and for problem solving, in that, for the variables *ideas, discourse* and *problem identification*, some of the informants perform in a similar manner to the G.7 informants and others in a similar manner to the G.13 informants.

Attention to aspects of writing in the English data. Table 4.6 gives the means and standard deviations for the English data. For attention to *language*, G.7 and G.10 do not seem to differ judging by the means, but there is a decrease in attention to *language* at G.13. As was the case for the Danish data, there is an increase in attention to *discourse, ideas* and for *concurrent attention* from G.7 via G.10 to G.13, and a decrease in attention to *procedure* from G.7 via G.10 to G.13.

As for the Danish data, the rank order of means for the variables at the three grade levels is not brought out in the post hoc tests. Whereas there were no significant differences with regard to attention to *language* in the Danish data, the English data shows significant differences for G.7 versus G.13 and for G.10 versus G.13, but not for G.7 versus G.10, which tallies with the impression from the means. In other words, there is more and the same level of attention to *language* for G.7 and G.10 than for G.13. Similar to the findings for the Danish data, the variable attention to *discourse* results in significant differences for G.7, on the one hand, and for G.10 and G.13, on the other hand, but not for G.10 versus

Table 4.6 Attention to aspects of writing: means and standard deviations for the *English* data

L2	Grade 7		Grade 10		Grade 13	
	Mean	SD	Mean	SD	Mean	SD
Language	34.40	5.60	34.20	5.10	29.55	6.00
Discourse	5.40	3.30	8.70	3.70	11.25	5.10
Ideas	32.35	8.20	33.75	6.40	37.75	6.60
Procedure	27.75	8.80	23.45	6.30	21.50	6.40
Concurrent attention	50.56	9.90	53.76	9.60	55.03	8.10

Writing in Two Languages 135

G.13. In other words, there is less attention to discourse for G.7 compared with the two other groups. Again, as for the Danish data, we find a significant difference for attention to *ideas* for G.7 versus G.13 only, with the latter group showing more attention to ideas. Unlike the results for the Danish data, there is a significant difference with regard to *procedure* for G.7 versus G.13 only, and no significant differences could be established for *concurrent attention* between any of the groups. The result for *concurrent attention* is again surprising in view of Cumming's (1989) study, in which a high degree of concurrent attention to several aspects of writing was found in expert writers. The fact that all three groups demonstrated similar levels of *concurrent attention* is in line with our finding that *concurrent attention* increased from L1 to L2 for G.7 and G.10. In other words, in our study, high degrees of *concurrent attention* do not seem to be related to writing expertise, a point we shall discuss in Sections 4.5.1 and 4.5.2.

For the L2 data, we also find that the G.10 informants have an intermediate position with regard to two of the variables relating to attention to aspects of writing: *ideas* and *procedure*. In both cases, some of these informants are similar to G.7 informants and others are similar to G.13 students and, for the variable *language*, the G.10 students show the same level of attention as G.7.

Problem solving in the English data. Compared with the Danish data, the means for problem solving in the English data, presented in Table 4.7, give a somewhat different picture of progression with regard to grade levels. Relatively speaking, we still find more problem solving for G.7 as reflected in the variable *no problem*, but there is no difference to speak of in the means for G.10 and G.13. For *problem solved quickly*, the means indicate that G.7 and G.13 are at the same level, whereas the mean for G.10 is somewhat higher than for the other two groups. The results for the last two variables, however, are similar to those found in the Danish data. For *heuristic searches with resolution*, we see an increase of this kind from G.7 via G.10 to G.13, and for *problem identification*, there is a decrease in means from G.7 via G.10 to G.13, again showing that G.7 are more likely to encounter problems that they have to leave unresolved.

In view of the comments on the means for problem solving, it is unsurprising that we find significant differences at $p < .05$ with regard to fewer variables in this data set compared with the Danish data. As for the Danish data, no significant differences were established for *problem solved quickly* and, here, the same applies to the variable *no problem*. For *problem identification*, we find significant differences for G.7 versus G.10 and G.13, but not for G.10 versus G.13. However, unlike for the Danish

136 *Vocabulary and Writing in L1 and L2*

Table 4.7 Problem solving: means and standard deviations for the *English* data

L2	Grade 7		Grade 10		Grade 13	
	Mean	SD	Mean	SD	Mean	SD
No problem	30.90	9.60	26.15	7.70	26.55	7.40
Problem identification	17.20	6.80	11.95	6.30	7.95	3.80
Problem solved quickly	40.75	9.00	42.85	7.20	40.70	8.60
Heuristic searches with resolution	7.80	6.00	14.40	5.50	20.35	8.60

data, we find significant differences between all the groups for *heuristic searches with resolution*. Hence, for the English data, differences between all three groups are established with regard to the measure that Cumming (1989) found to be characteristic of expert writers.

In sum, the answer to our research question is that, for the L1 data, only differences between the group of G.7 students and the other two groups were established, and no differences were found between G.10 and G.13. However, for the English data, we found significant differences between all the three grade levels for the problem-solving category *heuristic searches with resolution*. On most other counts, the pattern of significant differences was the same as for the Danish data.

Comparing product results across grade levels

For comparing the product results across grade levels, Table 4.8 gives the means and standard deviations for the assessments of the essays in both languages. For all the means, we see an increase in ratings from G.7 via G.10 to G.13. However, the difference in means for the last two groups is less pronounced.

The general finding for the Danish process data – that differences between grade levels are found for G.7 versus the other two grade levels, but not for G.10 versus G.13 – is reflected in the results for the assessment of the L1 essays. This finding applies to the results of the TOEFL assessment and the multiple traits assessments (see (1), (2) and (3) in Table 4.8) where we find significant differences at $p < .05$.

For the mean ratings for the English essays, given in Table 4.8, we find significant differences at $p < .05$ between the same grade levels as in the Danish data except for the *language control* assessment, for which the analysis has established significant differences between all the groups.

Table 4.8 Assessment ratings: means and standard deviations for the *Danish* data and the *English* data

Danish data	Grade 7		Grade 10		Grade 13	
	Mean	SD	Mean	SD	Mean	SD
TOEFL	5.35	2.00	8.10	1.20	9.05	1.70
(1) Ideas and argumentation	5.45	2.30	8.30	1.40	8.95	1.80
(2) Rhetorical features	5.00	2.00	7.80	1.40	8.30	1.70
(3) Language control	6.70	2.00	8.70	1.00	8.95	1.50
English data						
TOEFL	2.65	1.60	6.50	1.10	7.40	1.90
(1) Ideas and argumentation	3.35	1.80	6.95	1.20	7.95	1.50
(2) Rhetorical features	3.35	1.70	6.60	1.60	7.45	1.70
(3) Language control	3.10	2.20	6.00	1.60	7.55	1.60

In other words, it seems that the only feature that brings out a distinction between all three grade levels is our informants' command of the foreign language.

The answer to our research question for the Danish data is that there is a difference between the essays' assessment results for G.7 versus the two other groups, but no difference between G.10 and G.13. For the English data, we found a difference between the assessment results for all grade levels with regard to *language control*, but not for the other types of assessments.

4.3.4.3 Comparing process versus product results in L1 and L2

Having reported on the results of the informants' writing processes and of the assessments of their essays separately, we were curious to see if the process and the product results correlated. For this, we applied the Spearman correlation and the variable used for process results was *heuristic searches with resolution*. The results are reported in Table 4.9.

As is apparent from Table 4.9, no positive and significant correlations were found between the process measure and any of the assessment ratings of the essays in either language. Thus, we found no relationship between process and product for our informants; if anything, we found moderate negative correlations between process and product for the G.10 students in L2. As noted in Section 4.1.2, previous studies show conflicting findings with regard to the relationship between process and product, and we shall return to this issue in later sections.

138 *Vocabulary and Writing in L1 and L2*

Table 4.9 Spearman correlations for process versus product

L1 process with L1 product	Grade 7	Grade 10	Grade 13
Process with TOEFL	−.057	.174	−.148
Process with Ideas and argumentation	−.027	−.040	.046
Process with Rhetorical features	.128	.266	−.080
Process with Language control	.286	.344	−.110
L2 process with L2 product	**Grade 7**	**Grade 10**	**Grade 13**
Process with TOEFL	.078	−.454*	−.116
Process with Ideas and argumentation	−.010	−.498*	−.095
Process with Rhetorical features	−.110	−.475*	−.168
Process with Language control	.081	.148	.183

Note: Correlations found at the 0.05 level (*) (two-tailed)

4.3.4.4 The variables L2 proficiency and L1 writing skills

In this section, we shall first address the relationship between L2 language proficiency and L2 writing skills by correlating L2 proficiency measures with essay ratings and with L2 process results. Second, we will look into the relationship between L1 writing skills and L2 process measures. Language proficiency in L2 is here measured on a vocabulary test and a reading test, and writing skills in L1 are operationalized as the results obtained by our informants on the variable *heuristic searches with resolution* with regard to their L1 essay writing.

As reported in Chapter 2, all our informants were asked to complete Nation's Levels Test (Nation, 2001) and, in addition to this, G.10 and G.13 were given the Nelson–Denny Reading Test (Brown et al., 1993)[5] whereas the G.7 students were exposed to a different L2 reading test. The results of these tests and the process results of *heuristic searches with resolution* in L1 were correlated with the informants' L2 process and product results. For the former, we used results on *heuristic searches with resolution* and, for the latter, we used the holistic TOEFL rating and the *language control* measure of the multiple trait ratings. To investigate this, we applied Spearman's correlations for each grade level separately. The results are presented in Table 4.10.

Table 4.10 shows that L2 proficiency is more closely connected to the product results than to the writing process results. For the product

Writing in Two Languages 139

Table 4.10 Spearman correlations for the selected variables

L2 proficiency with L2 product	Grade 7	Grade 10	Grade 13
Nation with TOEFL	.493*	.230	.351
Reading with TOEFL	.534*	.349	.448*
Nation with Language control	.820**	.597**	.294
Reading with Language control	.693**	.628**	.286
L2 proficiency with L2 process	**Grade 7**	**Grade 10**	**Grade 13**
Nation with Heuristic searches with resolution	.224	.121	.130
Reading with Heuristic searches with resolution	.282	−.024	−.025
L2 process with L1 writing skills	**Grade 7**	**Grade 10**	**Grade 13**
L2 Heuristic searches with resolution with L1 Heuristic searches with resolution	.725**	.595**	.538*

Notes: Correlations found at the 0.01 level (**) or the 0.05 level (*) (two-tailed).

measures, the holistic assessment (see TOEFL) only correlates with Nation's Levels Test for G.7, whereas the language assessments of the essays show moderate to high correlations with Nation's test for G.7 and G.10, but no correlation for G.13. Similar correlations are established for the reading tests, the exception being the significant correlation between the reading test and the TOEFL ratings for G.13. For the L2 process measure, no correlations could be established with L2 proficiency at any of the grade levels; that is, neither with Nation's Levels Test nor with the L2 reading tests. However, we found moderate to high correlations between the L2 process and the L1 writing skills; that is, between the variables *heuristic searches with resolution* in L1 and L2.

Judging from these correlations, for G.7, L2 language proficiency is an important variable, in that it relates both to the specific language and to the holistic ratings of the essays, although more so to the former. For G.10, L2 language proficiency only plays a role for the specific language ratings of the essays, whereas L2 language proficiency, as measured here, is not an important variable for G.13. For G.13, only reading in L2 correlates with the holistic ratings of the essays.

4.3.4.5 Summing up the main findings

In this section, we shall first focus on the main findings with regard to the within-subjects data, comparing the informants' writing in the two

140   *Vocabulary and Writing in L1 and L2*

languages. Second, we deal with the main results with regard to the between-subjects data, comparing the informants across grade levels. Finally, we address our findings in relation to the results of the variables L2 language proficiency and L1 writing skills.

For the within-subjects data comparing L1 and L2, the analyses of the *verbal protocols* revealed that, overall, there were statistically significant differences for attention to aspects of writing and problem-solving behaviour between the two languages for the Grade 7 and Grade 10 students, but not for the university students. In other words, the university students seem to have reached a skill level that allows them to operate in similar ways in the two languages, whereas this is not the case for the informants from the other two grade levels.

For Grade 7 and Grade 10, the greater demands of the writing task in L2 result in an increase in *attention to language*, which occurred at the cost of *attention to discourse organization*. Furthermore, writing in L2 gave rise to more problems for Grades 7 and 10, which was also reflected in the fact that their problem solving led to more instances of mere *problem identification*. However, with regard to *heuristic searches with resolution*, we only found a significant difference between the two languages for Grade 10. The results for Grade 7 and Grade 13 were thus similar, but only apparently so. For Grade 7, the lack of difference in their case indicates that these informants use heuristic searches to the same limited extent in both languages, whereas the university students apply this type of processing to the same extensive degree in both languages. With the Grade 10 students, we might be seeing a group of informants who are in the process of development, in that they have acquired the ability to use heuristic searches in their L1 to a similar degree as the university students although they are not yet in a position to apply this ability to their L2 writing.

Similar to the findings for aspects of writing, for *concurrent attention* to several aspects of writing, we found statistically significant differences between L1 and L2 for Grades 7 and 10, but not for the university students. Grades 7 and 10 had a higher level of concurrent attention in L2 than in L1. This was an unexpected finding, since in Cumming's study of L2 writing at university level (1989), this measure turned out to discriminate between skilled and less skilled writers, in that the former had a higher percentage of concurrent attention to aspects of writing. However, since many of the constellations of two aspects of writing were concurrent attention to *language* and *ideas* and, hence, cover problem-solving formulation processes, this finding seems to tally with the finding that Grades 7 and 10 encounter more problems in their L2 than in their L1. We shall discuss this issue further in Section 4.5.1.

When comparing the *assessments of the essays* in L1 and L2, we found, overall, that the results of the process analysis corresponded to the results of the assessment of the essays. In other words, for Grades 7 and 10, there were significant differences between the two languages as to the quality of their essays. For the university students, we found no significant differences between the L1 and L2 assessments with regard, on the one hand, to *ideas and arguments* and, on the other hand, to *rhetorical features*. Only the language assessment reached statistical significance. In other words, the equal attention to *ideas* and to *discourse*, during the process, was brought out in an equal assessment with regard to ideas, argumentation and the organization of essays of the university students in both languages. Unsurprisingly, the university students, being non-native speakers of English, also lag behind when it comes to an assessment of their language in the L2 essays compared with their L1 essays. Although all informants differ with regard to their language ratings from L1 to L2, the essay assessments show that the university students seem to operate at a level of language proficiency in L2 that apparently does not affect their ability to produce coherent essays.

For the between-subjects data, comparing the results of the analyses of the *verbal protocols* across the three grade levels, the outcome is counterintuitive. Our general finding is that, out of all variables for the Danish data and all variables except one for the English data, we only find significant differences between Grade 7, on the one hand, and the other two grade levels, on the other hand. For *concurrent attention* to aspects of writing, again, our findings were unexpected compared with Cumming's results, in that we only found significant differences for Grade 7 versus the two other groups in the Danish data, but no differences between any of the groups in the English data.

Thus, on the majority of the measures, we are not able to establish significant differences between sixteen-year-old sixth-form college students and university students in their early twenties. The counterintuitive results of the process analysis might give rise to speculations that the analysis applied to the data is insufficiently sensitive to register differences between the two older groups. However, the results of the *essay assessments* also bring out the same lack of difference between Grade 10 and the university students, which might indicate that the two groups are, in fact, very similar. In other words, as we saw for the comparisons of the L1 and L2 data, the essay assessments tally with the findings for problem solving and attention to aspects of writing, in that, for the

142   *Vocabulary and Writing in L1 and L2*

Danish and the English essays, we find significant differences for Grade 7 versus the two other grade levels. Only with regard to the language assessment of the English essays do significant differences emerge between all three grade levels. This leads us to the conclusion that, at some fundamental level, the Grade 10 and the university students might be more alike than different. We shall return to this issue in our discussion in Section 4.5.1.

However, for the use of heuristic searches in the English protocols, we do find significant differences between all grade levels with regard to the use of *heuristic searches with resolution*, which is the type of processing that requires the full operation of the CDO process referred to in Section 4.3.2. Thus, the Grade 10 and the university students are not alike in all respects. For instance, we have seen that the use of *heuristic searches with resolution* is a processing feature that distinguishes between the two groups for the English data, and, with regard to the application of L1 writing skills to L2 writing, only the university students manage this. In Section 4.4, we shall look into possible additional qualitative differences between the two groups not captured by the results presented so far.

Turning to the role of L2 language proficiency and L1 writing skills, as noted in Section 4.1.2, previous studies of the L2 writing process have addressed the issue of the contribution of L2 language proficiency and L1 writing skills to L2 writing success. Phrased differently, the question is whether writing in L2 is a language problem or a writing problem. As we have seen, in this study, correlations were calculated in order to compare: (1) the informants' L2 proficiency with their L2 product; (2) the informants' L2 proficiency with their L2 process results; (3) the informants' L2 process results with their L1 process results. Our findings are similar to those reported by Cumming (1989), in that, overall, L2 proficiency correlated with the ratings of the essays and not with the quality of the L2 process for G.7 and G.10, whereas for G.13 no correlations could be established. As did Cumming, we found significant correlations between the L2 writing process and the L1 writing process for all the three grade levels. However, unlike in Cumming's study, there were no correlations between the product and process measures in any of the languages. In other words, for our informants, we did not find a close link between the quality of the writing process and the quality of the essays produced as a result of this process.

In sum, the comparison of L1 and L2 writing showed that the university students were able to apply the writing skills demonstrated in the L1 task to the L2 writing task. This was not the case for Grades 7 and 10. However, the Grade 10 students seemed to have reached a level of writing skills in L1 that was similar to that of the university students but, unlike the university students, they were as yet unable to apply their L1 writing skills to the L2 writing task. When it came to comparing our informants across the grade levels, we were surprised to find that, on many measures, no significant differences were found between Grade 10 and the university students. The lack of difference between these two groups is explored in the qualitative analysis in the following section.

4.4 A qualitative analysis of the verbalizations of three informants

Having provided the results of the statistical analyses, we shall now proceed to a qualitative analysis of selected informants. As we have seen, only a few differences were found between the sixth-form college and the university informants in the cross-sectional analysis. In this section, we shall look further into possible differences between the Grade 10 and the university informants that were not captured by the statistical analyses of the students' writing in the two languages. For this, we have decided to give a detailed description of what happens in the L1 and L2 protocols of two students from Grade 10 and of one university level student.

We have chosen three informants who obtained very similar results for problem solving with the use of *heuristic searches with resolution in L1* (see Table 4.11), since we wished to look into the degree to which informants with a similar level of writing expertise managed when writing in L2. One informant is a university student (G.13 – Rebecca) and the other informants are two Grade 10 students (G.10 – Sarah and G.10 – Kate). Sarah and Kate were selected because of their similarities and differences with regard to Rebecca on other counts.[6] Generally speaking, of the two Grade 10 informants, Sarah rather than Kate has more in common with Rebecca, as seen in Table 4.11.

With regard to the other L1 measures, Rebecca has a somewhat higher figure for *attention to discourse* than do the Grade 10 students, and Kate has obtained lower essay ratings than the other two students. However, for L1, all three students have close to identical results for the two parameters that, according to Cumming (1989), distinguish expert writers; that is, *heuristic searches with resolution* and *concurrent attention*. Below, we shall look into the possible reasons for Kate's lower ratings on her essay.

144   *Vocabulary and Writing in L1 and L2*

Table 4.11   Results for three informants

Informants	G.13 Rebecca	G.10 Sarah	G.10 Kate
Heuristic searches with resolution L1 (%)	26	25	24
Problem identification L1 (%)	8	11	7
Concurrent attention L1 (%)	45.8	43.6	45.1
Attention to discourse L1 (%)	19	13	12
Length of essay L1	534	549	724
Ideas & arguments L1	10	10	7
Rhetorical features L1	10	10	7
Language control L1	10	10	8
Heuristic searches with resolution L2 (%)	20	13	12
Problem identification L2 (%)	7	16	25
Concurrent attention L2 (%)	49.5	52.3	74.2
Attention to discourse L2 (%)	13	10	15
Length of essay L2	449	482	484
Ideas and arguments L2	10	9	7
Rhetorical features L2	6	8	5
Language control L2	11	7	8
Levels test L1 (vocabulary test)	106	98	89
L1 reading score	29	26	13
Nation L2 (vocabulary test)	110	93	97
Reading L2 (Nelson–Denny)	36	28	28

As regards L2, Rebecca has obtained much higher percentages of heuristic searches than have the other two students and, for *concurrent attention*, we find that Rebecca and Sarah have similar results, whereas the percentage for Kate is markedly higher. For the essay assessments, Rebecca has obtained top ratings for *ideas and arguments* and *language control*, but a somewhat low rating for *rhetorical features*; and Sarah has higher ratings than Kate on two of the assessments. We shall look into these similarities and differences in our qualitative analysis of the three students.

For language proficiency, the L1 reading score reveals that Kate is the poorest L1 reader, which coincides with the fact that she has the lowest score on the L1 vocabulary test. Pertaining to L2 language proficiency, Sarah and Kate have similar scores on Nation's test and identical scores on the Nelson–Denny reading test. On both counts, Rebecca has obtained higher scores.

L1 composing: comparing the three students

As regards their L1 processing, Rebecca can be described as primarily an advance planner, and Sarah as an emergent planner (see Cumming, 1989). Kate, however, behaves in a very different manner, which might explain the difference between her essay ratings and those of the other two informants. Below, we shall address these issues.

Rebecca's initial planning is extensive, allowing her to set up a strong mental representation of her intended text. To this end, she produces a set of notes in the form of lists of pro- and con-arguments and, as seen in Extract 4.1 below, decides on her point of view, completing her initial planning by including a statement in her notes that gives the overall gist of her argumentation.

Extract 4.1
Rebecca: L1 protocol – translated from Danish

– what should I say now erm okay I'll just try and make an introduction to this weird thing what am I ... I suppose I am I could say that I agree that it should be forbidden to smoke and then I am going to choose to narrow it down to saying public places that is inside and then only I mean public places that is more like airports and erm like some train stations and funny stuff like that erm and then say that it is it ... erm so I guess I agree and then I am talking to some ... heavy smoker who does not agree with me and I have to make him change his point of view perhaps here you could stress ... that erm that non-smokers ... do not have to well ... it's sort of not orh what do you say it is ... non-smokers are do not have a choice but they should they – *should have a choice ... they are the ones who should give permission* <the ones who should give permission>

The strong mental representation of her text created in her initial planning probably enables her to introduce even global revisions when writing her fair copy. That Rebecca is in control of the task is further supported by the fact that, throughout her composing process, she refers to her notes, either to add to her lists of arguments or to consult them for how to proceed. Furthermore, she often returns to the writing prompt to ensure that she stays on topic. Another feature that helps her stay on track is her tendency to postpone the solution of language problems until later stages in her writing process, thus ensuring that her train of thought is not disrupted. In other words, in these instances, she identifies a problem only, but postpones the solution. It is this kind of behaviour that underlies her percentage for *problem identification*.

146 *Vocabulary and Writing in L1 and L2*

Throughout her protocol, Rebecca demonstrates not only a high level of awareness of textual organization, but also of the linguistic means that help bring out a coherent and stylistically acceptable text. The latter is exemplified in Extract 4.2.

Extract 4.2
Rebecca: L1 protocol – translated from Danish

<smokers have no right to force their smoke on others the smoke is not only annoying> – {or is it a nuisance} dah dah dah which is best I have just written nuisance so maybe I should stick with annoying –

The high ratings on the essay assessments of *ideas and arguments* and of *rhetorical features* are likely to be closely linked to her high level of awareness of these issues and to her processing. Furthermore, Rebecca's attention to language, which typically occurs concurrently with attention to ideas, is, in almost all cases, instances of upgrading rather than compensation, as seen in Extract 4.3.

Extract 4.3
Rebecca: L1 protocol – translated from Danish

it will always be impossible im pos si ble because erm the smoke will spread spread to – you can't say that it's not sort of like a plague or something like that so – <will no matter how much you try to shield smokers from non-smokers it will> *always be problematic* – problematic was a better word –

In other words, she makes an effort to identify the word or expression that best tallies with her intended meaning. This, in turn, coincides with her high rating for language with regard to her essay.

Sarah's differences from Rebecca mainly pertain to processing rather than to the quality of the essays. Sarah's planning behaviour is best categorized as emergent planning. Her initial planning is less extensive than Rebecca's, but still she produces a short list of pros and cons and defines her audience. Thus, initially, her mental representation of her intended text is not particularly elaborated. However, she compensates for this via planning episodes throughout her composing of the first draft. At these points, she most often plans at the local level of idea generation, but also at the more global level at the end of her draft. Also, as Rebecca, she frequently consults the writing prompt to ensure that she stays on track. In some of her planning episodes, she stops to recapitulate and evaluate what has been included up to a point, as seen in Extract 4.4.

Writing in Two Languages 147

Extract 4.4
Sarah: L1 protocol – translated from Danish

<they are completely ordinary people as well but the difference is that they have been styled for hours before the shooting to be perfect ... in this connection I cannot see how this would make our lives better> – I think this is quite a good way of erm sort of rounding off that section about there being people who disagree and then ss I sort of present that conclusion that I cannot see how this will make our lives better so I suppose that's okay ... erm – <cannot see how this will make our lives better ...>

Thus, instances such as the one in Extract 4.4 ensure continued updates of her mental representation of her text.

Although her verbalizations are less explicit than Rebecca's, Sarah also demonstrates a high level of awareness of textual structure. She considers the order of presentation, for instance, by deciding to start with the opponent's view and to state her own position in the introduction. Another example is her awareness that the title needs to correspond to the actual content of the essay and needs to catch the reader, as illustrated in Extract 4.5.

Extract 4.5
Sarah: L1 protocol – translated from Danish

– .... alright so I think I'm going to make a fair copy now erm ... because now well yes now I think it's okay ... nah I don't think I will call it { } just the title I suppose it's something to do with the influence of advertisements ... erm on the subconscious mind that's what I have written but I think that is stupid I think I'll just wri just call it but it also sounds a bit tame it sounds a bit tame to write the influence of advertisements ... erm the power of the advertising industry I might ... only that sounds somewhat dramatic [laughs] – *the power of the advertising industry* – but that just might catch somebody's attention –

Furthermore, at another point, she explicitly refers to text type when deciding not to use the expression 'the critical reader' by noting that her text is not a letter to the editor. These considerations, in combination with her processing, probably account for her high ratings on the essay with regard to *ideas and arguments* and to *rhetorical features*. Again, as Rebecca, Sarah's protocol reveals that her concurrent attention to ideas and language represents upgrading rather than compensation. She

148 *Vocabulary and Writing in L1 and L2*

makes an effort to identify the words and phrases that best tally with her intentions and the text type she has decided to produce. Thus, in Extract 4.6, in addressing the issue of children and advertising, her initial intention is to provide a vivid description of children with their arms full of toys. She discards her inclination to say *with their arms full of fire engines and Barbie dolls* (in Danish, there is alliteration, lost in the translation here) but decides to use the generic term *toys* instead, to avoid being sexist. This in turn is discarded as too dull, and she ends up with *bears and Barbie dolls*.

Extract 4.6
Sarah: L1 protocol – translated from Danish

<arms full of> – fire engines and Barbie dolls [laughs] nah that's sort of a bit too sexist {up} well {anyway} erm ss – <full of> -toys I suppose I could just say that ... - *toys ... .* <how many times have you seen ...> – nah that sounds too boring – *bears and Barbie dolls* [Deletes toys and replaces it with 'bears and Barbie dolls']

Thus, this kind of attention to language on Sarah's part coincides with her high essay rating for language.

Despite **Kate**'s similar percentage of heuristic searches with resolution, her processing is very different from that of the other two informants. Her initial planning is extremely extensive; she devotes almost half of her time to this. However, the quality of her planning does not live up to that demonstrated by the other two informants. A closer look at her planning reveals that, although she initially decides on her point of view and goes on to generate and list a few arguments for and against her position, the bulk of her planning is committed to paper in the form of a disjointed list-like text. At this stage, she spends a lot of time detailing the contents of her essay and her ideas; points and examples are written down as isolated sentences or short paragraphs. She refers to these pages as her draft, but they are rather like a list of more or less elaborately phrased points. What is conspicuous is that Kate does not reveal any awareness of the fact that these points are going to end up in a text. Although her percentage of attention to discourse is close to identical to Sarah's percentage, the quality of that attention is very different, only amounting to quick decisions, such as indenting for a paragraph. In other words, Kate's protocol gives very little indication of awareness of textual structure. That this might be a true picture of her knowledge of discourse is further supported by the fact that, in writing her fair copy, she picks at random from the pages of her 'draft' with the result that her final text lacks coherence. That this way of composing does not enable her to create a gist-like mental representation of her text is also supported by the observation that, in some cases, her notes are so short that she is unable to recall to what they refer. In other words, her processing and her very rudimentary attention to textual issues are reflected in her rather low ratings for *ideas and arguments* and for *rhetorical features*.

Finally, her attention to language is not very elaborate either. It mainly relates to quick choices between two options and, rather than attempting to identify a more precise word or expression, she presents her words and expressions in inverted commas, probably as a way of getting round finding appropriate expressions. The latter is illustrated in Extract 4.7, in which she realizes that she has used a direct translation into Danish of the English *hear somebody out*. She makes a quick decision to use the word *reasons* in inverted commas.

Extract 4.7
Kate: L1 protocol – translated from Danish

*in a telephone conversation both parties can speak and hear each other out ... * – you can only say that in English ... out hear me out hear each other what the hell do you say then each other's explanations each other's ... – *reasons in inverted commas*

Even though, on a number of occasions, she shows awareness of the need to avoid repeating the same words and expressions, she does not act on these observations. In other words, her solution to the language problems she encounters can be characterized as compensation rather than upgrading, which in turn corresponds with her essay rating for language.

In sum, Rebecca and Sarah both managed to write essays that obtained the same high ratings on all three traits evaluated. Our analysis of their planning shows that Rebecca is an advance planner and Sarah an emergent planner. In other words, they both arrive at the same results but through different equally appropriate routes. Further support for their identical essay ratings was found in the observations that they both have very similar levels of awareness of textual organization and of language use. Despite her high percentage for heuristic searches, Kate does not manage to build a mental representation of her text that can guide her through her efforts in producing an essay. Her poorer essay results go hand in hand with her markedly different way of planning her essay and with her obvious lack of considerations of textual organization and efforts to find appropriate solutions to her language problems.

150 *Vocabulary and Writing in L1 and L2*

L2 Composing: comparing the three students

When it comes to writing in their L2, the planning behaviour of the three students is close to identical to their planning behaviour for the L1 essays. If anything, the differences are a matter of degree rather than type. Comparing the L1 results to the L2 results presented in Table 4.11, we find marked changes from L1 to L2 for Sarah and Kate, but not for Rebecca.

However, Rebecca's L2 essay assessment for *rhetorical features* is very much lower than for her L1 essay, and lower than Sarah's L2 assessment. Despite Rebecca's awareness of textual structure, the L2 essay is less coherent than her L1 essay. Although her initial planning is extensive, it might here result in a weaker mental representation of her text than in L1. This interpretation is supported by the fact that, when summing up her initial planning, she explicitly states her doubts about some of the points entered in her notes, and her statement in Extract 4.8 lends further support to this interpretation.

Extract 4.8
Rebecca: L2 protocol

– erm ... I'm just gonna write ... straight form the heart now ... err can always ... you know put it back together afterwards so ... –

For Sarah and Kate, having to operate in the L2 results a marked decrease in use of *heuristic searches with resolution* (see Table 4.11). In fact, on most of the other counts, the two Grade 10 students do less well in L2 compared with L1. Still, Sarah's product results are better than Kate's when it comes to the essay ratings of *ideas and arguments* and *rhetorical features*. This is probably due to Sarah's better handling of planning and her efforts to organize her text; features, which are completely missing from Kate's protocol, also in L2. As in L1, Kate's focus is mainly on ideas and examples but, for her L2 protocol, we see an increase in attention to language. For Kate, the pronounced increase in attention to *concurrent aspects* from L1 to L2 covers the fact that she encounters many more problems expressing her ideas.

As previously indicated, the majority of instances of concurrent attention to aspects of writing covers the constellation of attention to *ideas* and *language*, and thus reflect the informants' formulation processes. The three informants behave very differently in this respect. Rebecca's concurrent attention typically covers problem solving of the upgrading kind, and this also applies to Sarah, although

Writing in Two Languages 151

her solutions are less elegant than Rebecca's due to the many gaps in her L2 linguistic knowledge. For Kate, the very high percentage of concurrent attention typically results in compensation rather than upgrading.

In Extract 4.9, Rebecca is searching for a more precise expression to replace *good things* and decides to look up the Danish equivalent of *advantages* (L1: '*fordele*'), but accesses the word *advantages* prior to identifying it in the dictionary.

Extract 4.9
Rebecca: L2 protocol

– erm … I guess … I should …. err hm hm hm … I mean are there any good things – *and are there any … * – good things erm I'm just gonna look it up then … fordele – §_fordele fordele … I know the word just orh I can't remember [informant hums] { } _ advantages_ there you go didn't even have to see it_§ *ad van ta ges advantages when it comes to commercials …*

In another instance, she is unhappy with the word 'vulnerable' and selects the word 'sensitive' from among the dictionary options 'receptive' and 'impressionable' for the sentence: 'Perhaps some people are more sensitive to commercials than others'.

Prior to Extract 4.10, Sarah has been struggling with the same problem; that is, the expression 'sometimes I take myself in sitting', which is a literal translation of a Danish expression. She considers 'grab myself', but discards it and has no luck in consulting the dictionary. Extract 4.10 shows her final solution to the problem, which she explicitly refers to as compensation. This illustrates that Sarah is inclined to upgrade her expression as she does in L1 and, even though she makes a real effort here, her language proficiency forces her to settle for less.

Extract 4.10
Sarah: L2 protocol – italic text translated from Danish

– *nah you can't say that* I take myself in sitting aj erm – <erm sometimes I take myself in sitting in f { }> – *what should I write* hm sometimes … I know that I sometimes … I know that I sometimes { } and I – *I know that I sometimes* <erm sitting in front of the television … I know … I know that I sometimes am sitting in front of the television thinking about all other things than what I am watching> – *like that you can avoid it in that way I think … can't you erm yes* –

152 *Vocabulary and Writing in L1 and L2*

As in her L1 protocol, Kate's concurrent attention to aspects of writing either leads to mere *problem identification* (see her high percentage for this in Table 4.11) and/or to compensation rather than upgrading, as illustrated in Extract 4.11. Although she does consult a dictionary, she quickly abandons her search and solves the problem by using the same dictionary entry by substituting the adjective with the verb form. In other instances, her typical comment when in doubt about an expression is 'I don't know if you can put it like that but never mind', thus clearly giving up on improving her text.

Extract 4.11
Kate: L2 protocol – italic text translated from Danish

at hospitals I understand that smoking is not allowed and I find it respectable – *you probably can't say that ... just going to look it up ...* – §r e s ... respect ... train time [yawns] _no can't find it_ ... respect able respectable ... _respectable_ ... § – *oh you can say that can't you ....* – <uh find it> *to respect [fiddles with paper] but I see no reason what so ever that we should try to decide whether people should smoke [45 minutes] or they shouldn't ...*

Finally, we wish to stress that, even though Sarah and Kate's L2 language proficiency is close to identical, as seen in their scores on Nation's vocabulary test and the Nelson–Denny reading test in Table 4.11, the two Grade 10 students still differ markedly in their L2 processing. In other words, this illustrates that it takes more than a high level of L2 language proficiency to operate a good writing process in L2.

Summing up
In the quantitative analysis, these three students had all obtained similar results with regard to their L1 writing processes. The qualitative analysis exemplified the difference that seems to exist in the group of Grade 10 writers. We thus saw that Kate behaved very differently from Sarah, not succeeding in setting up manageable goals for her composition, despite her similar level of heuristic searches. Although their type of planning differed, Sarah was, in fact, very similar to Rebecca in the qualitative as well as the quantitative analysis: they both managed to create strong mental representations of their intended texts, even if they arrived at this in different, but equally appropriate, ways. The fact that similar percentages of *heuristic searches with resolution* gave poor results for Kate further illustrates that the analysis applied here is insufficiently sensitive to capture qualitative differences between the informants. One

explanation for this might be that the resolutions the writers arrive at are resolutions with which they are satisfied or that they settle for, and thus might not be solutions that will go down well with the reader of the essay. Another explanation might be that concurrent attention to language and ideas covers upgrading as well as compensatory formulation. When it comes to writing in L2, the qualitative analysis also illustrated that the Grade 10 students do not manage to sustain the level of processing they demonstrate in their L1, whereas Rebecca manages to do so.

4.5 Discussion and implications

Below, we shall discuss our findings in relation to previous research. Initially, we address issues pertaining to the measures we have used and how our findings may be explained as a function of the types of informants with whom we operate. We shall proceed to addressing the issue of lack of differences between the grade levels in our L1 cross-sectional data. Finally, in 4.5.3, we present a conclusion and briefly suggest general implications for teaching.

4.5.1 Our findings versus previous research

Based on Cumming's results (1989), we expected the measure for *concurrent attention to aspects of writing* to reveal qualitative differences between our informants at the three grade levels. Cumming found that expert writers had a greater percentage of attention to multiple aspects of writing in L2 than the other groups of writers. For our L1 data, we did see an increase in means across Grade 7 through Grade 10 to the university, although only significantly different for Grade 7 versus the two other groups. However, when comparing the results on this measure between L1 and L2, we found a significant difference between the two languages for Grades 7 and 10, with an increase in percentages from L1 to L2. This finding goes against the initial assumption regarding this measure: that the percentages for *concurrent attention* would be higher in L1 than in L2, due to the expectation that students' writing processes are more advanced in L1 than in L2. When taking the cross-sectional L2 results for this measure into account, we found no significant differences between the three groups: they all had the same level of attention to multiple aspects of writing. These findings go against Cumming's results, in that this measure relates to writing expertise. With the caveat that the interpretation of multiple references might not be identical in the two studies, we see the difference in

154   *Vocabulary and Writing in L1 and L2*

results as a function of the types of informant groups used in the two studies.

Since the typical constellation of attention to two aspects of writing was attention to *ideas* and *language*, many instances underlying this measure are, in fact, cases of problem-solving formulation processes. Therefore, the fact that Grades 7 and 10 demonstrate an increase in this kind of processing from L1 to L2 seems easy to explain, in view of their lower levels of L2 language proficiency. However, how do we account for the fact that not only Grades 7 and 10, but also the university students have similar percentages for *concurrent attention* in L2? In their cross-sectional study, Roca de Larios et al. (2006) found an increase in upgrading problem-solving formulation processes from high school through university students to postgraduate informants. A possible interpretation of our results might, therefore, be that concurrent attention for Grade 7 covers compensatory formulation and for the university level represents upgrading formulation. In other words, because the variable of maturity and extreme differences in L2 proficiency were not issues in Cumming's study of university students, a high level of attention to multiple aspects of writing did, in fact, coincide with writing expertise. However, because we included much younger learners in our study, we found that this measure, in isolation, cannot be used to distinguish able from less able writers. Judging from our qualitative analysis, Grade 10 might again represent a mixed ability group. Thus, it is likely that the mean for concurrent attention for Grade 10 either covers some informants with more upgrading than compensatory formulation – as we saw for Sarah, or the other way round – as was the case for Kate or, alternatively, that Grade 10 have a mixture of upgrading and compensatory formulation processes.

Furthermore, also contrary to Cumming's findings (1989), there was no correlation in L2 between *heuristic searches with resolution* and the quality of the essays. As previously mentioned, resolution is seen from the informant's point of view. It is therefore likely that the relationship between process and product found by Cumming might be attributed to university students arriving at better resolutions than the informants in our study. Our assumption is that this is so due to the fact that our Grade 7 and 10 informants differ in age and educational experience from Cumming's subjects. Furthermore, our university group comprised students in the early months of their first year at university, whereas the students in Cumming's study were students in their first or second year and, more importantly, some were experienced professional writers in their L1. However, our findings correspond to the results in Pennington

Writing in Two Languages 155

and So (1993), who, in an observational study of the writing processes of university students *in their fourth year*, did not find a close relationship between process and product results either.

As noted on a number of occasions, we were surprised to find that, on most of the counts, we could not establish significant differences between the Grade 10 students and the university group, even though the two groups differ in age and educational experience. We also mentioned that this finding might be due to lack of sensitivity in the analyses applied, although, previously, the same system of analysis had established differences among university level students writing in their L2 (Cumming, 1989). In order to look further into this matter, we gave a detailed account of the three informants' verbalizations. This account highlights that the Grade 10 students are a mixed ability group, in that one Grade 10 student was clearly much closer to the university student in L1 processing than the other Grade 10 student. Naturally, this is not substantial evidence and there might be other explanations than the sensitivity of the system of analysis that we have applied.

Thus, we would tentatively suggest that, for L1, a ceiling level of procedural knowledge might be reached around the level represented by our Grade 10 students. This might specifically apply in our context since the Grade 10 students in our study represent the academically more able part of the teenage population, in that they are the ones who managed to be accepted for a sixth-form college education. In a study by Tarone et al. (1993), investigating Southeast Asian-American ESL students' writing abilities from grades 8, 10, 12 to university freshman level, no significant differences were found between *any* of the groups, with regard to ratings of their essays. In other words, their cross-sectional product data did not indicate that any development took place over a five-year period. The authors had included two additional university level groups: a group of international students and a group of native speakers. No differences could be established between any of the groups of Southeast Asian informants and the former group, whereas highly significant differences were found with regard to the native-speaker group and all the other groups. This unexpected finding might, of course, partly be a function of L2 language proficiency. On the other hand, the authors stress that they had expected that the essay ratings of organization and coherence would reveal differences between some of the groups as a reflection of difference in maturity. The study included one NS group only, and the authors discuss the possibility that this finding might also apply to non-ESL students and suggest the use of parallel data

156 *Vocabulary and Writing in L1 and L2*

from NS at all the grade levels. The results of our study with regard to the Danish data might indicate that the findings in Tarone et al. apply more generally than they expected.[7] An L1 study by Kroll (1986) seems to lend further support to this notion, and to the issue of the sensitivity of an analytical system. Kroll's cross-sectional study focused on written explanations of how to play a game, using grades 5, 7, 9 and 11 as well as college level students. On a measure of the adequacy of information included in the descriptions, the only point at which significant differences could be established was between grades 5 and 7 versus the three older groups. Only when analyzing the finer aspects of the descriptions, did he identify features that distinguished the two oldest groups (grade 11 and the college group) from the others. Thus, it seems that we need to get at the finer nuances, as we attempted to do in the qualitative account of three of our informants, in order to be able to show what characterizes the higher educational levels.

4.5.2 Research implications

On a number of occasions, we have drawn attention to some counterintuitive findings and to findings for the variable *concurrent attention* that do not tally with the results of other studies. We have queried whether our findings might be attributed to lack of sensitivity of the measures used when applied to new and different learner groups, as has been the case in our study.

Our qualitative analysis has lead us to the tentative suggestion that future research of students' writing processes should include analyses of strategies such as planning, and possibly revision, in addition to analyses of online problem solving, which have been the focus of our investigation. In addition, an analysis that, in a principled manner, relates the use of heuristic searches to, for instance, the quality of attention to discourse, might also be worth considering as a way of providing a yardstick for determining resolution. Such combination of analytical approaches is more likely to capture the actual differences underlying the processing of older groups of students as our Grade 10 and university students.

Furthermore, when operating with learners as different as the informants in our study, concurrent attention to language and ideas should be analyzed with a view to distinguishing between upgrading and compensatory problem solving. The challenge for future research is to identify ways in which these distinctions can be included in an analytical framework that allows for quantitative investigations of the quality of learners' attention.

4.5.3 Conclusion and teaching implications

We set out to investigate the relationship between writing in L1 and L2 for students at three grade levels. Our findings show that, for Grades 7 and 10, writing in the two languages differs, whereas this is not the case for our university informants. According to the cross-sectional analyses, there is no difference in L1 writing skills between Grade 10 and Grade 13, but this is the case for their L2 writing skills (see *heuristic searches with resolution*). The cross-sectional findings thus further support the interpretation that the Grade 10 students had reached a level of writing skills similar to the university students but, unlike the university students, they were unable to apply these skills in the L2 writing context. Furthermore, the Grade 7 students were clearly less skilled writers, compared with the other two groups, in both languages.

We thus see a pattern in the relationship between L1 and L2 writing as a function of grade level. At the most **basic level**, the Grade 7 students are still struggling with their procedural knowledge. In L1, their predominant attention to aspects of writing, next to *ideas*, is to *procedure* and the typical problem-solving category for this group is *no problem*. In other words, their processing has most features in common with the knowledge-telling approach to writing. When these writers turn to L2 writing, their attention patterns change. Attention to language predominates in L2, and they clearly run into more problems when writing in L2, which is reflected in the changed pattern of results for the problem-solving categories. However, they are still closer to knowledge telling in L2, in that they still only operate the full CDO process at the same limited level as in L1. At the **intermediate level**, the Grade 10 students demonstrate a more balanced attention to aspects of writing, and their problem solving is also more varied. They are, however, only in a position to apply the full CDO process to a high degree in their L1 writing. In addition to this, on a number of counts in L2, they are more similar to the younger basic writers than the older more advanced writers. This applies to most of their attention to aspects of writing and, when it comes to *heuristic searches with resolution*, they are clearly a middle group. At the **advanced level**, the university students are the closest we find in our data to operating a knowledge-transforming approach to writing. Unlike the intermediate group, having to operate in L2 while writing does not affect their ability to operate the full CDO process.

As demonstrated in studies, which have analyzed writing strategies in L1 and L2, the way in which individual learners approach a writing task is very similar in the two languages. In this study, we did not focus on phases such as planning and revision, or other types of writing strategies,

158   *Vocabulary and Writing in L1 and L2*

but rather on the way in which our informants deal with the issues they attend to while writing throughout the composing process. Even so, as illustrated in the qualitative analysis of three learners and based on our impressions from analyzing the many protocols, we find that, if writers start by making notes before writing the first draft in one language, they do so in the other language as well. Furthermore, if they revise extensively from first draft to final copy, they do so in both languages.

The present study, with its focus on problem solving, shows that, relatively speaking, the students process in their L2 either as well or as poorly as they do in their L1 and that, for the younger groups, having to operate in L2 has a constraining effect on their L2 processes. From a teaching perspective, this means that writing in L2 is both a language and a writing problem. Thus, EFL learners can only benefit from improved L2 language proficiency but, if their writing skills in L1 are poor, the chances are that they will be poor in L2 as well, despite an improved L2 proficiency.[8] We have seen how the Grade 10 students, as a group, obtained similar results to the university students with regard to processing in L1, but that their processing in L2 differed from that of the university students. This finding seems to imply that the foreign language is the obstacle that prevents them from applying their L1 process in the L2 context and that teaching geared to improving their L2 proficiency is called for. However, since we also need to address the learners' processing, the question is which type of language teaching should be employed. We saw, albeit only in the qualitative analysis, that the informants differ in two crucial respects, even in their L1; that is, in the way in which they handle language problems and in their awareness of text structure. We also saw that individual students behaved in very similar fashions with regard to these two issues when writing in their L2. For improving the students' L2 language proficiency, a fruitful teaching approach might therefore be to ensure raising the students' awareness of the link between language use and textual coherence, in composition classes in the native language and in the foreign language classroom. This type of awareness raising seems essential if we are to help students improve their writing processes in the foreign language, since we saw that two students who had obtained similar scores on the L2 vocabulary test and identical scores on the L2 reading test operated qualitatively very different writing processes. In other words, at school, the foreign language teacher and the mother tongue teacher should cooperate closely to ensure that students with poor L1 writing skills are given guidance that will help them improve their writing in both languages. Instruction of this kind would help the Grade 7 student, whose essay introduced this chapter, make better use of all the time she spent on her short and poor essay.

Notes

1 The main criterion for selecting this sub-set of informants was level of reading ability in L1 (see Chapter 1, for our selection criteria for the whole informant group). We chose the ten best and the ten poorest readers within each grade level. This criterion was, however, in a few cases overruled to obtain as fair a gender balance as possible (G.7: 10 males and 10 females; G.10: 4 males and 16 females; G. 13: 8 males and 12 females).

2 We wish to thank external lecturer Sanne Larsen for her invaluable assistance with the analyses of the verbal protocols, for her thoughtful comments on our research and for her critical reading of earlier drafts of this chapter. Any shortcomings are, of course, entirely our responsibility.

3 The label 'heuristic searches' is used 'to describe a strategic process of directing mental effort into deliberate evaluation of a particular problem' (Cumming, 1988: 90).

4 The zero score in the TOEFL scoring guide was disregarded in this case, since our data did not include essays of virtually no response.

5 For the Nelson–Denny reading test (Form G), a T-test comparing G.10 and G.13 reached a significance level of .003.

6 The names given here are pseudonyms.

7 In a study by Schoonen et al. (2002) comparing L1 and L2 essays written by Dutch students at grade 8, the learners comprised two groups; native speakers of Dutch and immigrant speakers of Dutch. The authors expected to find no difference between the two groups when writing in English (L2), and did not, but they did expect differences between the two groups when writing in Dutch. The study operated with essay assessments and looked into the degree to which a number of variables explained the variance in writing proficiency. Although they did find a significant difference between the essay assessments for the two groups, the difference was small, and, in addition to this, they found no differences between the two groups pertaining to the variance explained by the variables investigated. Extremely tentatively, the Dutch study might be taken to indicate that some bilingual students are not so very different from their monolingual counterparts.

8 Note that we found no positive correlations for L2 proficiency with L2 writing processes, whereas L2 writing processes correlated with L1 writing processes.

5
Lexical Knowledge, Lexical Inferencing and Writing

In the previous chapters, we have investigated different aspects of our learners' competence in their L1 and their L2. Chapter 2 was devoted to measures of declarative lexical competence, including an analysis of both the learners' vocabulary size (breadth) and their network knowledge (depth). In Chapter 3, issues relating to lexical competence were still in focus, but the interest here was shifted to the learners' lexical inferencing procedures and their ability to guess the meaning of unknown words in a number of short reading texts. In Chapter 4, the focus was moved away from our informants' receptive skills to their productive skills, describing their writing procedures when asked to produce argumentative essays. In all three studies, the learners from the three educational levels were given identical, or similar, parallel tasks in their L1 (Danish) and their L2 (English). The investigations presented in the preceding chapters primarily concerned differences and similarities with regard to the within-subjects data, comparing the learners' ability to cope in the two languages, and with regard to the cross-sectional data, comparing the three grade levels in English and in Danish, respectively.

In this chapter, we bring together the results from the three studies to investigate the degree to which similarities or differences have been found across the different aspects of ability studied for the same learner. First, we deal with the developmental patterns found in the results reported in the preceding chapters. Second, we report on the degree to which statistically significant correlations were established between the measures from the three studies. Here, we will also look at the measure for L2 reading proficiency,[1] which was included in our overall task battery. In Section 5.3, we address the issue of how individual learners fare across the studies, identifying typical learner profiles. Finally, we detail lexical profiles for three informants from Grade 10. As the results in the previous chapters have shown, this educational level turned out to be an interesting intermediate group, not only in terms of age and educational level, but also because some of the Grade 10 informants shared features found in the learner data of the younger Grade 7 informants, while others shared features with the older, more advanced Grade 13 students.

5.1 Bringing the three studies together

Let us first look at the overall results of the three studies by focusing on the measures that best discriminated between the informants in the various studies. In the writing study, the measure *heuristic searches with resolution* was singled out as the hallmark of complex processing. The procedure identified as complex processing in lexical inferencing was the category of *top-ruled processing with integration of linguistic cues*; that is, the measure referred to as *advanced processing*. Moreover, the measure *adaptability* was described as an important characteristic of good processing, covering the informants' ability to adapt their processing types to the features of individual words of which they had to guess the meaning. In both studies, product measures were also calculated; that is, the *language control* score for the assessments of the essays written by the informants, and the measure *inferencing success*, which captured the quality of the lexical guesses supplied by the informants on the lexical inferencing tasks. Finally, two of the overall scores from the lexical study, the *word association score* and the *vocabulary size score* will be included in the discussion.

5.1.1 Comparing the L1 and L2 results

For *heuristic searches with resolution* from the writing study, a significant difference between the two languages was only found for the Grade 10 informants, whereas no differences could be established for the two other grade levels. As discussed in Chapter 4, the Grade 7 informants exhibited very little use of this complex processing type in both languages, whereas the more advanced students from Grade 13 had adopted this processing strategy and used it equally extensively in their L1 and their L2. The intermediate group, the Grade 10 informants, were able to utilize this processing type in their L1 at a similar level to the university students, whereas they were not able to apply this skill to the same degree in L2. In other words, the results for this very complex processing type in a highly demanding productive task display the developmental pattern: (1) initial lack of ability in both languages; (2) developing ability and use in the native language, but with more

162 *Vocabulary and Writing in L1 and L2*

restricted use in the target language; and (3) equal use in both the L1 and the L2.

Interestingly enough, none of the other measures exhibits this pattern across the three educational levels. For *all* the other measures mentioned above, including the language scores for the essay evaluations, the L1 scores were significantly higher than the L2 scores, irrespective of grade level. At first glance, these results seem trivial and what one might expect when comparing informants' performance in a foreign language with their skills in their native language. Some of these results are, however, somewhat surprising, especially the results on the inferencing measure *advanced processing*, which is top-ruled processing with integration, and the results on the network task for the university informants. One would have expected that the more advanced university students, in line with the results found for the writing procedure, would have developed the ability to use advanced processing in the receptive task as frequently in their L2 as in the L1. Moreover, it was also unexpected that these very advanced informants did not perform equally well in the two languages on the word association task, which taps into their network knowledge of extremely high frequent nouns and adjectives. This result may reflect the very slow nature of network building and the need for extensive language exposure to develop native-like structural links in the mental lexicon. That the results for the processing measures of the writing and the lexical inferencing tasks differ might be attributed to the fact that processing with regard to lexical inferencing, by its very nature, is more sensitive to the informants' level of language proficiency, especially their vocabulary knowledge. This observation tallies with the results of the lexical network study and the essay assessments for language control, in that, on all these measures, the informants obtained significantly lower scores in L2 than in L1.

5.1.2 Cross-sectional results in L2 and L1

When looking at the *cross-sectional results for L2*, the same developmental pattern was found across most of the measures. The results for Grade 7 were significantly lower than the results for Grade 10 and Grade 13, and the results for Grade 10 were significantly lower than for Grade 13 (Grade 7 < Grade 10 < Grade 13); that is, the expected linear development was found across the three educational levels. Only the results from the word association task differed, in that here significant differences were found between Grade 7 and the two other grade levels, whereas no significant differences were found between Grade 10 and Grade 13 (Grade 7 < Grade 10 = Grade 13). As noted in Chapter 2, the network task targets high frequent items, and it could certainly be expected that the informants from the two older groups would manage to perform equally well on these tasks.

The *cross-sectional results for L1* are more mixed, in that no clear patterns could be found across the various measures. For the vocabulary size measure, the measure for inferencing success and the adaptability measure for lexical inferencing, the same linear pattern as described for the L2 measures was found (Grade 7 < Grade 10 < Grade 13). However, for *all* the other results (the results for word association, advanced processing in lexical inferencing, heuristic searches with resolution in writing and the language control assessments of the essays), the same pattern was found: Grade 7 < Grade 10 = Grade 13. In their native language, the Grade 10 informants clearly managed to achieve as well as the more advanced university students on these measures. These findings lend further support to the assumption discussed in Chapter 4 that, for this population, a ceiling level seems to have been reached at Grade 10 when it comes not only to processes in comprehension and production, but also to lexical competence in the L1.

When comparing the three studies, more similarities than differences were found. Thus, in all studies on most measures, students performed better in L1 than in L2. As to the cross-sectional data, on most measures, significant differences between Grade 10 and Grade 13 were established for L2, but not for L1.

5.2 Correlations across the studies

Up to this point, we have looked at similarities and differences across the three studies with regard to group results; however, we have not capitalized on the fact that these groups consist of the same people performing all the tasks across the studies. A first step with regard to exploring how individual learners managed was to apply correlation analysis. For our data, non-parametric Spearman correlations had to be used, which means that the rank orders of the informants on the various measures are compared. In other words, we set out to see whether significant correlations could be found between the different measures from the studies highlighted above in 5.1.

Correlations between measures within each of the studies have already been presented and discussed in the relevant chapters. Here, we shall limit the discussion to the measures from the three studies with regard to which it is *theoretically plausible* that significant positive correlations might be found. Moreover, we will include some

164 *Vocabulary and Writing in L1 and L2*

comparisons with L2 reading scores. The following research questions were addressed:

R1 Is there a significant positive correlation between the processing measures for writing and lexical inferencing?

R2 Is there a significant positive correlation between the measures for writing and the measure for lexical network knowledge?

R3 Is there a significant positive correlation between the measures for lexical inferencing and the measure for lexical knowledge?

R4 Is there a significant positive correlation between the scores for L2 reading ability and the measures for lexical inferencing, the measures for lexical network knowledge and vocabulary size?

First, we will look at the relationship between the two measures for complex processing in lexical inferencing and writing. Second, we shall consider the relationship between processes in writing and the measures for declarative lexical knowledge, before we proceed to the relationship between lexical inferencing and the lexical measures. Finally, the discussion will be expanded to include the informants' L2 reading skills, investigating the relationship between reading skills, declarative lexical knowledge and lexical inferencing.

5.2.1 Processing measures in lexical inferencing and writing

Predictions: A significant positive correlation was predicted between the measure *heuristic searches with resolution* (writing) and the measure *advanced processing* (lexical inferencing), based on the underlying assumption that both of these measures reflect the informants' ability to carry out complex problem-solving procedures.

Results and discussion: The answer to our first research question is negative with regard to processing in the two tasks. Contrary to our expectations, the predicted correlation between the two different measures, tapping into the informants' procedural knowledge (*advanced processing* in lexical inferencing and *heuristic searches with resolution* in writing), was not found. However, Grade 7 was exceptional in two respects. First, correlations could not be calculated between the two measures in L2 owing to the fact that most of the Grade 7 informants obtained a zero score for *advanced processing* in L2. Second, the L1 results for Grade 7 showed a moderate correlation (.469, at the p < .05 level) between the two measures. In all other cases, no correlations were found in either of the languages. Even though both measures tap into cognitive processes that involve complex instances of problem solving, the lack of correlations may be related to the fact that we are dealing with productive and receptive procedures that differ markedly in a number of respects. Writing is a more global, complex process, involving a number of sub-processes. *Heuristic searches with resolution* are defined as the procedures in which a problem is addressed and a solution reached by elaborating the nature of the problem to be solved. The procedure thus involves both problem identification and different types of attempts at problem solution. Lexical inferencing, on the other hand, is a more focused process, embedded in the process of reading. The goal for the activity is set in advance by the researchers – that is, finding the meaning of specific words underlined in the texts – and, hence, no process of initial problem identification is involved. The task requires that the informants come up with a proposal for word meaning, which means that no avoidance behaviour is possible, whereas the informants in the writing task control the goal setting and, therefore, may avoid potential problems. Furthermore, it should be noted that, unlike for the measure *heuristic searches with resolution*, results on the measure *advanced processing* are highly dependent on the informants' ability to arrive at a correct, or an approximately correct, guess and are, hence, sensitive to the informants' level of L2 proficiency, notably their lexical competence. The fact that no correlation was found could, therefore, be related to the different underlying cognitive processes and task demands related to the measures compared.

5.2.2 Writing and lexical knowledge

Predictions: As we have seen in Chapter 4, for L2 no correlations were found to exist between processing in writing and vocabulary size.[2] However, we still assumed that a significant positive correlation could be predicted between the measure *heuristic searches with resolution* and the measure for lexical network knowledge (the *word association* score). This assumption is based on the expectation that the quantity and quality of the lexical links tapped by the network measure would function as an important declarative knowledge base for complex processing in writing by providing more access routes to lexical items and, thus, freeing mental capacity for important higher-order processing. Moreover, since we had already found significant positive correlations between the *language control* score for the L2 essays and L2 vocabulary size for Grades 7 and 10, as described in Chapter 4, we assumed positive

166   *Vocabulary and Writing in L1 and L2*

correlations would also be found between the essay scores and results on the word association task for these two grade levels. A significant positive correlation was therefore predicted between the lexical network measure and the language scores awarded to the different essays, based on the underlying assumption that the informants' level of lexical network knowledge would be reflected in the quality of the written products.

Results for writing and lexical network knowledge: The answer to our second research question was negative with regard to correlations with the measure for the writing process, but partly positive as to correlations with the written product. Contrary to our predictions, no significant correlations were found between the processing in writing (*heuristic searches with resolution*) and the scores for lexical network knowledge in either language. Neither did we find any correlation between the *language control* scores for the evaluations of the essays written in Danish and the results on the L1 lexical network task. These findings tally with the results for the correlations with vocabulary size (see note 2). The lack of correlation between the measure *heuristic searches with resolution* and the lexical network measures possibly relates to the fact that this type of complex problem solving is also applied to issues other than lexical problems. At any rate, our assumption that greater processing capacity is a function of a more elaborated lexical network was not confirmed.

When comparing the writing product results and the lexical network results, no correlations were established for the L1 data and, for the L2 data, significant correlations were found for the Grade 7 students only (.827, p < 0.01). The results for Grade 7 tally well with the findings in previous studies, which have stressed the importance of lexical knowledge for language production. However, since no correlations were found for any of the grade levels in the L1 data, nor for the Grade 10 and Grade 13 informants in the L2 data, it could be argued that for native speakers, and for the more advanced foreign language users, the word association task employed in the study was insufficiently sensitive. Since this task was designed to measure the learners' network knowledge with high frequent words as stimulus words for their associations, the task might not capture the true quality of these learners' overall lexical network knowledge in L1 for all informants and in L2 for the older students. A quality measure based on vocabulary items from all major word classes and from a range of frequency bands across the lexicon is probably needed for the expected correlations to emerge.

5.2.3 Lexical inferencing and lexical knowledge

Predictions: A significant positive correlation was predicted between the three scores for lexical inferencing (*advanced processing, adaptability* and *inferencing success*) and the lexical measures. This prediction was based on the underlying assumption that a lexicon that is both large and well-structured functions as an important declarative knowledge base for advanced processing and adaptability with regard to the lexical inferencing process and for lexical inferencing success. In order to carry out optimal lexical inferencing in the form of integrated processing and to show adaptability in inferencing behaviour, the informants must draw on lexical cues in the unknown words themselves and must be able to utilize lexical cues in the surrounding context. The ability to employ optimal inferencing procedures and the ability to exhibit adaptability in relation to the different word types are expected to enhance the level of inferencing success. In other words, one could expect the measure for advanced processing, the adaptability measure and the measure for inferencing success to have a strong correlation with the informants' degree of lexical knowledge.

Results for lexical network knowledge and lexical inferencing: Research question R3 obtained only a partly positive answer with regard to correlations between the lexical inferencing measures and the lexical network measure (see Table 5.1).

As above, correlations were found for Grade 7 only, but, in this case, with regard to both the foreign language and the first language. As to the L2 results for these informants, we found moderate to strong correlations between the measures for adaptability and inferencing success, on the one hand, and the lexical network score, on the other

Table 5.1 Correlations between lexical inferencing and network knowledge for Grade 7

Lexical inferencing	WAT L1	WAT L2
Advanced processing	**.474	–[a]
Adaptability	**.607	**.573
Inferencing success	*.469	**.741

Notes: Correlations found at the 0.01 level (**) or the 0.05 level (*) (N = 29)
[a] Correlations could not be calculated in L2, since most of the Grade 7 informants obtained a zero score for *advanced processing* in L2

168   *Vocabulary and Writing in L1 and L2*

hand, whereas the correlation for L1 was more moderate for inferencing success and slightly higher for adaptability than in L2.

Again, these findings may be explained by the fact that the network task taps into relational knowledge of high frequent words and is therefore insufficiently sensitive to measure quality aspects pertaining to the larger and more advanced vocabulary of the two older informant groups. Furthermore, the fact that the lexical inferencing task required the informants to produce qualified guesses of the meaning of extremely low frequent words made correlations between lexical inferencing and network knowledge of high frequent words less likely for the older learners.

Results for lexical size and lexical inferencing: For research question R3, relating to correlations between the lexical inferencing measures and vocabulary size, the answer was positive.

As can be seen from the figures in Table 5.2, moderate and high correlations were found across the board in both languages between the lexical inferencing measures and the vocabulary size scores. Only the Grade 13 L1 scores for advanced processing did not correlate with this lexical measure. It is not surprising that the measure tapping into the informants' breadth of lexical knowledge correlated fairly highly with the various inferencing measures, since vocabulary knowledge is crucial not only for making optimal use of the co-text, but also for utilizing available cues in the unknown words themselves. The fact that the L2

Table 5.2 Correlations between vocabulary size and inferencing measures

L2 vocabulary size correlated with:	Grade 7	Grade 10	Grade 13
Advanced processing in L2	–[a]	**.638	**.526
Adaptability in L2	**.490	**.570	**.658
Inferencing success in L2	**.660	**.601	**.483
L1 vocabulary size correlated with:	**Grade 7**	**Grade 10**	**Grade 13**
Advanced processing in L1	**.753	**.681	.147
Adaptability in L1	**.685	**.696	*.396
Inferencing success in L1	**.762	**.819	**.693

Notes: Correlations found at the 0.01 level (**) or the 0.05 level (*)
(N = 29 for each grade level)
[a] Correlations could not be calculated in L2, since most of the Grade 7 informants obtained a zero score for *advanced processing* in L2

size score, contrary to the findings for the network measure, correlates with the lexical inferencing measures for the Grade 10 and Grade 13 informants may be due to the fact that the size test is more comprehensive, tapping into a much larger stratum of vocabulary knowledge. Unlike the network task, the vocabulary size test is, therefore, sufficiently sensitive to reveal significant correlations between language proficiency and language use for the more advanced learners.

5.2.4 Reading skills, lexical inferencing and lexical knowledge in L2

Predictions: The final correlations to be considered concern the relationship between reading in the L2 and the three measures for L2 lexical inferencing and the two measures for declarative lexical knowledge. As discussed in Chapter 2, previous studies have established a strong correlation between reading ability and lexical knowledge and, as pointed out in Chapter 3, studies of lexical inferencing have shown that reading ability and vocabulary size are strong predictors of lexical inferencing success. Therefore, we expected to find the same close relationship in our research between reading, lexical inferencing and lexical knowledge. Since the lexical inferencing procedures studied in the project are embedded in the process of reading a number of different written texts, it is highly probable that the ability to employ advanced inferencing procedures and the relative success achieved through this process will be strongly correlated with the informants' reading ability. Positive correlations were, therefore, also expected between the informants' L2 reading scores and the inferencing results and the lexical knowledge measures, respectively.

Due to the large age and proficiency span between the three educational groups, two different L2 reading tests were employed. As noted in Chapter 4, the Nelson–Denny reading test was used for the Grade 10 and the Grade 13 informants and a less rigorously validated L2 reading test was given to the Grade 7 informants.

Results for reading compared with measures for lexical inferencing and lexical knowledge: The fourth research question regarding the correlation between L2 reading ability and the lexical measures obtained a positive answer. For the correlations between reading in the L2 and the measures for L2 lexical inferencing and lexical knowledge, moderate to very strong relationships were found for all the three informant groups across a majority of the measures, as predicted. All the measures for the Grade 7 and Grade 13 informants correlated; only one of the measures for Grade 10 did not correlate.

170 Vocabulary and Writing in L1 and L2

Table 5.3 L2 reading, lexical inferencing and lexical knowledge

L2 reading correlated with:	Grade 7	Grade 10	Grade 13
Advanced processing L2	–[a]	*.414	**.486
Adaptability L2	**.516	.225	**.506
Inferencing success L2	**.719	**.539	*.468
Word association L2	**.749	**.722	**.492
Vocabulary size L2	**.732	**.798	**.751

Notes: Correlations found at the 0.01 level (**) or the 0.05 level (*)
(N = 29 for each grade level)
[a] Correlations could not be calculated in L2, since most of the Grade 7 informants obtained a zero score for *advanced processing* in L2

Over and above confirming the results reported in the literature with regard to correlations between reading ability and vocabulary size, as well as between reading and lexical inferencing, the results in Table 5.3 also show that reading ability correlates with the informants' lexical network knowledge. As discussed in Chapter 2, these results also mirror previous research findings, confirming the predicted relationship between quality of lexical knowledge and language learners' reading skills.

5.2.5 Summary, discussion and implications

For this summary, we shall focus on the results of the *correlations for L2*. Irrespective of grade level, correlations were found between the informants' reading skills and their lexical competence, both in relation to vocabulary size, their network knowledge and their lexical inferencing skills (process and product measures). Looking more closely at the three L2 lexical inferencing measures, correlations were also found across all grade levels between the learners' lexical inferencing ability and the size of their L2 vocabulary. However, correlations between the lexical inferencing measures and the lexical network measures were found only for the Grade 7 informants. Turning to the process and product measures of the writing study, it was found that the L2 vocabulary size scores only correlated with the essay evaluations for the Grade 7 informants and the Grade 10 informants; no correlations were found between these measures for the most advanced students. Finally, correlations were found between the network knowledge score for the Grade 7 informants and the essay evaluations. Our findings thus show that vocabulary size is crucial for process as well as product in lexical inferencing and for our informants' written products, corroborating previous research findings concerning the importance of a certain threshold level of L2 vocabulary knowledge for efficient language use.

However, the many instances of lack of predicted correlation should be addressed. In doing so, we shall deal with the issue of asking informants at different age and educational levels to perform the same tasks and with the issue of differences in cognitive demands across tasks.

The fact that identical tasks were given to all informants enabled a direct comparison of the ability level of the three groups of informants within each of the three studies. However, since the tasks had to be manageable for the youngest informants, the drawbacks were that some of the tasks were not sufficiently sensitive to distinguish between the two higher grade levels, notably with regard to the word association task. This finding also had implications when comparing the learners across the studies. We have no way of knowing how the overall network knowledge of the Grade 10 and the university students relates to the lexical inferencing process and to inferencing success, since the true quality of their overall network structure was not addressed in the lexical network task employed here. Another issue was that, even though great care had been taken in developing the lexical inferencing tasks, the youngest informants had difficulties decoding the texts and, hence, these learners were not able to demonstrate the true extent to which they could utilize contextual cues. In both cases, future research should consider a format of task construction in which the task becomes progressively more taxing for the informants, allowing the youngest students to demonstrate their abilities up to a point and ensuring that the older students get a chance to demonstrate their more advanced abilities. In other words, a format similar to Nation's Levels Test could be employed for all the tasks included.

As to differences in task demands, we assumed that the writing task and the lexical inferencing task would tap into similar levels of procedural knowledge. As mentioned above, the two tasks did differ on a number of points. For lexical inferencing, the problems the informants had to address were predetermined and well defined whereas, for writing, the issues to be addressed (such as goal setting) were decided on by the informants and were ill defined. That we found no relationship between complex processing in lexical inferencing and in writing, we attribute to the fact that the lexical inferencing task by its very nature calls for a high level of lexical competence, whereas in the productive writing task many more language and discourse abilities are at stake.

172 *Vocabulary and Writing in L1 and L2*

Thus, in writing, students have to generate ideas, organize these ideas with a view to their audience and express their ideas in the L2. For the latter, again, more is at stake than lexical knowledge; they also need to be able to produce correct sentences and, thus, have to draw on other aspects of their linguistic competence. For all these reasons, and due to the open nature of the task, they might be inclined to use avoidance when faced with lexical problems. These differences in task demands turned out to be crucial, in that the informants were in charge of their level of ambition in the writing task, whereas in the lexical inferencing task, they only had the options of dealing with the set lexical problem or giving up. The implications are that future research comparing processing in writing to lexical inferencing needs to operate with measures in lexical inferencing that are less dependent on objective success in outcome than the measures employed in the present study. In other words, measures should be included that focus more on the actual procedures employed regardless of whether the learner achieves a correct guess. Alternatively, the analyses of the writing process should include a measure that specifically targets the use of complex processing applied to lexical problems, thereby enhancing the possibility of comparing similar procedural skills.

5.3   Learner profiles

Having reported on the degree of correlations between the three studies, the second step in our quest to trace the same learner across the three studies is addressed in our last research question: Is it possible to set up profiles of the informants as a function of how well-developed their knowledge and skills are within the areas studied? To answer this question, we shall turn to a qualitative investigation of our data.

5.3.1   Typical profiles of individual informants across the studies

Our aim in this section is to take a closer look at the results of individual informants to establish the extent to which the various aspects of their performance are developed to a similar degree, or the extent to which some aspects are more developed than others. In other words, we wish to obtain an assessment of how far individual learners have developed their abilities with respect to three main areas: that is, (1) their procedural skills; (2) their declarative knowledge; and (3) the degree to which they were able to apply their skills and knowledge to obtain successful products.

Lexical Knowledge, Lexical Inferencing and Writing   173

As a yardstick for assessing individual informants' level of development, we used the means for the whole population for a number of selected measures. For procedural skills, we included the measures *heuristic searches with resolution* in L1 and L2 writing and *advanced processing* in L1 and L2 lexical inferencing. For declarative knowledge, the measures were *word association* for L1 and L2 network knowledge and *vocabulary size* in L1 and L2, and, for product results, the measures were *language control* for L1 and L2 writing and *lexical inferencing success* in L1 and L2.

For each measure, we grouped the results by calculating the mean for all the informants irrespective of grade level, and identified three ranges of results by subtracting half a standard deviation from the mean and by adding half a standard deviation to the mean, thus identifying a lower range, a mid-range and an upper range of scores. For each of the three areas discussed, each informant was thereby given a combination of four score ranges. One informant might have all four scores within the lower, mid- or upper score range or two within the low and two within the mid- score range, or perhaps an even more mixed profile such as one within the low, two within the mid- and one within the upper range. The results of this procedure are presented in Tables 5.4 to 5.6.

We are, of course, dealing with a cline from low score ranges on all four measures to an increasing number of scores on the mid- and upper score ranges to four scores on the upper ranges. To see how the informants from the three educational levels are quantitatively grouped on various parts of a developmental cline, we have divided the combinational patterns into three developmental sections: a lower section, a middle section and an upper section. In order to be placed on the middle or the upper sections, at least two of the four scores for each area investigated must belong to the middle section or two to the upper section, respectively.[3] We will first look at the four process scores from the writing and the inferencing studies, then we will discuss the four vocabulary measures and, finally, we will focus on the four product scores.

The four process scores

Table 5.4 shows that the Grade 7 informants perform poorly on the measures for processes. The majority of the learners in this group, 18 informants, fall within the lower or middle section of the developmental cline, with 12 informants obtaining scores on the lower range on three, or even all four, of the process measures. Unsurprisingly, only one informant from Grade 7 reaches the upper section with two mid-range and two upper range scores. For the university level, the majority of the informants – 14 students – have a least two scores within the upper

174   *Vocabulary and Writing in L1 and L2*

range and, therefore, fall within the upper section of the developmental cline. Three of the university students have scores in the upper range for all four processes. In the mid-range, four university students fall just short of the criteria for belonging to the upper section, with two or three scores within the mid-range and one within the upper score range.

The results for Grade 10 indicate that this is the middle group. In Table 5.4, the Grade 10 informants are distributed almost evenly on the middle and the upper sections of the score range. At the low end of the developmental cline, we only find two Grade 10 students, one with low range scores for all four processes and one with three low range scores and one mid-range score.

The four vocabulary scores
The results for the four vocabulary measures, presented in Table 5.5, show an almost similar overall distribution with regard to the number of informants within the lower, mid- and upper sections to that found in Table 5.4 for the writing and inferencing process results. However, there is a minor difference, in that a few more informants from each grade level have proceeded further along the developmental cline.

The four product scores
The results for the four product measures from the writing and inferencing studies, presented in Table 5.6, show the same distribution with regard to the number of informants within the lower, mid- and upper sections to that found in Table 5.4 for the process results and in Table 5.5 for the vocabulary scores. Again, we see that the Grade 7 informants primarily fall within the lower and the mid- sections, with most informants in the lower section. The Grade 10 informants are almost evenly distributed on the mid- and the upper sections, whereas the majority of the Grade 13 informants fall within the upper section.

The figures in the three tables show how the students in each of the three sections (lower, mid- and upper) perform in both languages with regard to processing in lexical inferencing and writing; size and breadth of lexical knowledge; and lexical inferencing success and language control in writing. However, the figures do not tell us whether the same person is represented in a given cell across the three tables. We need to trace the individual informants on all these measures in order to set up profiles of the relative development of the various skills covered by the measures. Therefore, we will investigate whether or not individual learners fall into the lower, mid- or upper sections with regard to all three

Table 5.4 Combinations of the four process results

	Grade 7	Grade 10	Grade 13
Lower section			
Lower 4	9	1	
Mid 1 Lower 3	3	1	
	12	2	0
Middle section			
Mid 2 Lower 2	3		
Mid 3 Lower 1	1	1	
Mid 4	1	2	
Upper 1 Mid 1 Lower 2	1		
Upper 1 Mid 2 Lower 1		2	2
Upper 1 Mid 3		4	2
Upper 2 Lower 2			1
	6	9	5
Upper section			
Upper 2 Mid 1 Lower 1		2	4
Upper 2 Mid 2	1	5	3
Upper 3 Mid 1			4
Upper 4		1	3
	1	8	14
N	19	19	19

Key: Lower: range from 1/2 SD below the mean;
   Mid: range from 1/2 SD below to 1/2 SD above the mean;
   Upper: range from 1/2 SD above the mean.

areas: their procedural knowledge, their declarative lexical knowledge and the results obtained on the product measures.

Comparing across the three tables

When tracing how individual learners fare across the three areas of processing, vocabulary knowledge and product results, we find the following when collapsing the results within the three main sections of ability combinations (see the sections labelled *lower*, *mid-* and *upper* in Tables 5.4, 5.5 and 5.6). *For Grade 7*, ten informants obtained results within the lower section on all the measures in both languages (see Table 5.7). In other words, these learners demonstrate a low level of ability with regard to procedural and declarative knowledge, which, in turn, results in poor product results. Three students had scores in the mid-section on all measures. *For Grade 10*, one informant also has scores within the lower section on all measures. Four informants in this

176 *Vocabulary and Writing in L1 and L2*

Table 5.5 Combinations of the four vocabulary results

	Grade 7	Grade 10	Grade 13
Lower section			
Lower 4	8		
Mid 1 Lower 3	2	1	
Upper 1 Lower 3	1		
	11	**1**	**0**
Middle section			
Mid 2 Lower 2	2	1	
Mid 3 Lower 1	4	2	
Mid 4		1	
Upper 1 Mid 1 Lower 2		1	
Upper 1 Mid 2 Lower 1	1	2	2
Upper 1 Mid 3	1		1
	8	**7**	**3**
Upper section			
Upper 2 Mid 1 Lower 1		1	3
Upper 2 Mid 2		6	
Upper 3 Lower 1		1	
Upper 3 Mid 1		3	6
Upper 4			7
	0	**11**	**16**
N	**19**	**19**	**19**

Key: Lower: range from 1/2 SD below the mean;
Mid: range from 1/2 SD below to 1/2 SD above the mean;
Upper: range from 1/2 SD above the mean.

group have reached results within the mid-section on all measures, demonstrating intermediate ability in all three areas. Finally, three informants have obtained results within the upper section on all measures, showing that they belong to the most able students in this population with regard to the three ability areas. *For the Grade 13 level,* one inform-ant has results within the mid-section on all measures. However, ten university informants have obtained results within the upper section on all measures, revealing that they have reached the highest level of ability with respect to procedural and declarative knowledge, and that they are able to utilize these knowledge sources in generating successful prod-ucts. For the thirteen informants from Grade 7, the eight Grade 10 learn-ers and the twelve Grade 13 students, the ability profiles are straightforward. They demonstrate either the same low level or the same mid-level or the same high level of ability within the three areas.

Lexical Knowledge, Lexical Inferencing and Writing   177

Table 5.6   Combinations of the four product results

	Grade 7	Grade 10	Grade 13
Lower section			
Lower 4	6	1	
Mid 1 Lower 3	6	1	
	12	2	0
Middle section			
Mid 2 Lower 2	1		
Mid 3 Lower 1	1		
Mid 4	1	1	
Upper 1 Mid 2 Lower 1	1	4	1
Upper 1 Mid 3	2	3	3
	6	8	4
Upper section			
Upper 2 Mid 1 lower 1	1		1
Upper 2 Mid 2		3	4
Upper 3 Lower 1			1
Upper 3 Mid 1		3	3
Upper 4		3	6
	1	9	15
N	19	19	19

Key: Lower: range from 1/2 SD below the mean;
   Mid: range from 1/2 SD below to 1/2 SD above the mean;
   Upper: range from 1/2 SD above the mean.

Table 5.7   Informants with results within the same sections for all L1 and L2 measures

	Grade 7	Grade 10	Grade 13
Lower section	10	1	
Middle section	3	4	1
Upper section		3	10
Total	13 = 68%	8 = 42%	11 = 58%

Note: (N = 19 for each grade level)

The remaining students at each grade level have different and more complex ability profiles. When looking into these patterns, we were not able to establish typical combinations of level of ability with regard to processes, vocabulary knowledge and product results, that distinguished each of the three grade levels. Since the majority of the Grade

178   *Vocabulary and Writing in L1 and L2*

10 students – that is, 58 per cent – showed a mixture of ability levels, we shall only comment on some typical combinations of abilities for this group. Out of these eleven Grade 10 students, four informants demonstrated the same upper level of ability with regard to vocabulary knowledge and product results, but mid-section results for processes. In other words, despite their mid-level procedural ability, these students seemed able to apply their declarative knowledge successfully to the products they were required to produce in both languages (essays and degree of inferencing success). Three Grade 10 informants showed the same level of ability with regard to processing and vocabulary knowledge – again, in all cases within the upper sections – but demonstrated mid-level ability for their product results. It seems that these three students were not able to apply their high levels of procedural and declarative knowledge to obtain successful products.

In response to our question regarding profiles, the answer seems to be that, for the majority of the Grade 7 and Grade 13 students, similar levels of abilities have been reached for processing, vocabulary knowledge and the production of products. For the former group, the ability levels are low and, for the latter group, we find high levels of ability. That the group of Grade 10 informants is a mixed ability group, is also demonstrated here, in that the majority of these informants did not have similar levels of abilities with regard to procedural and declarative knowledge, and with regard to producing successful products. For these students, a mixture of ability profiles with no predictable developmental patterns was found.

5.3.2   Lexical profiles

Since the results of the correlations between the measures from the three studies yielded most instances of correlations for the various measures pertaining to our informants' lexical knowledge, we shall now attempt to draw up some lexical profiles for different learner types. As outlined in Section 5.3.1, many of the informants from Grade 7 were weak on all the lexical measures in both languages. A majority of the Grade 13 students did fairly well across the various measures in both L1 and L2, whereas the Grade 10 informants turned out to be a group with mixed results, both across the different measures and across the two languages. We will therefore focus on the Grade 10 informant group, from which three learners have been selected: one representing the upper, one the middle and one the lower level of this mixed ability group. Each profile will be based on the informant's quantitative results, both in terms of the process and product measures related to lexical inferencing and the declarative lexical knowledge scores, followed by a more qualitative

Lexical Knowledge, Lexical Inferencing and Writing   179

illustration of the three informants' actual guessing procedures in the L1 and the L2 lexical inferencing task.

We shall start by presenting the quantitative results for all three informants, referred to in the following as Karen (a low-level informant), Mike (a mixed profile learner) and Peter (a high-level informant). In Table 5.8, we include the mean results for Grade 7 and Grade 13 as points of comparison for these three Grade 10 informants. Karen is a learner who operates similarly to the Grade 7 level in both languages. In contrast to this, for Peter the upper limit set by the means for Grade 13 is a more appropriate yardstick for both his L1 and L2 measures. Mike's scores are mixed with the results for L1 being close to the Grade 13 means, and the L2 results closer to the means of the Grade 7 informants than to those of the Grade 13 informants. This approach serves the purpose of highlighting the pronounced inter-learner variability found within the group of Grade 10 informants.

Table 5.8   Lexical results for the three Grade 10 informants

	Grade 7 (N = 29)	Karen	Mike	Peter	Grade 13 (N = 29)
Advanced processing L1 (%)	16.7	23	57	50	41.3
Advanced processing L2 (%)	1.6	0	7	23	21.7
Adaptability L1 (%)	38.5	40	71	53	61.3
Adaptability L2 (%)	17.5	23	23	47	45.9
Inferencing success L1 (%)	29.4	21	61	56	58.7
Inferencing success L2 (%)	16.8	13	34	46	48.3
Intralingual cues L1 (%)		50.7	69.6	45.5	
Intralingual cues L2 (%)		11.1	37.5	48.2	
Vocabulary size L1	50.2	50	111	90	102.1
Vocabulary size L2	33.8	30	89	101	94.8
Frequency level L1		1	3	2	
Frequency level L2		0	1	3	
Word association L1	217.9	238.6	279.5	228.7	239.2
Word association L2	151.8	172.6	220.8	238.9	221.8
Canonical links WAT L1 (%)	37.5	47.9	37.5	27.0	37.0
Canonical links WAT L2 (%)	27.4	31.5	39.6	35.4	32.6
Low freq. links WAT L1 (%)	13.3	12.5	24.0	17.7	16.3
Low freq. links WAT L2 (%)	5.1	3.3	9.4	15.6	12.8
Lexical variation WAT L1	84.4	87.3	94.4	88.6	87.9
Lexical variation WAT L2	80.5	91.3	90.5	89.1	87.2
Reading L1		7	24	23	21.1
Reading L2		7	33	31	29.6

180 *Vocabulary and Writing in L1 and L2*

With regard to the lexical measures presented in Table 5.8, these have all been introduced in Chapters 2 and 3. The three hallmarks of high quality lexical inferencing are the two procedural constructs of *advanced processing* and *adaptability*, as well as the product measure of *lexical inferencing success*. Moreover, we have added figures for the number of *intralingual cues* activated by the informants while working on the lexical inferencing task, since we wish to relate the learners' activation of these cues to the word association measures tapping lexical organization.[4] Finally, we quote the reading scores, since reading skills have been found to correlate highly with declarative and procedural measures of lexical competence, both in previous studies and in the present study.

Karen: an example of an overall low level informant
Karen is low across many of the measures, both in L1 and L2. With regard to lexical inferencing, the L1 procedural measures of advanced processing and adaptability are fairly close to the Grade 7 level means, and the product measure for inferencing success is even a little below this level. For L2, the same tendency for low-level scores close to the Grade 7 means is found, with, for example, a total absence of advanced processing and a score for L2 *intralingual cues* a mere quarter of her L1 score.

Turning to the declarative measures for lexical knowledge, the L1 word association score is surprisingly high, if we consider the rather low score this informant obtained on the Danish vocabulary size test; a score mirroring the mean vocabulary size score for Grade 7. On the L1 size test, she only managed to reach the cut-off point for frequency Level 1; that is, a vocabulary of around 5000 words, which is the word level most of the Grade 7 learners also reached for their first language. A qualitative analysis of the L1 responses to the WAT task shows that the majority of the associations are semantically related to the stimulus words, many in the form of canonical links. The measure for lexical variation of the responses given is above the Grade 13 mean, but it is notable that only about 12.5 per cent of the responses supplied are in the form of low frequent words. In other words, Karen had no problem providing associations in the first language and in varying her response pattern, but the responses are primarily in the form of high frequent lexical items. The consistency in being able to respond semantically and to supply canonical links, however, enabled the informant to reach a rather high WAT score, reflecting a small vocabulary with good organizational properties for the high frequent nouns and adjectives tested. This mirrors the overall cross-sectional results reported in

Chapter 2, showing that significant differences were found in relation to L1 vocabulary size between the Grade 10 and the Grade 13 informants, whereas no differences could be detected for the WAT scores between these two grade levels. In other words, even if some of the Grade 10 learners (such as Karen) have a smaller vocabulary size than the Grade 13 informants, words from the high frequent bands of their L1 vocabulary did not seem to be less well organized than those of many of the older informants. This applies both in terms of network density and in relation to their ability to supply meaning based responses; for instance, in the form of canonical links.

In comparison to the L1 measure, the L2 word association score is very low, and much closer to the Grade 7 mean than to the Grade 13 mean. A qualitative analysis of the response types shows that 21 of the 96 potential associations are empty, which means that Karen very often failed to supply a second association to a given stimulus word. Again, most of the responses given are high frequent semantically related links, but fewer canonical links are supplied compared with the L1 data. The lexical variation score is surprisingly high, in that the informant managed to vary her response pattern. However, the responses given are limited to high frequent words and, often, the informant found it difficult to access more than one associative link to the stimulus words; that is, the lexical variation score must be viewed with the fewer associations given in mind. These results mirror the informant's extremely low scores on the L2 vocabulary size test; a result very close to the Grade 7 means. It is therefore unsurprising that Karen also failed to reach the cut-off point for frequency Level 1 on the L2 test. In other words, this weak Grade 10 informant has an estimated vocabulary size in English below 2000 words. Moreover, in terms of density of lexical links and the response types given, this learner seemed to have a different and much weaker organizational structure of high frequent lexical items in the L2 compared with the L1.

We can conclude that Karen is weak, both on procedural and declarative lexical knowledge. Let us take a close look at this learner's lexical inferencing protocols. Irrespective of the fact that she is one of the weak Grade 10 informants, it is still highly remarkable that not one instance of advanced processing was found in her L2 lexical inferencing data. Although her score for L1 is close to the Grade 7 means, she demonstrates in a few instances that she is able to employ this procedure to some degree for words with potential linguistic cues to meaning, as seen in Extract 5.1 from her L1 protocol. The learner here addresses the test word *'vankundige'* ('uninformed'), which appears in a text about

182 *Vocabulary and Writing in L1 and L2*

dinosaurs in the context (in translation): 'Many ordinary people find it exciting to read about dinosaurs, but compared to the experts we are of course **uninformed**.'

Extract 5.1 Karen, L1

TA (The informant starts by reading aloud the above sentence) this could mean that we don't know the first thing about it or something – but compared to the experts – they are the ones that know something about a particular topic – and in this situation it is the dinosaurs – and then we say that we are probably not knowledgeable (Danish: *kyndige*) that we don't know anything about it.

It is evident from the think-aloud protocol that the informant makes good use of contextual cues, especially the comparison between 'us' and 'them'; that is, the experts who 'know something about a particular topic'. A linguistic cue, the word '*kyndige*' (knowledgeable), is also activated and contributes to the proposal for word meaning, which is 'we do not know anything about it', a paraphrase assessed as an accurate guess. In sum, the protocol illustrates that this informant is occasionally capable of employing advanced processing in her L1 and shows some degree of adaptability by making use of one of the potential linguistic cues to meaning.

However in the L2, a different procedure is employed, in that she adopts two ways of tackling a test word with linguistic cues to meaning; she either sticks to pure top processing – that is, depending solely on contextual cues – or she uses bottom-ruled processing – as demonstrated in a short example with the test word 'olfactory' (see Extract 5.2). This word appears in one of the texts dealing with the human senses of sight, touch and smell, and the extract from her TA protocol points to bottom-ruled processing.

Extract 5.2 Karen, L2

TA ... olfactory – old – er factories (giggles) no I don't know – I think it means old something or other.

It appears that Karen divides the target word into two parts, 'ol' and 'factory', and with respect to 'ol' she pays exclusive attention to formal similarity between 'ol' and 'old', arriving at a proposal for word meaning that is 'old something or other'. In short, this informant, instead of using advanced processing, either employs an ineffective type of processing, resulting in a wrong proposal for word meaning that does not make sense in the context, or relies on pure top processing. Such an approach, which

Lexical Knowledge, Lexical Inferencing and Writing   183

shares many features with Grade 7 inferencing procedures, may account for the low figures found for both adaptability and inferencing success. It is very likely that Karen's inability to make more extensive use of advanced processing in the L1 and her reliance on either pure top processing or on bottom-ruled processing in the L2 is related to her weak declarative knowledge base in both the L1 and the L2, especially in terms of vocabulary size. Moreover, the extremely low reading scores in both languages also suggest that she was probably bogged down considerably by her weak reading skills in the lexical inferencing task.

Mike: an example of a mixed profile informant

Focusing first on the measures for lexical inferencing, we find that the difference between his performance in L1 and L2 is extremely marked. The figures for L1 indicate that, on the three hallmarks of lexical infer-encing, Mike performs at a higher level than the average Grade 13 informant, whereas there is a clear drop for the same measures in L2, especially regarding the two process measures. A similar tendency is found with regard to figures for *intralingual cues*, which are high for L1 and markedly lower for the L2.

When looking at the other lexical measures, we see that Mike obtained an extremely high WAT score in L1 and a lower score in L2, although the L2 score is in line with the Grade 13 means. Looking at the results for L1 first, the vocabulary size score is far above the Grade 13 mean. The informant managed to reach the cut-off point for frequency Level two and is just below the cut-off points for Level three and Level four; scores reflecting an L1 vocabulary size far above the 5000-word level. Unsurprisingly, the informant found it easy to supply semantically related links, both in the form of canonical links and other types of meaning based associations. Moreover, it is worth noting that almost one quarter of the associations given are low frequent vocabulary items, and the measure for lexical variation is very high. In other words, this informant was able to vary his response pattern and give associations that reflect the wide frequency range of vocabulary items found in his L1 vocabulary.

Turning to the L2 results, the vocabulary size score is below the Grade 13 mean but far above the mean for Grade 7. In relation to fre-quency bands, Mike only reached the cut-off point for frequency Level one, reflecting a vocabulary size of roughly 2000 words, but it must be pointed out that he is very close to the cut-off point for both Levels two and three. These results might indicate a vocabulary approaching the 5000-word level, but without a firm knowledge base

184 *Vocabulary and Writing in L1 and L2*

of the words covering the frequency bands from the 2000- up to the 5000-word level. The somewhat high WAT score reflects the informant's ability to access meaning based links and the ability to supply a large number of canonical links. The measure for lexical variation is also high, so he clearly managed to vary his response pattern. However, compared with the L1 data, far fewer low frequent vocabulary items are found. In other words, even if Mike is not able to do as well in the L2 compared with the L1 on the WAT and the size scores, the above average result on the two L2 measures reflects a somewhat large vocabulary with a well-organized structure for high frequent nouns and adjectives in both languages. Interestingly enough, this is not borne out in relation to the lexical inferencing results, where the L2 scores are surprisingly low. One explanation for this might be found in Mike's failure to reach the 5000-word level on the vocabulary size test; a threshold level described in the research literature as a crucial declarative knowledge base for transfer of procedural skills from the L1 to the L2. Moreover, he seems to have fewer links to low frequent items in his word store.

What is notable about Mike is that he exhibits a mixed learner profile, with a clear imbalance between the first and the foreign language, especially in relation to the three lexical inferencing measures with very high figures for L1 and much lower figures for L2. We shall now illustrate how this difference between the two languages is reflected in his lexical inferencing protocols.

For lexical inferencing in L1, Extract 5.3 from the protocol for the test word '*akvatiske*' ('aquatic') is a typical example of Mike's very competent use of advanced processing, where he even demonstrates use of a Latin cue.

Extract 5.3 Mike, L1

TA (The informant starts by reading aloud from the text) <Finally there are the ictosaura which are aquatic reptiles whose body made them perfectly adapted to catch fast swimming prey> – aquatic – that must be something with acqua – which is water – – so this must be – <aquatic reptiles> – that is reptiles who lived in the water – I think the word means – when something is in the water – so – the reptiles live in water.

Re aquatic – it was something in the text and also the word itself because of aqua you know – water in Latin – this – this helped me – you see like in a fish tank – and then it also said something about the ictosaura – and that was – their bodies were perfectly adapted to catch

Lexical Knowledge, Lexical Inferencing and Writing 185

fast swimming prey – this means that they had to be reptiles that lived in water – so what helped me was especially aqua – and then the text helped me.

From his TA protocol, it appears that the informant pays attention to 'aqua' meaning 'water', and the Re protocol confirms, first, that it is an interlingual cue stemming from Latin and, second, that he also sees a link between 'aqua' and the Danish word '*akvarium*' ('fish tank'). That contextual cues have been activated is revealed in the Re protocol, in which Mike spells out how he used a passage from the co-text to help him arrive at his proposal for word meaning. Moreover, he states in general terms that what helped him was the word 'aqua', as well as the text. In other words, the informant's use of advanced processing – that is, top-ruled processing with integration of a central linguistic cue – results in a proposal that achieves a high level of inferencing success, and the informant demonstrates a high level of adaptability by using the optimal processing type for a word with potential linguistic cues to meaning. His ability to activate *intralingual cues,* reflected in the figure of 69 per cent, is much higher than the L1 figures found for the two other informants, which tallies with his extremely high L1 scores for both vocabulary size and lexical organization.

Turning to L2 inferencing, we pay particular attention to Mike's low level of adaptability as part of the explanation for the L1–L2 differences described above. His L2 protocols show that, in relation to target words with potential linguistic cues to meaning, he often uses either pure top processing – depending exclusively on contextual cues to meaning – or top-ruled processing with activation but no integration of linguistic cues. Considering his rather high scores on the vocabulary size test, we wonder why he does not spot relevant linguistic cues such as, for instance, the verb 'cure' for the target word 'curative'. Looking for potential explanatory factors to this shortcoming, we note that his top-down approach tallies with the lower number of activated linguistic cues and the relatively lower word association score in the L2, with few low frequent associations given. We tentatively suggest that Mike may be aware that his lexical knowledge in L2 is weaker than in his L1 and, therefore, he adheres to the use of contextual cues, relying on his very advanced reading skills in the L2. Using pure top processing for words with linguistic cues is a potentially effective strategy, but it can only be regarded as a 'second best strategy', as it hardly ever leads to accurate guesses; that is, to a high level of lexical inferencing success. However, judging from Mike's verbal protocols, it does lead to approximate

186 *Vocabulary and Writing in L1 and L2*

guesses in quite a few cases, which may explain why the success measure does not drop as dramatically as the processing measures.

Let us finally illustrate the second approach adopted by Mike, which is top-ruled processing with activation but no integration of linguistic cues, as illustrated in Extract 5.4. The test word is 'indiscriminately' which appears in the following context about helping plants to grow (in translation): 'families were shown how to place animal dung in holes in the ground instead of spreading it **indiscriminately**'.

> **Extract 5.4 Mike, L2**
> TA the way the word is used here it probably just means spreading it pell-mell – – there is of course to discriminate and in – – then it is the opposite – it could mean in – something or other – but – it does not quite fit into the sentence – so I have to guess – I am not sure but I think this word means something about spreading something all over the place.

In this case, Mike activates relevant linguistic cues, the verb 'discriminate' and the prefix 'in-'. However, he seems to reject the latter cue, because it does not fit the context ('it does not quite fit into the sentence'), and his proposal for word meaning is based on the contextual cues that he had already spotted at the outset, as expressed initially in the phrase 'the way the word is used here'. This type of processing shares features with the pure top processing strategies discussed above. Unlike pure top processing, in this protocol we see activation of linguistic cues. This means that Mike has moved closer to being able to use advanced processing in the L2, in that he activates potential linguistic cues to meaning. However, he does not use advanced processing, which requires the individual's ability to integrate activated cues into the proposal for word meaning, thereby creating a synthesis. In the L1, Mike obtains high scores on the three hallmarks for quality lexical inferencing, indicating that his procedural skills, his declarative lexical knowledge and the interaction between them seem to be operative in the first language. However, for the L2, we suggest that he lacks one aspect of advanced processing; that is, the ability to let knowledge sources interact in a way that leads to the integration of linguistic cues. In his case, the ability to create a synthesis is less developed in the foreign language.

Peter: an example of a high level informant
As described above, Karen was rather weak in both languages, both in relation to measures for lexical inferencing and vocabulary size. In

comparison, Mike did well on the L1 tasks and performed less well on the L2 tasks. Our last informant, Peter, is an example of a Grade 10 informant who managed to do as well as the Grade 13 students on most of the lexical measures in both languages.

In relation to the three L1 measures selected as hallmarks of quality lexical inferencing, this informant obtained scores bordering on those of the average Grade 13 informant. As for L2 inferencing, the three inferencing measures are even closer to the Grade 13 means than for the L1 results. Almost similar figures for cue activation are found across the two languages and, again, we see that the L2 figures are slightly higher. Thus, Peter's lexical inferencing procedures in the L1 and the L2 are largely in balance.

Turning to the other lexical measures, the L1 vocabulary size score is below the mean for Grade 13 but above the mean for his peer group. In relation to frequency bands, the informant reached the cut-off point for frequency Level two, reflecting a vocabulary size far above the 5000-word level. Considering the WAT score, it is surprising that this inform-ant gets a lower score than the mean for Grade 13. One reason is that, in eight out of the 96 potential responses, the informant failed to write down a second association to the stimulus word. The comparatively low L1 WAT score may, therefore, be due to the large number of empty responses in combination with relatively few canonical and low fre-quent links, as well as a lower measure for lexical variation.

Turning to the L2 data, Peter's vocabulary size score is above the mean for Grade 13, and he managed to reach the cut-off point for frequency Level three, reflecting a vocabulary size in English of roughly 5000 words. The WAT score is also high, far above the Grade 13 mean and very close to the Grade 13 mean for L1. However, 5 per cent of the responses are still unqualified links (empty, ragbag or translations) but, compared with the L1 data, many more canonical links are given. The number of low frequent responses given is almost as high as for L1, and the measure for lexical variation is slightly higher for the L2 data. All in all, the result is a higher overall WAT score in the L2 compared with the L1; a result that closely mirrors the scores found for the L1 and L2 size measures.

In comparison with Karen and Mike, Peter is able to utilize advanced lexical inferencing procedures in both languages. The informant's high level of inferencing skills will, therefore, be illustrated exclusively by an example of his processing of an L2 test word with potential linguistic cues to meaning (see Extract 5.5). The target word is 'curative', appear-ing in a text about health and disease in the sentence: 'Of course doctors should be interested in the **curative** effect of medicine. '

188 *Vocabulary and Writing in L1 and L2*

Extract 5.5   Peter, L2

TA (The informant starts by reading the above sentence aloud) – I think this word curative is something like to cure I – I think the beginning of that cure and then it also says doctors and medicine and that must have something to do with the healing effect – yes it must be healing.

Re so curative – what helped me was the word and then also the text – much helped by cure from the beginning of the word.

In Extract 5.5, the protocol is very informative. In the think aloud, the intralingual cue, the verb 'cure', is activated, involving meaning reflections evident from the translation of this cue into Danish '*kurere*'. That contextual cues are used, is revealed in the utterance 'it also says doctors and medicine' and is supported by the retrospection. We see the proposal for word meaning, which is 'healing', as a result of top-ruled processing with integration of a central linguistic cue; in other words, an example of advanced processing. As for adaptability, Peter is rewarded for the use he makes of the word's potential linguistic cues and, because his result is a precise guess, this protocol extract reflects the learner's generally high level of lexical inferencing success. Off-hand, it is difficult to explain why Mike and Peter operate so differently in the L2, compared with their L1 inferencing procedures. Across the board, Mike does better on the L1 scores than Peter, but their reading scores in both languages are very similar. The exceptionally high scores for both learners are above the mean for Grade 13. However, a closer comparison of their results for lexical declarative knowledge may give a hint as to why Peter is able to make better use of his lexical inferencing skills in the foreign language. His L2 vocabulary size score is higher, and he manages to reach the cut-off point for frequency Level three, reflecting a vocabulary size of at least 5000 words. Moreover, his L2 word association score is, as noted earlier, well above the Grade 13 mean and close to the L1 mean for the Grade 13 group. Finally, his score for low frequent links in the word association task is much higher in L2 compared with that of Mike. All in all, this may explain why Peter is able to activate more linguistic cues in the L2 inferencing task and to make better use of them in lexical inferencing than can Mike.

Procedural skills versus declarative knowledge

We have seen that Mike and Peter are similar, in that they both demonstrate a high level of procedural skills in lexical inferencing, but they differ in this respect in relation to the two languages. Mike is clearly more capable in L1, whereas Peter demonstrates a similar level of procedural skills in both languages. For a tentative explanation of these different characteristics of the two informants, we shall look into the quality of their declarative lexical knowledge and link this to their figures for activation of *intralingual cues* while performing lexical inferencing. The rationale for linking quality of lexical knowledge with activation of cues is the assumption that a well-structured lexicon that includes links to many low frequent items gives the learner access to a large number of lexical cues for comprehension across a wide range of frequency bands in the mental lexicon.

In the case of Mike, we have seen that, in the L1, his scores for declarative lexical knowledge are extremely high with regard to both vocabulary size and lexical organization. For size, his score is above the mean for Grade 13, and he reaches Level three on the frequency bands. As to organization, his WAT score is far above the mean for Grade 13 and the quality of his lexical network is high. Notably, he is able to give very many responses in the form of low frequent links. His high level of declarative knowledge tallies with his procedural skills, and the link between the two types of knowledge is nicely reflected in his very high figure for activation of *intralingual cues*. For the L2, however, a different picture is found. The figures for low frequent links, as well as for the activation of *intralingual cues*, drop considerably from L1 to L2. We see this as one of the potential explanatory factors behind the difference in Mike's inferencing behaviour across the two languages.

The balance between the two languages observed for Peter in relation to inferencing results appears to be related to the fact that his declarative lexical knowledge is even higher in L2 than in L1. With regard to L2, his vocabulary size is very high and he reaches Level three in relation to frequency bands. As to lexical organization, his score for WAT is above the mean for Grade 13, and so is his high score for low frequent links; a result that corresponds with the finding that he has the highest figure for activation of *intralingual cues* among the three learners in L2.

Based on the detailed lexical profiles of the three Grade 10 learners, we have attempted to account for some relations between declarative lexical knowledge and the application of that knowledge in a lexical inferencing task that requires interaction between declarative and procedural knowledge. As discussed in Chapter 3, it is a common finding that L2 vocabulary size is closely linked to lexical inferencing success in L2. However, it has only recently been shown, in a study by Nassaji

190 *Vocabulary and Writing in L1 and L2*

(2004), that a relationship exists between depth of vocabulary knowledge, lexical inferencing success and strategy use. Based on our analysis and discussion of the three profiles, we tentatively propose that the quality of the lexical network, notably the degree to which it includes low frequent links, may have a strong bearing on an informant's inferencing procedures; for example, in relation to the ability to activate and utilize linguistic cues to meaning.

5.4 Summary and discussion of main findings

Our project design has enabled us to investigate several aspects of our learners' communicative competence, in both their native and foreign language. In this chapter, we have brought together the results from the individual studies and have attempted to trace how individual learners fare across the studies.

We shall highlight the most interesting findings. First, we shall deal with the cross-sectional results; second, with the within-subjects results with regard to the L1–L2 dimension; and, finally, address the question of the level of development found for individual learners across the three areas studied.

Performance across grade levels

In designing our study, we tried to ensure a wide range of ability by selecting our informants from three very different educational levels. Therefore, we included 13 to 14 year-olds from comprehensive schools, 16 to 17 year-olds from sixth-form colleges, and 20 to 22 year-olds from the first year of university education. We felt somewhat confident that we had identified three developmentally different groups. By and large, this was the case when comparing the performance of these groups in the foreign language, in which we found the expected significant differences between all three groups. However, in the first language no significant differences could be established between the two older groups on most counts. Despite great differences between the sixth-form and the university students with regard to age and educational experience, these two groups of students did not demonstrate significantly different levels of knowledge and skills in their L1. As pointed out in Chapter 4, the lack of difference between groups of very different educational and maturity levels is a finding that is not unique to this study. For the informants in our study, a ceiling level of development seems to have been reached at Grade 10 for their performance in their first language.

Performance across the first and the foreign language

Comparing our informants' performance across the two languages, we found, as expected, that the informants in all three studies did better in their native language than in their foreign language on most of the tasks, and in relation to most of the measures discussed, irrespective of educational level. The exception was the writing study, in which no significant differences were found between L1 and L2 for the Grade 7 and the Grade 13 groups with regard to their ability to carry out complex processing while writing. As discussed, the younger informants had not developed the ability to carry out the highly demanding procedure of advanced problem solving in the productive essay-writing task in any of the languages, whereas the university students had developed this ability to a similar level in their L1 and their L2. The intermediate learners from Grade 10 employed this advanced writing procedure to a lesser degree in the L2 task than in the L1 task. In comparison, it is surprising that the university students did not use advanced processing in the lexical inferencing task as frequently in the L2 as in the L1, as was the case in the writing task. Our tentative interpretation of this finding is that proficiency in the foreign language is a factor that plays a greater role in the task of lexical inferencing than in the writing task, as these tasks have been operationalized in this study. Our assumption at the outset of our study was that, in both tasks, we were tapping into comparable procedural knowledge. Below, we shall report further evidence as to why this was not the case.

Pertaining to the word association task, contrary to our expectations, we did find significant language differences across all three learner groups, although this task taps into organizational knowledge of extremely high frequent nouns and verbs. It is, of course, unsurprising that the younger learners, who have had fewer years of foreign language instruction and have had less exposure to the foreign language, managed to do far better in their L1 than their L2 on both the size and the network knowledge measure. However, it was not expected that even the sixth-form and university students did better in L1 than in L2 on this task. We take this finding as a clear demonstration of how slow and laborious the process of lexical network building is. Acquiring lexical items and developing an organizational structure in the lexical store is a demanding process, which requires considerable exposure to the target language – exposure that foreign language learners will always be in lack of compared with native speakers.

Level of development for individual learners across the three areas studied

Having exposed our informants to the many different tasks, we were curious to see how the individual learner performed across the tasks. Our first attempt at investigating this issue was the use of correlations. As discussed above, very few correlations were found across the studies. Therefore, some of the predicted correlations were not found, for instance, between the measures for complex processing in lexical inferencing and in writing. This finding underlines the assumption that, although procedural knowledge was at stake in both instances, the task demands and the way in which processes were analyzed in the two studies tapped into different types of procedures that were not directly comparable. As mentioned above, the lexical inferencing task is more closely dependent on the informants' level of lexical knowledge. This assumption was further supported by the correlations between the vocabulary size measures, on the one hand, and complex processing in lexical inferencing and in writing, on the other hand. Vocabulary size showed moderate to high correlation with lexical inferencing, but not with writing procedures. In other words, in our study, vocabulary size was found to be crucial for lexical inferencing processes and also for lexical inferencing success. The latter finding corroborates previous research findings that a certain threshold level of L2 vocabulary knowledge is essential for efficient language use in the target language.

Our second attempt at tracing the development of individual learners across the areas studied was to draw up ability profiles. This was done in relation to three areas of ability: one in relation to the learners' procedural skills (writing and lexical inferencing); another with regard to their declarative lexical knowledge (size and depth); and a third pertaining to the two product measures (inferencing success and the language control score of the essay assessments). The reason for setting up these profiles was that we wished to investigate how far individual informants had developed their knowledge and skills of the various aspects studied in the two languages. For a majority of Grade 7 and university students, similar levels of abilities had been reached in the three areas investigated. For the former group, the ability levels were low and, for the latter group, ability levels were high across all three areas. That the group of Grade 10 informants is a mixed ability group, was again demonstrated, in that the majority of these informants did not show similar levels of abilities with regard to procedural and declarative knowledge, and with regard to producing successful products. For these students, we saw a mixture of ability profiles with no predictable developmental patterns.

Since correlations were most in evidence with regard to lexical knowledge, our third attempt at investigating individual learner development was to set up lexical profiles for three Grade 10 learners. These profiles clearly illustrated the pronounced intra-learner and inter-learner variability found in the Grade 10 data. The weak Grade 10 informant shared many developmental features with the Grade 7 informants, in both languages. The intermediate learner was on his way in his L1 but still failed to apply his skills to the foreign language tasks. Finally, the advanced Grade 10 informant obtained a more balanced result in the two languages and was able to do as well on most of the lexical tasks as many of the older university students. The lexical profiles also led us to hypothesize that network knowledge might play a crucial role with regard to lexical inferencing procedures, as reflected in the link between the informants' use of intralingual cues and their generation of low frequent links in the word association task. This finding, in turn, might help explain why we found a significant difference between the results on the word association tasks in L1 and L2 for Grade 10 and the university students; a difference that we had not expected, since the starting points for the associations were high frequent nouns and verbs. In other words, despite the high frequent prompting words in the association tasks, the older students had a tendency to supply low frequent links and, of course, they were better able to do so in their first language.

In our study of the same learners' performance in the first and the foreign language on a number of tasks, we have shown that individual learners do better in their L1 than in their L2. However, when using means for the whole group as yardsticks, we also found that, relatively speaking, most informants perform at similar levels in the two languages across the skills studied. In other words, if students perform well in L1, they also do so in L2 and, if they obtain positive results with regard to one area studied, they do so too for the other areas. In cases where students did not perform at similar levels across the areas studied, we had expected to find some patterns of development that tallied with common notions of which abilities are mastered prior to other abilities. However, we did not consistently find that, for instance, receptive skills were more developed than productive skills, or that declarative knowledge was more developed than procedural knowledge. Rather, our findings show that, in these cases, the developmental routes individual learners took were very different.

Notes

1 The measure for L1 reading was used as a general proficiency measure to select the informants included in the study, so it is only relevant to make comparisons between the L2 reading scores and a range of L2 measures.
2 The same applies to the L1 data, apart from Grade 10 (.684, p < .001).
3 The combination of two lower range and two upper range scores was allotted to the mid-section. This combination applies to one informant in Table 5.4. The combination of one upper, one mid- and two lower range scores was also placed in the mid-section, applying to one student in Table 5.4 and one in Table 5.5.
4 As outlined in Chapter 3 (see Section 3.2.2.1 on Knowledge Sources), the category of 'Linguistic cues' is sub-divided into two sub-categories: 'Intralingual' and 'Interlingual'. For the present purpose, we have chosen to quote figures based exclusively on the informants' use of intralingual cues; that is, the number of activated Danish linguistic cues in relation to the L1 inferencing task, and the number of English linguistic cues for the L2 task. The reason for doing so is to make this inferencing measure comparable with the word association measure, for which the informants are required to provide intralingual responses, thus ensuring that we compare measures within the same language.

6
Implications for Research and Instruction

In this book, we have presented a multifaceted project in which the same informants were exposed to a number of tasks in both their first and their foreign language. In Chapter 1, we detailed the overall design of our study and, in Chapters 2, 3 and 4, the studies of lexical knowledge, lexical inferencing, and writing were dealt with, respectively. In Chapter 5, we traced the development of individual learners across the tasks from the three main areas studied. In this chapter, we shall round off our discussions by summing up what we have learnt with regard to research design, detailing what we would do were we given a second chance. Finally, with the caveat that instruction has not been the focus of our study, we shall draw attention to insights from our investigation that might be of interest in the context of language teaching.

6.1   Research implications

In order to investigate our informants' performance in L1 and L2, it was essential to compare like with like. Therefore, we gave the same types of tasks in the two languages within all three studies. In addition, to mini-mize the number of confounding variables, the exact same tasks were administered across the three grade levels. As detailed in Section 5.2.5, the fact that we had to give identical tasks to informants of very differ-ent age and educational levels, resulted either in tasks that were too difficult for the younger students or that were insufficiently taxing for the older students, the lexical inferencing and the lexical network tasks being cases in point, respectively. Future research in lexical inferencing should ensure that the design allows for tasks that become progressively more demanding and, thus, enable young students to demonstrate their true abilities in the first parts of the tasks, while still preserving the

196 *Vocabulary and Writing in L1 and L2*

opportunity for more able young pupils to show their superior abilities compared with their peers. With respect to lexical network tasks, such a design would ensure that older students would be given the opportunity to demonstrate the type of network knowledge they might have, not only in relation to high, but also to low frequent words. At the same time, the design would allow the young pupils to reveal the level of their network knowledge of the frequent words that they do have in their vocabulary.

Another aspect of our research design relates to our informants' procedural skills. This was investigated with regard to both the lexical inferencing and writing tasks and, therefore, we expected to see some connection between the levels of procedural skills revealed in the two tasks for the same individuals. As reported in Chapter 5, we found no correlations between the results of these two tasks. We attributed this to the fact that the lexical inferencing task is a more closed task, with preset problems that the informants have to solve, whereas the writing task is an open task, in which the informants themselves define the issues to which they attend. In addition, the lack of correlation might also be a function of the difference in the sensitivity of the tasks to the learners' level of declarative lexical knowledge, which is crucial for lexical inferencing but less so for writing. There is no doubt that an investigation of our informants' reading processes would have been a better candidate for comparing the receptive and productive processes of our informants. This type of data was, in fact, envisaged in our original research design, from which it had to be omitted, partly for financial reasons. Reading process data from the same informants would, no doubt, have been an asset, not only with regard to the receptive/productive distinction, but also in connection with the relationship between reading and lexical inferencing.

With regard to the relationship between declarative and procedural knowledge, we found a close relationship between declarative lexical knowledge and processing in lexical inferencing, but not in writing. However, our qualitative analysis of the writing protocols of a few learners indicated that these learners did, in fact, work with their language in qualitatively different ways, a feature not covered by the analytical category *attention to language*. The analysis of three learners showed that, when dealing with language problems, the more able learners tended to upgrade their expressions by not settling for their first impulse, and the less able learners used compensation, either by accepting an expression they were not happy with or by avoiding the issue altogether. Thus, an analytical taxonomy that captures the distinction between compensatory and upgrading problem solving applied by student writers to language issues might give results that would show a closer correlation between writing and declarative lexical knowledge. We base this on the assumption that learners who have a well-developed lexical network will be in possession of the type of knowledge needed for performing upgrading of their language, since they have more access routes to related words. Naturally, we would have stood a better chance of seeing a relationship between declarative and procedural knowledge in writing, had we included other aspects of communicative competence than our informants' lexical knowledge in our design; that is, more aspects of their linguistic knowledge and their discourse knowledge. Moreover, the learners' declarative knowledge with regard to lexical network knowledge only correlated with lexical inferencing for Grade 7. We attribute the lack of correlation for the two older informant groups to differences in task demands. The lexical inferencing task requires that the target words are *unknown* to all informants, including the university group, which meant that exclusively low frequent words were included as target words in this task. The lexical network tasks require the opposite, in that, all stimulus words must be *known* to students of all grade levels. In other words, a better balance between high frequent and low frequent words in the lexical network tasks might have given different results with regard to correlations between lexical inferencing procedures and lexical network knowledge for the two older groups.

Finally, we have talked about development partly based on cross-sectional findings and found that, in the first language, the two older groups obtained results that were not statistically different on a number of the measures investigated. This led us to the conclusion that, for the learners of this study, a ceiling level of development seems to be reached at the Grade 10 level. However, development should, of course, be investigated in a longitudinal rather than a cross-sectional design. We did collect data from the same Grade 7 and Grade 10 informants on whom we report in this book after an interval of about 18 months. However, these data could not be analyzed in time for this publication. Only such longitudinal data will reveal the degree to which individual Grade 10 learners change or remain at the same level and, hence, give a better indication of whether or not a ceiling level has, in fact, been reached by these learners in their L1.

In sum, in future research employing a cross-sectional and multi-task design, a progression in demands should be an inherent feature of the tasks employed in the study, and the methods of analysis applied to various sub-studies should be coordinated to ensure that the

198   *Vocabulary and Writing in L1 and L2*

analytical categories capture comparable features. Finally, analyses of development across grade levels should be supplemented with analyses of longitudinal data.

6.2   Perspectives on instruction

Our discussion of perspectives on instruction is based on the conviction that one of the important knowledge sources for language teachers is the study of how learners manage the tasks they have to perform in the foreign language. Although teachers are surrounded by learners performing in the foreign language in their classrooms and give feedback on many written products, they do not often have the time and opportunity to collect and systematically analyze learner data. Such data can help them understand what their students are actually doing and thinking, for instance, while reading or writing in the foreign language. The research context has allowed us to do just that but, as mentioned, we have not studied our informants in an instructional setting.

In the following, we shall single out the findings from our three studies that throw light on the L1–L2 dimension, and consider possible implications for teaching. Since the many verbal protocols have revealed that students who reflect extensively while working on the tasks perform better than those who do not, the approach we recommend is awareness raising about language and processes; that is, developing students' meta-communicative awareness of strategies in production and reception. This recommendation tallies well with the suggestions put forward by Wolff (1994) in his discussion of procedural knowledge (see Chapter 1, Section 1.8.1). He argues that lack of explicit awareness of L1 procedures, and of the transferability of skills from L1 to L2, impedes L2 learners when faced with real life tasks in the foreign language. Language teachers should therefore direct students' attention to their own production and reception processes; for instance, by introducing introspective procedures and group activities that engage learners in demanding task types. In this way, their own processing behaviour is made explicit in the verbal interaction between the learners.

Starting with *writing skills*, we shall first mention the findings of our study to be considered here. As to procedural knowledge, we have shown how important it is that students master complex processing and, with regard to the L1–L2 dimension, we have seen that complex processing must be developed in the L1 before it can be applied to the L2. Thus, we saw that the Grade 7 informants had not yet developed this ability in L1 and, hence, had few procedural skills to transfer to L2. For

Grade 10 informants, who had the skills in L1, it was found that having to operate in an L2 context had a constraining effect on their L2 processes, and only the university students had achieved the same high level of writing skills in both languages. We, therefore, suggest that, when focusing on writing, teachers should address the question: Does the problem for a particular student in their class appear to be primarily a writing problem or a language problem? Answering this question is regarded as an important first step in the teacher's planning process, since it provides the basis for deciding which type of potentially fruitful feedback and guidance of the student that is to follow. From our perspective, there can be no doubt that teaching should emphasize processes and, as mentioned above, awareness raising is considered an approach that lends itself well to the teaching of procedural knowledge.

Naturally, improvement of the foreign language should also be addressed in writing instruction. In our qualitative analyses of three learners, a distinction was made between upgrading and compensation with regard to the students' language-related problem solving. We found that a distinctive feature of problem solving that resulted in a good essay was that it included upgrading rather than compensation with regard to attention to language, thus emphasizing that a writing task not only poses a challenge to the learners' processing, but also to their handling of language problems.

Has our writing study anything to offer with regard to the teaching of different groups of school learners? For the younger learners, process instruction should be in focus, and we see close cooperation between the foreign language and the mother tongue teacher as an ideal way to ensure that students who are poor writers in L1 are encouraged to improve their writing in both languages. Such teaching could include raising awareness about writing processes in L1, which are developed first. Thus, building L2 teaching on the foundation laid in mother tongue teaching seems, to us, a fruitful approach. For the older learners, instruction should focus on language development in order to enable these learners to apply their L1 writing skills to L2 writing. In our qualitative analysis, it was evident that, during the writing process in both L1 and L2, some students quickly settle for a vague expression rather than engaging in a keen search for the precise word. They need to be challenged, and a focus-on-form approach (for instance, Doughty and Williams, 1998) that highlights the importance of lexical precision might work well in both first and foreign language teaching. Introducing examples of good writing practice to the classroom in the

200 *Vocabulary and Writing in L1 and L2*

form of verbal protocols might be one way of raising students' awareness, not only of writing processes, but also of how language is addressed during writing.

Moreover, the study of our informants' writing skills corroborates the teaching recommendations put forward in other studies, suggesting that writing in the foreign language is a task that, by its very nature, ensures that students focus on form. In other words, it caters for the noticing dimension of Swain's output hypothesis (Swain, 1995). Thus, writing tasks not only offer opportunities for learners to improve their writing skills, but also their command of the foreign language.

Turning to *lexical inferencing*, for procedural knowledge, it was found that mastering complex processing is extremely important and that, as for writing, this ability must be developed in L1 before it can be applied in an L2 context. Even for our university students, their L2 processing was not at the same high level as their L1 processing. Looking at the product of our learners' inferencing attempts – that is, the quality of their word guesses – we see a similar pattern; namely, that the level of inferencing success is higher in the L1 than in the L2. Finally, it was found that, in relation to both complex processing and inferencing success, students' L2 lexical knowledge base was crucial for their L2 performance.

Due to the nature of lexical inferencing, which requires close interaction between procedural knowledge and declarative lexical knowledge, there can be no doubt that instruction should focus on developing both types of knowledge. However, it may be important for the teacher to take our findings with regard to the different grade levels into account. The young students at the basic level need to have acquired processing skills in the first language before this ability can be transferred to the foreign language and, since good word guessing strategies share many features with good reading strategies, we suggest that they are taught in combination. Linking the two through awareness-raising activities is expected to enhance learners' understanding of the common principles of interactive processing in reading and lexical inferencing. With regard to students at the higher levels, focus should be shifted to intensive teaching of breadth, and especially depth, of vocabulary knowledge. This recommendation is supported by insights from our qualitative analyses, which suggest a close relationship between a lexical network characterized by many low frequent links and our learners' ability to use intralinguistic cues to meaning in lexical inferencing.

In our view, a fruitful approach to the teaching of procedural knowledge is raising students' awareness of what constitutes effective processing. For instance, with regard to word guessing strategies, an example of the kind of awareness-raising activity that we find useful is a pair work task, in which students are supplied with learner data and are instructed to identify particular features in these data, while reflecting and discussing with their partner. These data could be drawn from verbal protocols of the type used in our lexical inferencing study, which, in our experience, provide a good basis for a discussion of effective and ineffective word guessing strategies. Support for a similar approach that allows students to investigate their own processes and decide on which strategies work for them comes from a study of reading instruction by Auerbach and Paxton (1997).

Pertaining to *lexical knowledge*, we found that students at all grade levels did better with regard to size and depth of vocabulary knowledge in L1 than in L2. For our cross-sectional data, we found significant differences between all three grade levels for size in L2 but, for network knowledge, only the Grade 7 group differed from the other two groups. Our description of the lexical profiles of three learners, however, indicated that older students also differ in the quality of their network knowledge as a function of the number of low frequent links included in their associations.

Similar to our recommendations for the teaching of procedural knowledge, we suggest, in view of our findings, that instruction in declarative lexical knowledge should also be addressed in first language instruction. This suggestion is supported by our findings with regard to the correlations found between the L1 and L2 scores in the lexical study (see Section 2.7) and the developmental profiles, which indicated that informants who have a large and well-structured vocabulary in L1 also tend to belong to the group with a well-developed vocabulary in L2. Moreover, our impressions from the writing protocols, in which we observe that students who upgrade their expressions in L1 also do so in their L2, lend further support to this. In other words, not all learners seem successful in acquiring a large and well-structured vocabulary in their L1 through implicit instruction based on extensive reading. For these disadvantaged learners, network building activities typically developed for L2 instruction – for example, sorting and gradation tasks, which direct learners' attention to relations between lexical items – might also be very useful in first language teaching, and could thus serve as an example of ideas from foreign language teaching that could be taken up by all language teachers.

Moreover, the fact that, even for the university students, we found a significant difference between their lexical network in L1 and L2 suggests

202 *Vocabulary and Writing in L1 and L2*

that the network building process proceeds very slowly, as suggested by Aitchison (1987) for L1 acquisition and by Greidanus and her colleagues (2001, 2004, 2005) for L2 learners. Previous studies on receptive network knowledge have shown that non-native speakers lag behind native speakers, but the present study, which measures L1 and L2 for the same learners, documents this on both receptive and productive tasks that tap into knowledge of very high frequent items. Many of the Grade 7 informants found it difficult to supply an associative link in L2, which suggests that explicit vocabulary training in the foreign language classroom must first ensure development of their vocabulary in terms of size, but this should be supplemented with work with network tasks that aim at developing links between the targeted vocabulary items. The present study documents that many of the Grade 10 and Grade 13 students do not show stability in their mastery of the high frequency bands. The older informants must therefore be encouraged to keep developing their vocabulary, both in terms of consolidating their basic vocabulary, and also in terms of acquiring more low frequent items. The findings in this study thus suggest that the older learners may also benefit from more systematic vocabulary instruction in line with some of the vocabulary enhancement activities outlined by Paribakht and Wesche (1996) within the framework of a reading based approach. This could be achieved by including task types that not only aim at increasing learners' vocabulary size, but which also support the development of their network knowledge.

Based on our findings, we have argued that it appears fruitful to view foreign language development as a process that is rooted in and builds on what students bring with them from mother tongue teaching. Therefore, we have pointed to the potential advantages of intensifying cooperation between mother tongue teaching and foreign language teaching. Moreover, we have stressed that instruction should include awareness-raising activities, because such activities might make students aware of the close relationship between procedural skills and declarative knowledge.

Appendices

A.1 Statistics

A.1.1 Description of the statistical procedures

The same types of statistical analyses were used in the studies of declarative lexical knowledge (Chapter 2), lexical inferencing (Chapter 3) and writing (Chapter 4).

For the *within-subjects data*, comparing L1 and L2, two types of analyses were carried out. For the first analysis, we used the GLM Repeated Measures procedure of SPSS in mixed 2 (L1 vs L2) × 3 (G.7 and G.10 and G.13) ANOVAS. This procedure was used for each variable in the respective studies for all grade levels combined. Only the variables that conformed to the demands of this procedure were included in the second type of analysis. For the second type of analysis, the repeated-measures procedure was used for each variable for each grade level separately in one-way (two levels) within-subjects ANOVAs. The results obtained from the second type of analysis are the ones reported in Chapters 2, 3 and 4.

For the *between-subjects* data, comparing the three grade levels, the data were subjected to one-way (three levels: G.7 and G.10 and G.13) between-subjects ANOVAs. Homogeneity of variance was demonstrated by the Levene's test and many of our variables lived up to the test. In these cases, for the subsequent post hoc comparisons, Tukey's HSD test with an α level of 0.05 was used. For the variables for which homogeneity of variance could not be assumed, we used the non-parametric Kruskal–Wallis procedure and, for the subsequent post hoc comparisons, in these cases, the Tamhane test had to be used.

A.1.2 Statistical details for Chapter 4

Results for the within-subjects data, comparing L1 and L2

Attention to aspects of writing

Language:
ANOVA: $p < .001$; levels (G.7: F $(1, 19) = 43.743$; G.10: F $(1, 19) = 50.919$); $p < .176$; level G.13: F $(1, 19) = 1.974$

Ideas:
ANOVA: $p < .667$; level G.7: F $(1, 19) = .191$; $p < .556$; level G.10: F $(1, 19) = .398$; $p < .868$; level G.13: F $(1, 19) = .029$

204   *Appendices*

Discourse:
ANOVA: p < .010; level G.7: F (1, 19) = 8.256; p < .001; level G.10:
F (1, 19) = 17.799; p < .0.56; level G.13: F (1, 19) = 4.131

Procedure:
ANOVA: p < .018; level G.7: F (1, 19) = 6.693; p < .069; level G.10:
F (1, 19) = 3.730; p < .821; level G.13: F (1, 19) = .052

Concurrent attention:
ANOVA: p < .001; level G.7: F (1, 19) = 40.696; p < .036; level G.10:
F (1, 19) = 5.079; p < .405; level G.13: F (1, 19) = .727

Problem solving:
No problem:
ANOVA: p < .001; level G.7: F (1, 19) = 36.178; p < .002; level G.10:
F (1, 19) = 12.519; p < .437; level G.13: F (1, 19) = .629

Problem identification:
ANOVA: p < .001; levels (G.7: F (1, 19) = 37.423; G.13: F (1, 19) = 14.454);
p < .002; level G.10: F (1, 19) = 12.237

Problem solved quickly:
ANOVA: p < .003; level G.7: F (1, 19) = 11.745; p < .006; level G.10:
F (1, 19) = 9.477; p < .795; level G.13: F (1, 19) = .070

Heuristic searches with resolution:
ANOVA: p < .181; level G.7: F (1, 19) = 1.926; p < .004; level G.10:
F (1, 19) = 10.960; p < .220; level G.13: F (1, 19) = 1.609

Heuristic searches with no resolution:
ANOVA: p < .374; level G.7: F (1, 19) = .827; p < .328; level G.10:
F (1, 19) = 1.007; p < .607; level G.13: F (1, 19) = .273

Essay assessments:
TOEFL:
ANOVA: p < .001; levels (G.7: F (1, 19) = 51.111; G.10: F (1, 19) = 17.127);
p < .006; level G.13: F (1, 19) = 9.710

Ideas and arguments:
ANOVA: p < .001; level G.7: F (1, 19) = 24.009; p < .002; level G.10:
F (1, 19) = 13.700; p < .059; level G.13: F (1, 19) = 4.043

Rhetorical features:
ANOVA: p < .001; level G.7: F (1, 19) = 19.687; p < .020; level G.10:
F (1, 19) = 6.423; p < .151; level G.13: F (1, 19) = 2.240

Language control:
ANOVA: p < .001; levels (G.7: F (1, 19) = 42.164; level G.10: F (1, 19) = 47.598);
p < .004; level G.13: F (1, 19) = 10.826

Appendices 205

Results for the between-subjects data, comparing across grade levels

Variables for which no differences could be established between any of the grade levels in the post hoc tests are not reported below.

Attention to aspects of writing in L1

Discourse:
G.7 vs G.13 – Tukey: p < .030

Ideas:
G.7 vs G.13 – Tukey: p < .015

Procedure:
G.7 vs G.10 – Tukey: p < .006; G.7 vs G.13 – Tukey: p < .001

Concurrent attention:
G.7 vs G.10 – Tukey: p < .001; G.7 vs G.13 – Tukey: p < .001

Problem solving in L1

No problem:
G.7 vs G.10 – Tukey: p < .002; G.7 vs G.13 – Tukey: p < .001

Problem identification:
G.7 vs G.13 – Tukey: p < .003

Heuristic searches with resolution:
G.7 vs G.10 – Tukey: p < .001; G.7 vs G.13 – Tukey: p < .001

Essay assessments in L1

TOEFL:
G.7 vs G.10 – Tukey: p < .001; G.7 vs G.13 – Tukey: p < .001

Ideas and arguments:
G.7 vs G.10 – Tukey: p < .001; G.7 vs G.13 – Tukey: p < .001

Rhetorical features:
G.7 vs G.10 – Tukey: p < .001; G.7 vs G.13 – Tukey: p < .001

Language control:
G.7 vs G.10 – Tukey: p < .001; G.7 vs G.13 – Tukey: p < .001

Attention to aspects of writing in L2

Language:
G.7 vs G.13 – Tukey: p < .021

Discourse:
G.7 vs G.10 – Tukey: p < .038; G.7 vs G.13 – Tukey: p < .001

206 *Appendices*

Ideas:
G.7 vs G.13 – Tukey: p < .049

Procedure:
G.7 vs G.13 – Tukey: p < .023

Problem solving in L2
Problem identification:
G.7 vs G.10 – Tamhane: p < .045: G.7 vs G.13 – Tamhane: p < .001

Heuristic searches with resolution:
G.7 vs G.10 – Tukey: p < .010; G.7 vs G.13 – Tukey: p < .001; G.10 vs G.13 – Tukey: p < .022

Essay Assessments in L2
TOEFL:
G.7 vs G.10 – Tukey: p < .001; G.7 vs G.13 – Tukey: p < .001

Ideas and arguments:
G.7 vs G.10 – Tukey: p < .001; G.7 vs G.13 – Tukey: p < .001

Rhetorical features:
G.7 vs G.10 – Tukey: p < .001; G.7 vs G.13 – Tukey: p < .001

Language control:
G.7 vs G.10 – Tukey: p < .001; G.7 vs G.13 – Tukey: p < .000; G.10 vs G.13 – Tukey: p < .026

A.2 Description of response types in the word association data

Code	Type	Definition and examples
E	Empty	No response is given, but SW is known
R	Repetition	SW is repeated ('beautiful' triggers 'beautiful')
T	Translation	The response is a translation of SW or a response given in the native language ('mountain' triggers '*vulkan*')
RB	Rag bag	The response is impossible to code because it is indecipherable, or it is difficult to decide whether a Danish and English response has been given ('sweet' triggers '*rinze*'; 'soldier' triggers '*Thomas*')
F	Form-related	The response mirrors formal features of SW ('slow' triggers 'snow')
CH	Chaining	The response is related to previous responses which have been given and not to SW (stimulus: 'foot' triggers response 1 'soldier' which triggers response 2 'helicopter')

Code	Type	Definition and examples
CAH CAL	High or low frequent canonical links	The response is a semantically related link and it is one of the five most frequent responses given by our baseline informants (CAH: 'short' triggers 'long'; CAL: 'sour' triggers 'acid')
OSH OSL	High or low frequent, other semantically related links	The response is a semantically related link but it is NOT one of the five most frequent responses given by our baseline informants (OSH: 'short' triggers 'man'; OSL: 'short' triggers 'dwarf')

Key: SW = the stimulus word

A.3 Lexical inferencing

A.3.1 Think-aloud instructions (translated from the Danish original)

(Prior to giving the instructions below, the instructor had shown the informants two examples of how the meaning of words could be inferred. Without saying so explicitly, the instructor made use of cues from the main categories of cue types.)

Now you have seen a few examples, and in a moment it is your turn. You should begin thinking aloud as soon as you turn on the tape recorder. **It is very important that you say out loud everything that occurs to you; all the ideas you have concerning the meaning of a particular word in this context. Say it out loud even if you are not sure if it is correct or if it is a good proposal. You simply need to offer YOUR proposal.**

The oldest of you who might know a couple of the words printed in bold can say the following on the tape: 'I know this word; it means this and that.'

The youngest of you will probably feel that the words are extremely difficult – and yes, the words are really strange! But do not give up – TRY! Take up the challenge!

We need to hear all your thoughts about and suggestions for how you find the meaning of **the words that are printed in bold**. You might consider several different suggestions for the meaning of a word, but you need to end by suggesting one meaning. So **for each word** we ask you to **end up saying**: 'So **I think the word means: xxxxx.'** I will write it on the blackboard so you can remember it.

Any questions?

Now you may turn the page, start the tape recorder and start solving the task. You have 32 minutes to solve the entire task with 5 texts.

208 *Appendices*

A.3.2 The L2 lexical inferencing task

Introductory note: the task includes five short texts of which three are quoted below.

ON HEALTH IN THE RICH WORLD AND IN THE POOR

An American journalist, Dorothy Thompson, criticizes the rich world's health programmes in the poor world. She writes about her trip to Africa, where she got food poisoning and her friend got malaria:

'The town is very dirty. All the people are hot, they have dust between their toes, and there is a strong smell of **sewage** in the air. We both fell ill, and my friend had **bouts** of diarrhoea. At ten o'clock in the morning, I got frightened and took her to the only private hospital in town. After we had been treated by a doctor, we decided to take the next plane home.

When we came back to the States, we thought a lot about our reaction to this meeting with a poor country. In the rich world, we often forget how important it is to have money for food and clean water to drink. In the poor world, people are killed by the conditions they live under, the **squalor** and the lack of food and money. Of course doctors should be interested in the **curative** effect of medicine, but it is even more important that they analyze why people get the disease in the first place.

In the rich world, many diseases are caused by **affluence**. Other diseases are the result of pollution. Try to imagine the typical American worker on his deathbed: every cell **permeated** with such things as chemicals and radioactive materials. Such symptoms are true signs of an unhealthy world.'

ON THE ZULU PEOPLE

At the beginning of the 19th century, the Zulu clans of South Africa all belonged to the Zulu nation. But later the Zulu empire fell apart. It started with **dissension** among the blacks themselves and ended in conflicts with the whites.

Today there are still many problems for the Zulu people, including health problems. A serious health problem is malnutrition, and there are many **contributory** causes to this. First of all the Zulus do not get the right kind of food that can give **sustenance** to the body. Other causes are diseases such as tuberculosis. Before the whites came, the Zulus grew different kinds of corn, with millet being **prevalent**. Today the Zulus mainly get maize cooked in many different ways, as well as dried beans, **negligible** amounts of milk and now and then some meat.

To help the Zulus, a food programme was set up. One of the important principles of this was to make the best of what you had, with for example tomatoes and green peppers. In order to help the plants to grow, families were shown how to place animal dung in holes in the ground instead of spreading it **indiscriminately**. All household **refuse** could be placed directly in these holes and would help to produce better vegetables.

Appendices 209

ON REACHING THE SOUTH POLE

The first European explorers who reached the poles risked their lives in the masses of snow, and some of them never came back. Robert Scott from England set out to find the South Pole. Scott and four of his men reached the pole on January 18th 1912, but they were awfully disappointed to find out that Roald Amundsen had found the pole one month earlier.

The weather on Scott's return journey was extremely bad. They had too little food left for the five of them and for the dogs pulling the sledges. So in order to help the others, one of the men decided to crawl out of the tent into a snowstorm, which he knew would kill him. But what happened was that later the other men were hit by another storm that lasted for days. With quiet **fortitude** they waited for death in the tent. Later in the year of 1912, other explorers found the tent and the frozen bodies, as well as Scott's diaries and **copious** notes with much important information.

Today many things are easier because of modern ships and helicopters. But even if explorers of the pole have better clothing than Scott, they have to endure the low **ambient** temperatures, and the dogs, which are still needed, can be as **recalcitrant** as ever.

What Scott discovered has been developed by others. Today, scientists are working on the **undergirding** of theories about the South Pole area as well as on the **dissemination** of that knowledge.

A.3.3 Description of the interscorer procedure for lexical inferencing

The calculations of interscorer reliability are based on nine informants; that is, 10 per cent of the informant population. Three informants were selected from each educational level. From the Grade 7 group, we chose two informants with the lowest scores on the L1 reading test to be sure that this level was well represented. Correspondingly, we chose two high proficiency informants from the top level (the Grade 13 group) in order to have the highest level well represented. We chose informants from the Grade 10 level randomly, regardless of proficiency. The informants were each analyzed for: (1) knowledge sources; (2) processing types; and (3) inferencing success by two separate researchers, and their results were compared.

The calculation of interscorer reliability *for knowledge sources* was done in the following way: each attempt to guess one of the thirty test words was analyzed for the different types of knowledge sources used. Often, several analytical categories were allotted to each instance of word guessing. Interscorer reliability was calculated for each word as follows: the number of knowledge sources agreed on by the two researchers was divided by the mean number of sources (the identified number of knowledge sources divided by two). The scores for each word were added up and divided by the number of valid items for each informant, and the average score for all nine informants was calculated.

210 *Appendices*

Table A.3.1 Interscorer reliability

Aspect	L1		L2	
	Interscorer reliability	Valid items	Interscorer reliability	Valid items
Knowledge sources	82.23 %	269	82.14 %	254
Processing types	.87	241	.91	210
Inferencing success	.80	260	.74	235

A different method was used for the calculations of interscorer reliability for processing types and inferencing success, since each item only received one coding. The formula used for these aspects was Cohen's Kappa.

The results of these calculations and the number of valid items for each calculations are repeated in Table A.3.1.

A.4 Writing

A.4.1 Writing prompts

1 Do you agree or disagree with the following statement? Telephones and email have made communication between people less personal.

You are writing to somebody who disagrees with you. Try to win the reader over to your point of view. Use specific reasons and examples to support your opinion.

2 Some people say that advertising makes us buy things we really do not need. Others say that advertisements tell us about new products that may make our lives better. Which viewpoint do you agree with?

You are writing to somebody who disagrees with you. Try to win the reader over to your point of view. Use specific reasons and examples to support your position.

3 In some countries, people are no longer allowed to smoke in many public places and office buildings. Do you think this is a good rule or a bad rule?

You are writing to somebody who disagrees with you. Try to win the reader over to your point of view. Use specific reasons and details to support your position.

4 Do you agree or disagree with the following statement? Television has destroyed communication among friends and family.

You are writing to somebody who disagrees with you. Try to win the reader over to your point of view. Use specific reasons and examples to support your opinion.

Appendices   211

A.4.2   Transcription conventions for verbal protocols in the writing study

The coding system covers the following categories:

- * * = actual writing sequences
- < > = reading aloud of already produced text or the writing prompt
- << >> = reading aloud by translating into L1
- – – = comments/verbalization of thinking
- { } = inaudible, or partly inaudible, portions of protocol (if partly audible, text represents transcriber's best guess; if totally inaudible, blank space provides rough indication of length)
- [ ] = indicates: 1) coughing, laughing, sighing etc. 2) transcriber's comments to help clarify the transcription for the reader (for example, 'rising intonation' only in cases where the syntax leaves doubt), 'sound of annoyance', 'turns/ fiddles with paper', 'corrects something' etc. 3) time and interruptions.
- [[ ]] = the transcriber's queries
- § § = consultation of dictionary; within this category, the code _xxx_ is used to indicate comments – what is not coded within this category represents reading aloud of the dictionary
- *italics* is used to indicate emphasis
- ... or .... or ...... = rough indication of length of pause

All extracts from L1 protocols appear in translation. As to the extracts from L2 protocols, the verbalization in Danish has been translated. The parts of the L2 protocols that were originally in Danish are in italics.

A.4.3   Interscorer reliability for the analysis of the verbal protocols and for the assessment of the essays

For the analysis of the verbal protocols, two coders worked independently on the data. The procedure for obtaining interscorer reliability involved initial training on protocols from the pilot data. When a fair level of agreement on the pilot data had been reached, the analysis of the data proper was carried out. Interscorer reliability was calculated on ten percent of the data: six L1 protocols (two from each grade level) and six L2 protocols (two from each grade level). For identification of episodes, the disagreements were too few to mention. For aspects of writing, the agreement was 90 per cent on 2313 codings (range for the 12 protocols: 81–99 per cent). The percentage of agreement, $\Sigma POA/N$, was arrived at as follows: for each episode, the mean of aspects of writing detected by the two coders was normed by the number of aspects common to the two coders, yielding a percentage of agreement (POA) for each episode. The sum of the POAs, ΣPOA, was divided by the total number of episodes, N. For problem solving, the agreement was 0.79 Cohen's Kappa on 1369 decisions (range for the 12 protocols: Cohen's Kappa 0.75–0.95).

For the assessments of the essays, two raters were trained for the actual scoring of the essays. They were presented with model essays, taken from our pilot data,

212 *Appendices*

which served as illustrations of prototypical assessments on the various scales. Trial sessions using other essays from our pilot data were conducted to ensure that the raters performed as stipulated in the procedures. For the scoring, the raters worked over a period of three weeks independently on batches of essays, and met to compare their assessments; disagreements were resolved by discussion. A total number of 180 essays were assessed, 90 in each language, of which the results of 120 essays are included in this account. The raters were not informed about the individual writers' grade level, nor could they identify which L1 and L2 essays had been written by the same person: each essay was identified by a random number.

References

Aitchison, J., *Words in the Mind: An Introduction to the Mental Lexicon* (Oxford: Blackwell, 1987).

Adolphs, S. and Schmitt, N., 'Vocabulary Coverage According to Spoken Discourse Context', in P. Bogaards and B. Laufer (eds), *Vocabulary in a Second Language* (Amsterdam: John Benjamins, 2004), 39–49.

Akyel, A. and Kamisli, S., 'Composing in First and Second Languages. Possible Effects of EFL Writing Instruction', *Odense Working Papers in Language and Communication* 14 (1997), 69–105.

Albrechtsen, D., 'One Writer Two Languages: A Case Study of a 15-Year-Old Student's Writing Process in Danish and English', *International Journal of Applied Linguistics* 7(2), (1997), 223–50.

Arndt, V., 'Six Writers in Search of Texts: A Protocol-Based Study of L1 and L2 Writing', *ELT Journal* 41 (1987), 257–67.

Arnaud, P. and Savignon, S.J., 'Rare Words, Complex Lexical Units and the Advanced Learner', in C. Coady and T. Huckin (eds), *Second Language Vocabulary Acquisition* (Cambridge: Cambridge University Press, 1997), 157–73.

Auerbach, E.R. and Paxton, D., '"It's not the English Thing": Bringing Reading Research into the ESL Classroom', *TESOL Quarterly* 31(2), (1997), 237–61.

August, D. and Shanahan, T. (eds), *Developing Literacy in Second Language Learners* (Mahwah, NJ: Lawrence Erlbaum, 2006).

Bagger Nissen, H., *Ordassociationer på Dansk og Engelsk* (Unpublished MA Thesis from the Department of English, Germanic and Romance Studies, University of Copenhagen, 2002).

Bagger Nissen, H. and Henriksen, B., 'Word Class Influence on Word Association Test Results', *International Journal of Applied Linguistics* 16(3), (2006), 390–407.

Bensoussan, M. and Laufer, B., 'Lexical Guessing in Context in EFL Reading Comprehension', *Journal of Research in Reading* 7(1), (1984), 15–32.

Bereiter, C. and Scardamalia, M., *The Psychology of Written Composition* (Hillsdale, NJ: Lawrence Erlbaum Associates, 1987).

Bengeleil, F.B. and Paribakht, T.S., 'L2 Reading Proficiency and Lexical Inferencing by University EFL Learners', *The Canadian Modern Language Review* 61(2), (2004), 225–49.

Bergenholtz, H. *Dansk Frekvensordbog, Baseret på Danske Romaner, Ugeblade og Aviser 1987–1988* (København: Gad, 1992).

Bonk, W., 'Second Language Lexical Knowledge and Listening Comprehension', *International Journal of Listening* 14 (2000), 14–31.

Bossers, B. 'On Thresholds, Ceilings and Short-Circuits: The Relation between L1 Reading, L2 Reading and L2 knowledge', *AILA Review* 8 (1991), 45–60.

Brown, J.I., Fishco, V.V., and Hanna, E., *Nelson–Denny Reading Test. Forms G,* (Itasca: Riverside Publishing, 1993).

Brown, G. and Yule, G., *Discourse Analysis* (Cambridge: Cambridge University Press, 1983).

214   *References*

Case, R. *Intellectual Development: Birth to Adulthood* (Orlando, FL: Academic Press, 1985).

Chenoweth, N.A. and Hayes, J.R., 'Fluency in Writing: Generating Text in L1 and L2', *Written Communication* 18(1), (2001), 80–98.

Coady, J., Magoto, J., Hubbard, P., Graney, J. and Mokhtari, K., 'High Frequency Vocabulary and Reading Proficiency in ESL Readers', in T. Huckin, M. Haynes and J. Coady (eds), *Second Language Reading and Vocabulary Learning* (Norwood, NJ: Ablex, 1993), 217–26.

Cumming, A., *Writing Expertise and Second Language Proficiency in ESL Writing Performance* (Doctoral Dissertation, University of Toronto, 1988).

Cumming, A., 'Writing Expertise and Second Language Proficiency', *Language Learning* 39 (1989), 81–141.

Cumming, A., 'Theoretical Perspectives on Writing', *Annual Review of Applied Linguistics* 18 (1998), 61–78.

Cumming, A., 'Learning to Write in a Second Language: Two Decades of Research', in R.M. Manchón (ed.), 'Writing in the L2 Classroom: Issues in Research and Pedagogy', *International Journal of English Studies* (Special Issue) 1(2), (2001), 1–23.

Cumming, A., Rebuffot, J. and Ledwell, M., 'Reading and Summarizing Challenging Texts in First and Second Languages', *Reading and Writing: an Interdisciplinary Journal* 2 (1989), 201–19.

de Bot, K., Paribakht, T.S. and Wesche, M., 'Toward a Lexical Processing Model for the Study of Second Language Vocabulary Acquisition: Evidence from ESL Reading', *Studies in Second Language Acquisition* 19(3), (1997), 309–29.

Deese, J., *The Structure of Associations in Language and Thought* (Baltimore: John Hopkins University Press, 1965).

Doughty, C. and Williams J. (eds), *Focus on Form in Classroom Second Language Acquisition* (Cambridge: Cambridge University Press, 1998).

Dufour, R. and Kroll, J., 'Matching Words to Concepts in two Languages: A Test of the Concept Mediation Model of Bilingual Representations', *Memory and Cognition* 23, 2 (1995), 166–80.

Egan, K. *Romantic Understanding: The Development of Rationality and Imagination, Ages 8–15* (New York: Routledge, 1990).

Ellis, N. and Larsen-Freeman, D. (eds) 'Language Emergence: Implications for Applied Linguistics', *Applied Linguistics* (Special Issue) 27 (4), (2006).

Entwistle, D.R., *Word Associations of Young Children* (Baltimore: Johns Hopkins University Press, 1966).

Ericsson, K.A. and Simon, H.A., *Protocol Analysis. Verbal Reports as Data* (Cambridge, MA: MIT Press, 1993).

Ervin, S., 'Changes with Age in the Verbal Determinants of Word Association', *American Journal of Psychology* 74 (1961), 361–72.

Fagan, W.T. and Hayden, H.M.R., 'Writing Processes in French and English of Fifth Grade French Immersion Students', *Canadian Modern Language Review* 44 (1988), 653–68.

Flower, L. and Hayes, J., 'Images, Plans and Prose: The Representation of Meaning in Writing', *Written Communication* 1 (1984), 120–60.

Færch, C. and Kasper, G., 'Plans and Strategies in Foreign Language Communication', in C. Færch and G. Kasper (eds), *Strategies in Interlanguage Communication* (Harlow: Longman, 1983), 20–60.

References 215

Galbraith, D. 'Writing as a Knowledge-Constituting Process', in M. Torrance and D. Galbraith (eds), *Knowing How to Write: Conceptual Processes in Text Production* (Amsterdam, NL: Amsterdam University Press, 1999), 139–60.

Gardner, H., *Frames of Mind: The Theory of Multiple Intelligences* (New York: Basic Books, 1983).

Gass, S. 'Discussion: Incidental Vocabulary Learning', *Studies in Second Language Acquisition*, 21 (1999) 319–33.

Gelderen, A. van, Schoonen, R., Glopper, K. de, Hulstijn, J., Simis, A., Snellings, P. and Stevenson, M. 'Linguistic Knowledge, Processing Speed and Metacognitive Knowledge in First and Second Language Reading Comprehension; A Componential Analysis', *Journal of Educational Psychology*, 96 (1), (2004), 19–30.

Grabe, W., 'Notes toward a Theory of Second Language Writing', in T. Silva and P.K. Matsuda (eds), *On Second Language Writing* (Mahwah, NJ: Lawrence Erlbaum Associates, 2001), 39–57.

Grabe, W. and Kaplan, R.B., *Theory and Practice of Writing* (New York: Longman, 1996).

Grabe, W. and Stoller, F.L., *Teaching and Researching Reading* (Edinburgh: Longman, 2002).

Greidanus, T., Bogaards, P., Van Der Linden, E., Nienhuis, L. and De Wolf, T., 'The Construction and Validation of a Deep Word Knowledge Test for Advanced Learners of French', in P. Bogaards and B. Laufer (eds), *Vocabulary in a Second Language* (Amsterdam: John Benjamins, 2004), 191–208.

Greidanus, T. and Nienhuis, L., 'Testing the Quality of Word Knowledge in L2 by Means of Word Associations: Types of Distractors and Types of Associations', *The Modern Language Journal* 85 (2001), 567–77.

Greidanus, T., Beks, B. and Wakely, R., 'Testing the Development of French Word Knowledge by Advanced Dutch- and English-Speaking Learners and Native Speakers', *The Modern Language Journal* 89(2), (2005), 221–38.

Haastrup, K., *Lexical Inferencing Procedures or Talking about Words: Receptive Procedures in Foreign Language Learning with Special Reference to English* (Tübingen: Gunter Narr, 1991).

Haastrup, K. and Henriksen, B., 'Vocabulary Acquisition: from Partial to Precise Understanding', in K. Haastrup and Å.Viberg (eds), *Perspectives on Lexical Acquisition in a Second Language* (Lund: Lund University Press, 1998), 97–124.

Haastrup, K. and Henriksen, B., 'Vocabulary Acquisition: Acquiring Depth of Knowledge through Network Building', *International Journal of Applied Linguistics* 10 (2000), 221–39.

Haastrup, K. and Henriksen, B., 'The Interrelationship between Vocabulary Acquisition Theory and General SLA Research' in S. Foster-Cohen and A. Nizegorodcew (eds), *EUROSLA Yearbook.* (Amsterdam/Philadelphia: John Benjamins, 2001), 69–78.

Haastrup, K. Albrechtsen, D. and Henriksen, B., 'Lexical Inferencing Processes in L1 and L2. Same or Different? Focus on Issues in Design and Method', *Angles On The English-Speaking World* 4 (2004), 111–28.

Hall, C., 'Managing the Complexity of Revising Across Languages', *TESOL Quarterly* 24 (1990), 43–60.

Hamp-Lyons, L., 'Holistic Writing Assessment for LEP Students', *Proceedings of the Second National Research Symposium on Limited English Proficient Student Issues: Focus on Evaluation and Measurement. OBEMLA* (1992).

216 *References*

Hartmann, C., *Ordassociationer på engelsk – fokus på verber* (Unpublished MA Thesis from the Department of English, Germanic and Romance Studies, University of Copenhagen, 2004).

Henriksen, B., 'Three Dimensions of Vocabulary Development', in M. Wesche and T.S. Paribakht (Guest Eds), Incidental L2 Vocabulary Acquisition: Theory, Current Research and Instructional Implications, *Studies in Second Language Acquisition* (Special Issue) 21(2), (1999), 303–17.

Henriksen, B, Albrechtsen, D. and Haastrup, K., 'The Relationship between Vocabulary Size and Reading Comprehension in the L2', *Angles on the English-Speaking World* 4 (2004), 129–40.

Hornberger, N. (ed.), *Continua of Biliteracy: An Ecological Framework for Educational Policy, Research, and Practice in Multilingual Settings* (Clevedon, UK: Multilingual Matters, 2003).

Horst, M., Cobb, T. and Meara, P., 'Beyond a Clockwork Orange: Acquiring Second Language Vocabulary through Reading', *Reading in a Foreign Language* 11(2), (1998), 207–23.

Hu, M. and Nation, P., 'Unknown Vocabulary Density and Reading Comprehension', *Reading in a Foreign Language* 13 (2000), 403–30.

Huckin, T. and Coady, J., 'Incidental Vocabulary Acquisition in a Second Language: A Review', in M. Wesche and T.S. Paribakht (Guest Eds), 'Incidental L2 Vocabulary Acquisition: Theory, Current Research and Instructional Implications', *Studies in Second Language Acquisition* (Special Issue) 21(2), (1999), 181–93.

Hulstijn, J.H., 'Towards a Unified Account of the Representation, Processing and Acquisition of L2 Knowledge', *Second Language Research* 18(3), (2002), 193–223.

Janssen, D., van Waes, L. and van den Bergh, H., 'Effects of Thinking Aloud on Writing Processes', in C.M. Levy and S. Ransdell (eds), *The Science of Writing Theories, Methods, Individual Differences, and Applications* (Mahwah, NJ: Lawrence Erlbaum Associates, 1996), 233–50.

Jiang, N., 'Lexical Representation and Development in a Second Language', *Applied Linguistics* 21(1), (2000), 47–77.

Jiang, N., 'Form-meaning Mapping in Vocabulary Acquisition in a Second Language' *Studies in Second Language Acquisition*, 24 (2002), 617–37.

Jiang, N., 'Semantic Transfer and Its Implications for Vocabulary Teaching in a Second Language', *The Modern Language Journal* 88 (3), (2004), 416–32.

Joe, A., 'Text-Based Tasks and Incidental Vocabulary Learning', *Second Language Research* 11 (1995), 149–58.

Jones, S. and Tetroe, J., 'Composing in a Second Language', in A. Matsuhashi (ed.), *Writing in Real Time: Modelling Production Processes* (Norwood, NJ: Ablex Publishing, 1987), 34–57.

Jourdenais, R., 'Cognition, Instruction and Protocol Analysis', in P. Robinson (ed.), *Cognition and Second Language Instruction* (Cambridge: Cambridge University Press, 2001), 354–75.

Kintsch, W., *Comprehension: A Paradigm for Cognition* (Cambridge: Cambridge University Press, 1998).

Koda, K., *Insights into Second Language Reading* (Cambridge: Cambridge University Press, 2005).

Koda, K. (ed.) *Reading and Language Learning* (Malden, MA: Blackwell Publishers and *Language Learning*, 2007).

References 217

Krings, H.P., 'Schreiben in der Fremdsprache – Prozessanalysen zum Vierten Skill', in G. Antos, and H.P. Krings (eds), *Textproduktion: Ein Interdisziplinärer Forschungsüberblick* (Tübingen: Max Niemeyer Verlag, 1989), 377–436.

Kroll, B.M., 'Explaining How to Play a Game: The Development of Informative Writing Skills', *Written Communication* 3(2), (1986), 195–218.

Kroll, J.F. and de Groot, A.M.B., 'Lexical and Conceptual Memory in the Bilingual: Mapping Form to Meaning in Two Languages', in A.M.B. de Groot and J.F. Kroll (eds), *Tutorials in Bilingualism: Psycholinguistic Perspectives* (Mahwah, NJ: Lawrence Erlbaum Publishers, 1997), 169–99.

Kroll, J.F., and Tokowicz, N., 'Models of Bilingual Representation and Processing: Looking back and to the Future', in J.F. Kroll and A.M.B. de Groot (eds), *Handbook of Bilingualism: Psycholinguistic Approaches* (New York: Oxford University Press, 2005), 531–53.

Laufer, B., 'How Much Lexis is Necessary for Reading Comprehension?', in P.J.L. Arnaud and H. Béjoint (eds), *Vocabulary and Applied Linguistics* (London: Macmillan, 1992), 126–32.

Laufer, B., 'The Lexical Plight in Second Language Reading', in J. Coady and T. Huckin (eds) *Second Language Vocabulary Acquisition* (Cambridge: Cambridge University Press, 1997a), 20–34.

Laufer, B., 'What's in a Word that Makes it Hard or Easy?: Some Interlexical Factors that Affect the Learning of Words', in N. Schmitt and. M. McCarthy (eds), *Vocabulary: Description, Acquisition and Pedagogy* (Cambridge: Cambridge University Press, 1997b), 140–55.

Laufer, B. and Hulstijn, J., 'Incidental Vocabulary Acquisition in a Second Language: The Construct of Task-Induced Involvement', *Applied Linguistics* 22, (2001) 1–26.

Leech, G., Rayson, P. and Wilson, A., *Word Frequencies in Written and Spoken English: based on the British National Corpus* (London: Longman, 2001).

Leki, I., Cumming, A. and Silva, T., 'Second-Language Composition Teaching and Learning', in P. Smagorinsky (ed.), *Research on Composition: Multiple Perspectives on Two Decades of Change* (New York and London: Teachers College Press, Columbia University, 2006), 141–69.

Levelt, W.J.M., *Speaking: From Intention to Articulation* (MIT Press: 1989).

Manchón, R.M., 'Trends in the Conceptualizations of Second Language Composing Strategies: A Critical Analysis', in R.M. Manchón (ed.), 'Writing in the L2 Classroom: Issues in Research and Pedagogy' (Special Issue), *International Journal of English Studies* 1(2), (2001), 47–70.

Meara, P., 'Learners' Word Associations in French', *Interlanguage Studies Bulletin* 3, (1978), 192–211.

Meara, P., 'The Dimensions of Lexical Competence', in G. Brown, K. Malmkjær and J. Williams (eds), *Performance and Competence in Second Language Acquisition* (Cambridge: Cambridge University Press, 1996), 35–53.

Meara, P. and Wolter, B., 'V_Links: Beyond Vocabulary Depth', *Angles on the English-speaking World* 4, (2004), 129–40.

Mecartty, F., 'Lexical and Grammatical Knowledge in Reading and Listening Comprehension by Foreign Language Learners of Spanish', *Applied Language Learning* 11, (2000), 323–48.

Mellow, J. and Cumming, A. 'Concord in Interlanguage: Efficiency or Priming?' *Applied Linguistics* 15 (4), (1994), 442–73.

218   References

Mori, Y., 'Individual Differences in the Integration of Information from Context and Word Parts in Interpreting Unknown Kanji Words', *Applied Psycholinguistics* 23 (2002), 375–97.

Murphy, M.L., *Semantic Relations and the Lexicon: Antonymy, Synonymy, and other Paradigms* (Cambridge: Cambridge University Press, 2003).

Namei, S., *The Bilingual Lexicon from a Developmental Perspective. A Word Association Study of Persian-Swedish Bilinguals* (Centre for Research on Bilingualism: Stockholm University, 2002).

Namei, S., 'Bilingual Lexical Development: A Persian-Swedish Word Association Study', *International Journal of Applied Linguistics* 14(3) (2004), 363–88.

Nassaji, H., 'The Relationship between Depth of Vocabulary Knowledge and L2 Learners' Lexical Inferencing Strategy Use and Success', *Canadian Modern Language Review* 61(1), (2004), 107–34.

Nation, I.S.P., *Teaching and Learning Vocabulary* (Massachusetts: Newbury House, 1990).

Nation, I.S.P., *Learning Vocabulary in another Language* (Cambridge: Cambridge University Press, 2001).

Nation, P. and Waring, R., 'Vocabulary Size, Text Coverage and Word Lists', in N. Schmitt and M. McCarthy (eds), *Vocabulary: Description, Acquisition and Pedagogy* (Cambridge: Cambridge University Press, 1997), 6–19.

Newton, J., 'Task-Based Interaction and Incidental Vocabulary Learning: A Case Study', *Second Language Research* 11 (2), (1995), 159–77.

Nielsen, J.C. and Møller, L., *Tekstlæseprøverne TL 1–5* (København: Dansk Psykologisk Forlag, 1998).

Nurweni, A. and Read, J., 'The English Vocabulary Knowledge of Indonesian University Students', *English for Specific Purposes* 18(2) (1999), 161–75.

Palermo, D.S. 'Characteristics of Word Association Responses Obtained from Children in Grades One through Four', *Developmental Psychology* 9 (1971), 118–23.

Paribakht, T.S., 'The Influence of First Language Lexicalisation on Second Language Lexical Inferencing: A Study of Farsi-Speaking Learners of English as a Foreign Language', *Language Learning* 55(2005), 701–48.

Paribakht, T.S. and Wesche, M., *Vocabulary Enhancement Activities and Reading for Meaning in Second Language Vocabulary Acquisition* (The Tenth World Congress of Applied Linguistics (AILA), Amsterdam, 8–14 August, 1993).

Paribakht, T.S. and Wesche, M., 'Vocabulary Enhancement Activities and Reading for Meaning in Second Language Vocabulary Acquisition', in J. Coady and T. Huckin (eds), *Second Language Vocabulary Acquisition: A Rationale for Pedagogy* (Cambridge: Cambridge University Press, 1997), 174–200.

Paribakht, T.S. and Wesche, M., '"Incidental" L2 Vocabulary Acquisition through Reading: An Introspective Study', in M. Wesche and T.S. Paribakht (Guest Eds), Incidental L2 Vocabulary Acquisition: Theory, Current Research And Instructional Implications, *Studies in Second Language Acquisition* (Special Issue) 21(2), (1999), 195–224.

Paribakht, T.S. and Wesche, M.B., 'Enhancing Vocabulary Acquisition through Reading: A Hierarchy of Text-Related Exercise Types', *Canadian Modern Language Review* 52 (1996), 155–78.

Partnership for Reading, *Adolescent Literacy: Research Needs* (Washington, DC: National Institute for Literacy, 2004).

References 219

Pennington, M.C. and So, S., 'Comparing Writing Process and Product across Two Languages: A Study of 6 Singaporean University Student Writers', *Journal of Second Language Writing* 2(1), (1993), 41–63.

Politzer, R.B., 'Paradigmatic and Syntagmatic Associations of First Year French Students', in V. Honsa and M.J. Hardman-de-Bautista (eds), *Papers on Linguistics and Child Language* (Ruth Hirsch Weir Memorial Volume, Mouton, 1978), 203–10.

Postman, L. and Keppel, G., *Norms of Word Associations* (New York: Academic Press, 1970).

Quian, D.D., 'Assessing the Roles of Depth and Breadth of Vocabulary Knowledge in Reading Comprehension', *Canadian Modern Language Review* 56 (1999), 282–307.

Quian, D.D., 'Investigating the Relationship between Knowledge and Academic Reading Performance: An Assessment Perspective', *Language Learning* 52 (2002), 513–36.

Read, J., 'The Development of a New Measure of L2 Vocabulary Knowledge', *Language Testing* 10 (1993), 355–71.

Read, J., 'Validating a Test to Measure Depth of Vocabulary Knowledge', in A. Kunnan (ed.), *Validation in Language Assessment* (Mahwah, NJ: Lawrence Erlbaum, 1998), 41–60.

Read, J., *Assessing Vocabulary* (Cambridge: Cambridge University Press, 2000).

Read, J., 'Plumbing the Depths: How should the Construct of Vocabulary Knowledge be Defined ?', in P. Bogaards and B. Laufer (eds), *Vocabulary in a Second Language* (Amsterdam: John Benjamins, 2004), 209–27.

Richards, J., 'The Role of Vocabulary Teaching', *TESOL Quarterly* 10 (1976), 77–89.

Ringbom, H., 'On the Distinctions of Item Learning vs System Learning and Receptive Competence vs Productive Competence in Relation to the Role of L1 in Foreign Language Learning', in H. Ringbom (ed.), *Psycholinguistics and Foreign Language Learning* (Publications of the Research Institute of the Åbo Akademi Foundation, 86, 1983), 163–73.

Roca de Larios J., Marín, J and Murphy, L., 'A Temporal Analysis of Formulation Processes in L1 and L2 Writing', *Language Learning* 51(3), (2001), 497–538.

Roca de Larios, J., Murphy, L. and Marín, J., 'Critical Examination of L2 Writing Process Research', in S. Ransdell and M.L. Barbier (eds), *New Directions for Research in L2 Writing* (Dordrecht/Boston/London: Kluwer Academic Publishers, 2002), 11–47.

Roca de Larios J., Manchón, R.M. and Murphy, L., 'Generating Text in Native and Foreign Language Writing: A Temporal Analysis of Problem-Solving Formulation Processes', *The Modern Language Journal* 90 (1), (2006), 100–14.

Sasaki, M., 'A Multiple-data Analysis of the 3.5-year Development of EFL Student Writers', *Language Learning*, 54(3), (2004), 525–82.

Sasaki, M. and Hirose, K., 'Explanatory Variables for EFL Students' Expository Writing', *Language Learning* 46(1), (1996), 137–74.

Scardamalia, M. and Bereiter, C., 'The Development of Evaluative, Diagnostic and Remedial Capabilities in Children's Composing', in M. Martlew (ed.), *The Psychology of Written Language: Developmental and Educational Perspectives* (Chichester/New York/Brisbane/Toronto/Singapore: John Wiley and Sons, 1983), 67–95.

220 References

Scardamalia, M. and Paris, P, 'The Function of Explicit Discourse Knowledge in the Development of Text Representation and Composing Strategies', *Cognition and Instruction* 2(1), (1985), 1–39.

Schmitt, N., 'Quantifying Word Association Responses: What is Native-Like?', *System* 26, (1998), 389–401.

Schmitt, N, Schmitt, D. and Clapham, C., 'Developing and Exploring the Behaviour of Two New Versions of the Vocabulary Levels Test', *Language Testing*, 18(1), (2001), 55–88.

Schoonen, R. and Verhallen, M., 'Ennis Van Woorden: De Toetsing Van Diepe Woordkennis' (Knowledge of Words: The Testing of Deep Word Knowledge) *Pedagogische Studiën* 75, (1998), 153–68.

Schoonen, R., Gelderen, A. van, Glopper, K. de, Hulstijn, J., Snellings, P, Simis, A. and Stevenson, M., 'Linguistic Knowledge, Metacognitive Knowledge and Retrieval Speed in L1, L2 and EFL Writing; A Structural Equation Modeling Approach' in S. Ransdell and M.L. Barbier (eds), *New Directions for Research in L2 Writing* (Dordrecht: Kluwer Academic Press, 2002), 101–22.

Schoonen, R., Gelderen, van A., Glopper, de K., Hulstijn, J., Simis, A., Snellings, P., and Stevenson, M., 'First Language and Second Language Writing: The Role of Linguistic Knowledge, Speed of Processing, and Metacognitive Knowledge', *Language Learning* 53(1), (2003), 165–202.

Singleton, D., *Exploring the Second Language Mental Lexicon* (Cambridge: Cambridge University Press, 1999).

Skibniewski, L., 'The Writing Processes of Advanced Foreign Language Learners in their Native and Foreign Languages: Evidence from Thinking-Aloud and Behavior Protocols', *Studia Anglica Posnaniensia* 21 (1988), 177–86.

Skibniewski, L. and Skibniewska, M., 'Experimental Study: The Writing Processes of Intermediate/Advanced Foreign Language Learners in their Foreign and Native Languages', *Studia Anglica Posnaniensia* 19 (1986), 143–63.

Skriver, S., *Struktur i det Mentale Leksikon. En Undersøgelse af Densitet i Ordassociationsnetværk* (Unpublished MA Thesis from the Department of English, Germanic and Romance Studies, University of Copenhagen, 2005).

Smagorinsky, P., 'Think-Aloud Protocol Analysis: Beyond the Black Box', in P. Smagorinsky (ed.), *Speaking about Writing. Reflections on Research Methodology*, (Thousand Oaks/ London/ New Delhi: SAGE Publications, 1994) 3–19.

Stevenson, M., Schoonen, R. and de Glopper, K., 'Revising in Two Languages: A Multi-dimensional Comparison of Online Writing Revisions in L1 and FL', *Journal of Second Language Writing* 15(2006), 201–33.

Stratman, J.F. and Hamp-Lyons, L., 'Reactivity in Concurrent Think-Aloud Protocols: Issues for Research', in P. Smagorinsky (ed.) *Speaking about Writing. Reflections on Research Methodology* (Thousand Oaks/ London/ New Delhi: SAGE Publications, 1994), 89–112.

Stæhr Jensen, L., *Vocabulary Knowledge and Listening Comprehension in English as a Foreign Language: An Empirical Study Employing Data Elicited from Danish EFL Learners* (Unpublished PhD Thesis, Copenhagen Business School, 2005).

Swain, M., 'Three Functions of Output in Second Language Learning' in G. Cook and B. Seidelhofer (eds), *Principle and Practice in Applied Linguistics* (Oxford: Oxford University Press, 1995), 125–44.

Söderman, T., 'Word Associations of Foreign Language Learners and Native Speakers: The Phenomenon of a Shift in Response Type and its Relevance for

Lexical Development', in H. Ringbom (ed.), *Near-Native Proficiency in English* (Åbo: Åbo Akademi, 1993), 91–182.

Tarone, E., Downing, B., Cohen, A., Gillette, S., Murie, R. and Dailye, B., 'The Writing of Southeast Asian-American Students in Secondary School and University', *Journal of Second Language Writing* 2(2), (1993), 149–72.

Thorson, H., 'Using the Computer to Compare Foreign and Native Language Writing Processes: A Statistical and Case Study Approach', *The Modern Language Journal*, 84(2), (2000), 155–70.

TOEFL, *TOEFL Information for Computer-Based Testing 2001–2002* (Educational Testing Service, 2001).

Uzawa, K., 'Second Language Learners' Processes of L1 Writing, L2 Writing, and Translation from L1 to L2', *Journal of Second Language Writing* 5(3), (1996), 271–94.

Van Daalen-Kapteijns, M., Elshout-Mohr, M. and de Glopper, K. 'Deriving the Meaning of Unknown Words from Multiple Contexts', *Language Learning*, 51(1), (2001), 145–81.

Verhallen, M., Özdemir, L., Yüksel, E. and Schoonen, R., 'Woordkennis Van Turkse Kinderen', in De Bovenbouw Van Het Basisonderwijs. Een Vergelijkend Onderzoek Bij Één- En Tweetalige Turkse Leerlingen, *Toegepaste Taalwetenschap*, in Artikelen 6 (1), (1999), 21–33 (with an English summary).

Waring, R. and Nation, P., 'Second Language Reading and Incidental Vocabulary Learning', *Angles on the English Speaking World*, 4 (2004), 97–110.

Wesche, M. and Paribakht, T.S., 'Incidental L2 Vocabulary Acquisition Through Reading: An Introspective Study' (Paper Presented at the Second Language Research Forum (SLRF), Ithaca, Cornell University, 29 September–1 October, 1995).

Wesche, M. and Paribakht, T.S. 'Assessin.g Second Language Vocabulary Knowledge: Depth versus Breadth'. *Canadian Modern Language Review* 53(1996), 13–40.

Whalen, K. and Ménard, N., 'L1 and L2 Writers' Strategic and Linguistic Knowledge: A Model of Multiple-Level Discourse Processing', *Language Learning* 45, (1995) 381–418.

Wilks, C. and Meara, P., 'Untangling Word Webs: Graph Theory and the Notion of Density in Second Language Word Association Networks', *Second Language Research* 18, (2002), 303–24.

Wolff, D., 'Importance of Procedural Knowledge in Second Language Comprehension, Production and Learning', in G. Bartelt (ed.), *The Dynamics of Language Processes: Essays in Honour of Hans W. Dechert* (Tübingen: Narr, 1994).

Wolter, B., 'Comparing the L1 and the L2 Mental Lexicon', *Studies in Second Language Acquisition* 23, (2001), 41–69.

Wolter, B., 'Assessing Proficiency through Word Associations: Is there Still Hope?' *System*, 30(3), (2002), 315–29.

Wong, R.Y.L., 'Strategies for the Construction of Meaning: Chinese Students in Singapore Writing in English and Chinese', *Language, Culture and Curriculum* 6, (1993), 291–301.

Index

Note: Page numbers in *italics* denote figures/tables/appendices.

awareness raising, 27, 64, 109–10, 158, **198–201**

Bereiter, Carl, **118–19**, 122, 127

Cumming, Alister, xi, xiii–xvii, 114, 117, 122–23, 127, 135–36, 140–45, 153–55, 159 n.3

design
counterbalancing, 12, 40, 121
data collection procedures, 11–12, 40–4, 74–5, 121–22
experimental setting, 11, 122
field testing, 41, 43, 65, 74, 110 n.3, 111 n.7, 121
identical tasks, 11, 73, 171, 195
open-closed tasks, 43, 120, 171–72, 196
order of presentation, 11, *12*, 40, 121
parallel tasks L1/L2, 11, 20, 21, 40, 73, 74–5, 121
pilot study,123, *211–12*
task instructions, 12, 40–2, 58, 74–5, 121, *207, 210*
time for reflection, 32, 43, 62
time on task, 40–2, 74–5, 112
training of informants, 9, 12, 121
transcriptions, 75–6, 111 n.6, 122, 123, *211*
development, across grade levels
across studies, 162–63
lexical inferencing study, in, 92–4, 94–6
lexical study, in, 44–5, 51–5, 58–61
writing study, in, 132–37, 139–43

elicitation tasks, 10–11, *12*
essay writing tasks, 121, *210*

lexical inferencing tasks, 73, *208–9*
reading tests, 11
vocabulary size test, 57–8
see also vocabulary size
word association task, 40–1
see also word association task
word connection task, 41–2
see also word connection task

Færch, Claus, xi, 13–14, 77

Galbraith, David, **16–17**, 119
Greidanus, Tine, 36, 37, 38, 42, 56, 63, 64, 65, 202

Haastrup, Kirsten, 67, 70, 71, 76, 77, 87, 88, 102, 103, 105, 106
Henriksen, Birgit, 26, 27, 64
Hultstijn, Jan, xi, 28, 69, 109

implications, research, 63–65, 108–10, 156, 195–98
implications, teaching, 63–65, 108–10, 157–59, 198–202
informants, 3–4, 6–9, *7*
grade 7 (beginners, comprehensive school), 4, 6–7
grade 10 (intermediates, sixth form college), 4, 7, 20
grade 13 (advanced, university students), 4, 7
low/high ability groups, 7–8
introspective methods, 9–10, 75–6, 119–20
ability to verbalize, 8–9
concurrent think aloud, 75, 120
reactivity, **120**, 122
retrospection, 40, 42, 47, 75–76, 120
validity, 75

Kasper, Gabrielle, 13–14, 77
Kintsch, Walter, **15–17**, 69, 77

Index 223

knowledge
  background
    (encyclopaedic/schema), 15,
      29–30, 31, 43
  declarative – procedural, 6, 11,
    13–15, 87–9, 97–8, 100, 109–10,
    164–65, 167, 172, 175–76, 178,
    181, 184, 186, **188–90**, 192–93,
    196–97, 200–2; declarative, **22**,
    100, 109, 160, 169, 173, 178,
    196–97; procedural, 13–15, 77,
    100, 102, 109, 155, 157, 164,
    171, 191–92, 198–200
  lexical, *see* vocabulary knowledge
  meta-semantic, 29–30, 31, 43
  vocabulary, *see* vocabulary
    knowledge

L1/L2, 5–6, **24**, 31, 38–9, 70, 114–16
  across studies, 161–62
  lexical inferencing study, in, 92–4,
    94–6
  lexical study, in, 44–5, 51–5, 58–61
  writing study, in, 129–31, 139–43
language proficiency and writing, 117,
    138–39
Laufer, Batia, 24, 25, 61, 68, 69, 71,
    106, 109
learner profiles
  across studies, 172–78; lexical,
    178–90
  lexical inferencing, 97–102
  see also verbal protocols, lexical
    inferencing, qualitative
    analysis
  writing, 143–53
  see also verbal protocols, writing,
    qualitative analysis
levels of representation, 29–32
  associative links, 30, 32
  lexical entries, 30, 35
lexical inferencing, **67**
  developmental continuum,
    102–105
  hierarchy of cue levels, *80*
  knowledge sources, 76–7
  processing types, 77–86; processing
    continuum, 80–6

Manchón, Rosa, M., 114, 115, **116**,
    154
Marín, Javier, 114, 115, **116**
Meara, Paul, 5, 27, 28, 32, 34, 37, 38,
    65, 71
Murphy, Liz, 114, 115, **116**, 154
Murphy, Lynne, 28, 29, 31, 34

Namei, Shidrokh, 32, 33, 34, 36, 46,
    47, 49, 54
Nation, Paul, 27, 47, 57, 138

Paribakht, Sima, T., 64, **69**, **71**, 106,
    107, 110 n.1, 202

Read, John, xi, 5, 25, 26, 36, 63
reading process, models
  construction-integration model,
    15–16, 17–18
  interactive models, 70, 77
  text base – situation model, 15
research questions, 18
  across studies, 164, 172
  lexical inferencing study, 72, 92,
    94, 95
  lexical study, 39
  writing study, 113, 128–29, 132
results
  across studies, 161–70,
    170–72
  lexical inferencing study, 91–6,
    96–7
  lexical study: network knowledge,
    44–55, 55–6; size, 58–61
  writing study, 128–39,
    139–43
Roca de Larios, Julio, 114, 115, **116**,
    154

Scardamalia, Marlene, **118–19**, 122,
    127
Schmitt, Norbert, xi, 33, 49, 57,
    66 n.11
Singleton, David, xi, 2, 28, 32,
    33, 35
Söderman, Tove, 32, 35, 53
statistical analysis, 45, 92–3, 125,
    128–29, 132, *203*

224 *Index*

statistical analysis – *continued*
ANOVA, 45, 51, 52, 53, 54, 59, 92,
93, 94, 95, 129, 132, 133, *203,
203–6*
correlations, 24–5, 61–2, 137–39,
142, 164–72, 172–90
interscorer reliability, 47–8, 92,
209–10, 211–12

verbal protocols, analyses, lexical
inferencing
adaptability of processing, 88–90
advanced processing, 87–8
lexical inferencing success, 90–1
qualitative analysis: mature
inferencer, 97–9; immature
inferencer, 99–100; L1–L2
dimension, 100–2
verbal protocols, analyses, writing
aspects of writing (attention to),
123, 124–25
problem solving, 123, 125–27
qualitative analysis: formulation
(compensatory, upgrading),
116, **146–53**, 154, 156;
planning (advance, emergent),
118–19, 123, **145–46, 148–49,
150, 152**, 156–57
sensitivity of analysis, 155–56
vocabulary acquisition
mapping, 27–8
network building, 27–8
vocabulary knowledge, **22**
breadth/size, *see* vocabulary size
depth, 24, 25, **26–7**, 37, 56, 106,
137, 190, 200
network knowledge (*see* word
association task; word
connection task): density of
network, 37–8; graph theory,
37–8; lexical network/word
web, 27–32; network building,
27–8
receptive vs. productive, 32–9
threshold, **24–5**, 47, 61, 171, 184,
192
vocabulary size, 5, **24–7**, 27, 37,
57–61, 64, 168, 200
predictions, 58

results, *44, 50*, 58–61: across
frequency bands, 59–60;
correlations (*see* statistical
analysis, correlations); overall
test score, 58–9
test formats, 57–8; Danish levels
test, 58; Nation's levels test, 57,
63–4

Wesche, Marjorie, 64, **71**, 107,
110 n.1, 202
Wolff, Dieter, 13–14, 77, 198
Wolter, Brian, 32, 35, 37, 49, 53, 65
word associates task, 25, 36–7, *36*, 42,
64
word association task, 22–4, 25, **32–6,
40–1**
associations/links/relations/
responses, **32–5**, *33, 48*;
analytic, 30, 36,
65 n.1; canonical
(prototypical), 28, 30, 32, **33–4**,
35, 38, **43–5**, 46–7, 49–50,
53–4, 55, 61, 65 n.5, 180–81,
184, 187; form related vs.
semantically related, 32, *33*, 35,
38, 45, 53; high-frequent vs.
low frequent, 24, 32, **34–5**, 47,
48, 49, 50, **53–4**, 55;
idiosyncratic, 46; paradigmatic,
30, 31,32, *33*, 35, 36, 46;
semantic fields, 23, 30,
41, 64
coding procedure, 45–50, *48, 50,
206–7*
correlations (*see* statistical analysis,
correlations)
L1 vs. L2 links, 31–2, 38–9
overall word association score,
48–51, *51*, 55
responses: factors affecting
responses, 35–6; lexical
variation, 50, 66 n.1,
179, 180, 181, 183, 184, 187;
shifts in response behaviour,
28, 32, 35, 45–6,
49; unqualified responses,
47, 52, 55, 187; valid responses,
47, 48, 50; scores awarded, *50*

Index 225

word association task – *continued*
response type score, 50
results, 51–5, *51*, *52*
stimulus words, 35, 40–3, 53,
56, 64; concrete-abstract, 36;
frequency of, 35, *41*, 65 n.4,
66 n.9 166, 197; word
class, 36
word association – word connection,
42–3
word connection task, 39, 40, **41–2**,
42
correlations (*see* statistical analysis,
correlations)
results, 44–5, *44*
words, 42

word retrieval/access routes 22, 44,
165, 189, 197
writing process, models, 118–19
CDO process, **127**, 142, 157
knowledge-constituting model,
16–17, 17–18
knowledge telling, **118–19**, 126–27
knowledge transforming, 16, **119**,
126–27
writing, product
argumentative essays, 121
assessment of essays, 128, 131,
136–38, *211–12*
writing, product vs. process, 117,
137–38
writing prompts, 121, *210*

9781349520077

palgrave macmillan

Vocabulary and Writing in a First and Second Language is based on a large-scale empirical study. The innovative feature of the research was that the same students were asked to do the same tasks in both languages while reporting their thinking as they went along. Furthermore, they had to undertake the same tasks even though they were of very different experience, ranging from young children at school to university students. Three areas of learners' competencies and skills were explored: vocabulary knowledge, word-guessing strategies and writing. The authors further explore the relationship between the skills and describe the level of development for individual learners within the three areas. In all cases, statistical and qualitative analyses are offered based on the learners' own 'think-aloud' reports. Both researchers and teachers of language will find this in-depth approach useful in understanding the processes of both first and second language performance.

Dorte Albrechtsen is Associate Professor at the University of Copenhagen, Denmark. She has published on discourse analyses of learner texts and on processes in writing in the first and second language. She has been active in developing the field of foreign language acquisition at university level and has experience with in-service teacher training.

Kirsten Haastrup has held a Chair at the Danish University of Educational Studies and is currently Professor at the Copenhagen Business School. Her publications include a textbook on foreign language acquisition and a monograph on lexical inferencing. She has been active in establishing foreign language acquisition research in Denmark.

Birgit Henriksen is Associate Professor at the University of Copenhagen, Denmark. She has published on vocabulary acquisition and has co-authored a lexical task anthology. She has been active in developing the field of foreign language acquisition at university level and has given many courses for language teachers.

Jacket illustration 'random letters on black'
© thesupe87 (fotolia.co.uk).

ISBN 978-1-349-52007-7

9 781349 520077

www.palgrave.com